Sarah Amelia Scull

Greek Mythology Systematized

Sarah Amelia Scull

Greek Mythology Systematized

ISBN/EAN: 9783337246587

Printed in Europe, USA, Canada, Australia, Japan

Cover: Foto ©Thomas Meinert / pixelio.de

More available books at **www.hansebooks.com**

BY

S. A. SCULL.

PORTER & COATES,
PHILADELPHIA.

TO

Mrs. BISHOP SIMPSON

AND

Mrs. J. HERON FOSTER

THIS BOOK

IS GRATEFULLY AND AFFECTIONATELY

DEDICATED.

CONTENTS.

	PAGE
INTRODUCTION	9
SOURCES OF MATERIALS	27
GENEALOGICAL TABLES, BASED UPON HESIOD'S THEOGONY	31
KEY TO PRONUNCIATION OF GREEK NAMES	43
DORIC PORTICO, NAMING PARTS ORNAMENTED WITH MYTHOLOGICAL DESIGNS	44
PROGRAMME FOR STUDY OF MYTHOLOGICAL CHARACTERS	45
DEVELOPMENT OF MYTHOLOGY IN THE ORDER OF THE TABLES	47
CHARACTERS OUTSIDE OF HESIOD'S THEOGONY	329
LEGENDS OF HEROES	339
ABSTRACT OF GLADSTONE'S ANALYSIS OF HOMER'S MYTHOLOGY	316
GENEALOGICAL TABLES, BASED UPON GROTE'S HISTORY OF GREECE	371

ILLUSTRATIONS.

	PAGE
APHRODITE	280
APOLLO	146
ARES	140
ARIADNE	204
ARTEMIS	159
ATLAS	267
BELLEROPHON	342
CENTAUR	335
CERBERUS	215
CRONUS (HEAD OF)	59
DEMETER	105
DIANA OF EPHESUS	163
DIONYSUS	199
DORIC PORTICO	44
EROS	293
FATES, THE	314
FURIES	279
GANYMEDES AND THE EAGLE	191
HADES AND PERSEPHONE	99
HARPY, A	301
HEBE	144

	PAGE
HECATE	262
HELIOS	253
HEPHÆSTUS	233
HERA (HEAD OF)	92
HERACLES	209
HERMES	167
HESTIA	123
JUNO BARBERINI	97
LAOCOÖN	355
MEDUSA (HEAD OF)	227
MUSES, THE	179, 180
NIKE	265
NIOBE	194
PALLAS ATHENA	128
PAN	330
POSEIDON AND AMPHITRITE	119
PSYCHE	294
RHEA	62
SATYR (HEAD OF)	334
SILENUS	334
SISYPHUS, IXION, AND TANTALUS	195
TYCHE	325
ZEUS (HEAD OF), FROM DODONA	71
ZEUS	73
ZEUS FROM OTRICOLI	83

INTRODUCTION.

We should not study Mythology as we read fairy-tales—in a spirit of amused incredulity—for those who are prepared to speak to us will tell us that the theme is as comprehensive as are human interests, and as high as human aspirations. Its general scope may be indicated in general terms, but to grasp it in its depth, breadth, and suggestiveness one's knowledge must be deep, wide, and progressive.

Much meaning is given to a myth by Webster when he defines it as "a fabulous or imaginary statement or narrative conveying an important truth, generally of a moral or religious nature;" and certainly extensive ground is covered by his definition of Mythology as "a collective body of popular legends and fables respecting the supernatural actions of gods, divinities, and heroes." But this definition, wide as it is, would apply to Mythology regarded simply as a product of human thought, and therefore can scarcely be complete, for every mythologic system includes so much of religious belief and hope that it would seem that in its broadest sense Mythology comprehends man's search after religious truth.

Remembering that God alone can reveal spiritual truth, on the very threshold of the investigation of any mythic system these questions arise: First, What part of this system is the product of the human mind? Second, How far has it been modified by revealed truth?

If we simply consider what the mind of man can accomplish, endless fields of research open before us. We might notice the materials with which Nature furnishes him in sense-percepts as varied as are the objects and changes of the material universe. If we follow the results of the mysterious processes of his mind, we shall find him creating rich stores of new materials, believing in the supernatural, and then personifying what he believes.

As we follow through the grander processes of generalization, reasoning, and grouping into systems, we are not surprised that, in order to express the vast number of creations which a complex polytheistic system contained, it was said that in Athens "it were easier to find a god than a man."

Now, were man merely an *intellectual* being, Mythology would be synonymous with mental philosophy, and difference in mythic systems could be easily accounted for by saying that difference of location causes variety in the materials furnished by Nature, and that great variations in mental powers, in education, and in opportunities for culture cause all the weightier differences. But in order to make true and full answer to the question, Why do the systems of mythology so differ? we must give due attention to facts that have wider range than those that are merely intellectual—the facts that pertain to man as a *moral* being.

Man has a nature which makes him conscious that he is *governed*, yet is *free* to obey or to disobey—that, notwithstanding his freedom of choice, he is responsible to some being who holds the power of reward or punishment: he therefore seeks to propitiate the being or beings who can injure him, while he worships those who can help or enrich him; and though such beings be but the creation of his own thoughts, believed in, they become potent for good or for ill in all practical life.

Since the laws of man's moral nature have great uniformity, we might again ask, Why so many varieties of belief? For instance, how can the rainbow appear to the simple African a serpent lifted into celestial life and beauty; to the Greek, a shining pathway along which Iris came with heavenly messages; while the Hebrew lifted his eyes to it that he might there meet the gaze of God? There can be but one answer: Since the moral nature must have respect to truth and right, belief can be true only as it is enlightened by the oracles of God's truth, and no mode of teaching can be right unless it is in conformity with His moral law.

Might we not expect that the Being of whose will the moral law must be an expression would unfold to man unmistakably divine revelations of His character and of His purposes toward man? Have we reason to believe that such revelations have ever been made, and that they have influenced human beliefs and worships? In short, what is the relation of Mythology and Revelation?

There is but one Book in which is inscribed the world's whole history, and in which is indicated its whole destiny; and in the Bible alone can we find the materials for the adequate solution of the problems of religious life.

A writer of history has profoundly said, "He who in writing history ignores the fall of man cannot write philosophically;" and the assertion is just as profoundly true of the interpretation of Mythology. We never doubt that in the land watered this very hour by the Tigris and the Euphrates there once occurred an event that had stupendous meaning, for humanity was to choose between harmony with or rebellion against the sovereign will, of which the expression is that moral law whose penalty for disobedience is eternal loss, and whose reward for obedience is eternal good. We believe that in choosing disobedience man voluntarily separated himself from the "loving recognition" and the moral support of God: then, in accordance with the very laws of his being, having chosen the lower plane, the law of deterioration and the fearful influence of habit lowered the tone of his spiritual powers and tendencies, and he wandered into a darkness whose gloom may have sometimes shut out even the memory of the true God.

But He who created and gave laws to man, loves him; so, even while the child was "afar off" the Father implanted in his heart a heavenly home-sickness, or, as Pressensé has said, "a desire for reunion with Deity;" and, with the same writer, we believe that with a sense of guilt was always mingled a hope of pardon. Hence, wherever human beings have lived we find this mingling of fear and hope, this evidence of the spirit's consciousness of its divine origin and heavenly destination, taking pathetic expression in sacrifices, votive offerings, priesthoods, sacred fanes, and festivals. We admit that these were but indirect revelations, but we hold that they were God-given, and not the results of mental processes.

Further, we recognize as direct revelations the glory of the guiding-pillar, the Shekinah of the wilderness tabernacle, and the ritual of the Zion temple, which, sublime as it was in significance and suggestiveness, was to be dimmed into shadows in the presence of Him who in the express image of God's person was to reveal the world the "fulness of the Godhead."

If the existence of divine revelations be admitted, there arises the question, What has been their influence as world-forces? and the question of their acceptance or rejection brings us to a dividing-line in the interpretation of Mythology. Some thinkers (prominently Gladstone) assert the existence of *original external revelations*, and believe that mythological religions are only their modifications in more or less corrupted forms. On the other hand, there are those who deny external revelations, and believe that mythological religions are outgrowths of human development, a kind of spiritual Darwinism. May we not assume that these views, so opposite, are half truths, each needing the other as its complement? We admit that by the unfolding of his original endowments man may progress through ages of Stone, Bronze, or Iron, and even ripen by natural growth into the Silver and Golden Age; we know that mind can create systems of philosophy and belief so sublime that they seem God-wrought; but when we have to do with the problems into whose composition enter as elements man's relation to moral government, the inevitable consequences of choice, and the immortal destiny of souls, the adequate solution can come only from divine oracles. Hence it seems to us philosophical to say that a race or a nation is in a line of retrogression or of progression as it rejects or accepts divine revelations; and therefore when we investigate a mythic system we may know that however grand the temple or magnificent its service, it is all human in origin, and only mind-wrought, unless the worshipper is there taught that reunion with Deity may be attained only by the pure in heart and the blameless in life.

FORMS OF MYTHOLOGY.

Animism (*Nature-worship*).—If the truth of the foregoing principles be admitted, we need not be surprised that some peoples have looked no higher than Fetishism; for, as we have shown, simply by personification and belief in the supernatural objects and object-souls might be appreciated as beings who could harm or comfort, and who therefore should be propitiated or worshipped. By the natural process of generalization others deified the Nature-powers, worshipping in their blind way "a Heaven-Father," who, far above the visible sky, ruled and blessed his immortal attendants; while in some lands, as in China, they believed that nearer to human needs was a "terrestrial spirit," who royally ordained and controlled, but who tenderly bestowed the gifts of the days and of the seasons. In other nations the sun, correlating light, warmth, life, and growth, seemed a deity whose coming brought dawn and summer glory, but whose going was the signal for darkness and the winter. So, marshalling in splendid retinue planets and stars, we find a dazzling sun and astral-worship centring around the Chaldæan Baal or the Egyptian Osiris.

Animism presents greatly differing phases. The antagonisms of light and darkness, of growth and decay, suggested two distinct orders of worship—one of the *productive powers* of Nature, the other of its *destructive powers*. In this dual worship Pressensé finds a solution to the mythological paradox—the coexistence in the same cultus of rites extremely sensual and others revoltingly cruel. His solution may be thus briefly stated: Man imitates what he worships; his conceptions of the Deity determine his moral status. Now, when he yields to his corrupt nature, his once comparatively pure conceptions become degraded, and he sinks with his gods into sensualism. If he give way to his cruel passions, his deities become terrible monsters, that are pleased only with human torture and propitiated only with human blood.

Dualism.—The antagonisms of Nature, transferred to moral battle-fields, soon typified the conflict between right and wrong, good and evil; and this belief grew grand in Zoroastrianism. There, in the spotless glory of his exalted purity and power, shone Ahura-Mazda, the central figure of the bright constellation of his "good counsellors," and they were to have certain victory over all evil beings, led though these were by the mighty Ahriman.

The Soul's Immortality.—In Egypt the sublime truth of the soul's immortality was believed, and there men were taught that according as the soul is gross or pure its immortality would be one of gloom and of pain, or it would outshine Osiris's coming in splendor and rejoicing.

Any form of man's religious life should be of interest to man; and as with tenderness and with reverence we follow its outlines there will unfold much that might fascinate even the most superficial student, and more that will awe the most profound scholar. Therefore, as our researches grow deeper and subtler, and our spirit more sympathetic and enlightened by reason of that law of interdependence by which "all things sympathize with all," we shall find that every mythic creation has its symbol or archetype in Nature and its corresponding interest in human life; then shall we recognize in the Genius of Mythology a radiant form whose feet, indeed, press the very earth we tread, and whose heart is touched with every issue of this earthly life; but a spirit whose look is heavenward, and whose words shall have the savor of earthliness or of heavenliness according as they are born of the intoxication of earth-vapors or of the inspiration given by a "live coal" from the altar of divine truth.

GREECE IN COMPARATIVE MYTHOLOGY.

Before directing specific attention to Grecian Mythology we should ascertain its place in the study of Comparative Mythology; and here, again, we appeal to the universal Text-Book. When in prophetic vision God revealed Himself as "Governor among the nations," He said that in the line of Shem should be preserved His "name" and His "truth" until the coming of the Messiah. The Japhetic nations were to be "enlarged" by making the intellectual conquest of the world; then, returning with their world-harvests, they were to present them as offerings to God in the sacred tents of Shem. Even to the children of Canaan in their servitude (self-imposed because of evil-doing) there came a promise that in the very service of their brethren they should learn that truth which frees and ennobles.

Upon this great prophecy were based those wonderful genealogical tables that outlined not only the ground-forms of history, but also of philology and of mythology (Gen. x.). Hence, as to race, language, and belief, we may, in a general sense, regard a nation as SEMITIC, JAPHETIC (Aryan), or HAMITIC, though the latter term is generally merged in the more comprehensive one—the TURANIAN.

Leaving, on the one hand, the Turanian mythologies

with their earth-bound animisms, and on the other the Semitic with their special endowment of monotheistic tendencies, we give our attention to the mythologies of Aryan peoples. Even here we linger not in Persia nor in India, but we hasten to Greece, that land so glorious in creations that waken wonder until wonder almost merges into worship—Greece, grand in history, peerless in its art, its literature, and its mythology.

GRECIAN MYTHOLOGY.

Greece led the Aryan nations in the intellectual conquest of the world; but though she thought and wrought as has no other nation, it must needs have been under conditions and in accordance with general principles and laws. Then, if we would study the mythology simply of this one people, again would we find that our knowledge must be deep, wide, and progressive. We cannot have deep understanding of this great subject without careful analysis of its elements; and here, as in every mythic system, so many of its creations have a close association with Nature that it will be well to know much of the physical features of Greece—its mountains, valleys, and plains, its rivers, shores, and seas—for everywhere ministered a gentle nymph or ruled a mighty deity. The Greek national mind, acting upon these physical facts as does the individual mind, conceived new ideas that became beings. These were grouped and systematized until over every department of human life and action was installed a power that chastised or blessed the worshipper.

In our study of this great theme we should search for and expect to find development: we shall see on the part of the Greeks not only a recognition of the grand cosmological law—

> "From the indefinite comes the definite,
> From obscurity comes brightness"—

but an increasingly clear perception of mental and moral relations and duties. So that Uranus, the majestic central figure of the celestial firmament, together with all his retinue of sun and moon and stars, grew to be only a kind of brilliant symbolism of the higher glory that shone in the power, wisdom, and fatherhood of Zeus. In time, the "deities of *light*" conquered the "pythons" of *evil* as well as of darkness, and the hope of the soul's immortality, that had been solemnly whispered in Egypt, became at Eleusis a pæan of joy.

In following the growth of ideals we shall not be just and true if we rest satisfied with any that are below the highest conception to which the Hellenic thought attained. Now, when we study these ideals it will be necessary to discriminate between the beliefs that filled the heart and shaped the life of the people, and the exceptional visions of gifted ones who, like Homer, seemed to create the glory that they saw and sung.

Having thus in mind the ideals of the early times, whether they came through poets' visions or through the natural growth of mind, we shall be prepared rightly to estimate the inheritance of rich materials into which the later poets entered, and which they so grandly used.

Would we have wide knowledge of our subject we must be earnest students of the history of Greece. On the one hand, we must have in remembrance the ancient Pelasgic population, whose worship was scarcely more than a recognition of the gifts of Nature; from Zeus, on the other hand, we should note the magnificent creations and movements of the Hellenic mind and life. We must watch the great internal changes of Greece, particularly the Amphictyonic unions that became religious centres from which radiated wider and wider cycles of power; also the union of the people of different states in their religious festivals, and the subsequent union and extension of these festivals until they became pan-Hellenic and kings were competitors for their honors. Careful investigation will be necessary in following the changes that resulted from immigrations, bringing as they did new deities and worshippers, which often modified if they did not supplant the Hellenic. The momentous consequences of war enter into our study, for not alone from invading foes, but in distant fields where she gathered the laurels of conquest, Greece heard the names of unknown deities and felt the spell of strange "mysteries."

Causes other than war wrought important changes in Grecian Mythology—even those great tides of Oriental religions that overflowed Greece until her temple symbolism received new significance; and when Greece would stand forth as a pythoness, upon her bosom lay the Egyptian lotus and her robes were heavy with the poppy-dews of dreamy Ind and the perfumes of voluptuous Phœnicia, so that their odors intoxicated her and changed her utterances, even when the sacred foam was upon her lips. Then, if even Greece could not gather her magnificent robes about her and stand apart from her sister nations, surely we, who would be students of her mythology, must be earnest students of her history.

In addition to the elements, formations, and changes that we have been considering, it is essential that we have a thorough comprehension of the art-expression of Mythology — from the early years when artists wrought with still unskilled hands, but with such love and reverence that their works, like those of Dædalus, "though they were crude and inelegant to the view, had something of divine influence in them," through the grand periods when ideals grew sublime and interpreters more noble, until, through marvellous rivalry of architecture and sculpture, the earth wore in her crown the jewel of Parthenon perfection.

We ought to have also a wide knowledge of the language of Greece, for its words hold and reveal the mythic thoughts as does amber the imprisoned insect-forms that once had life and significance.

Progressive knowledge of our theme can be attained only in exchange for unceasing effort, not only in the varied departments already indicated, but in those inexhaustible mines that modern research is opening, as at Dodona, Olympia, Athens, and Mycenæ. Not alone around the temples that arose in her own soil clustered deep religious interests, but in the isles and on the shores of the Mediterranean, in Asia Minor, and wherever lay the highway along which Greece moved as she bestowed, through conquest or through colonization, the gifts of her culture and religion.

If we enter these sacred places, how few will be prepared to fully interpret the weird and solemn lessons there unfolded! Temples whose statues of deities are like yet unlike those of Greece; coins bearing familiar symbols, but unfamiliar names, or familiar names, but unknown symbols; sacred vessels for libations or for sacrifices of blood; votive offerings made in propitiation or in thanksgiving,—all these tell the story of human life in its highest phase—worship. All are touching expressions of that mingled sense of guilt and hope of pardon that fills the universal heart of man, and through which sacrifices and votive offerings became universal.

Would we know the name and nature of the deities with which those of the Hellenic system became identified, we must have knowledge of Comparative Philology and of Comparative Mythology, and only the rarest scholarship will enable us to understand the mingled worships of Greece and other nations.

Hitherto we have considered the mythologic system of Greece as a product of human thought, or at best as modified by the indirect revelations that are universally made to man's moral nature; but now a deeply-interesting question presents itself: To what extent was it modified by direct revelations? Though the answer to this question must be based upon *inferences*, it is not difficult to form a line of those that are so well grounded that they have much of the force of facts.

We can, however, reach no just conclusion without taking into consideration certain national characteristics of the Greeks. First, an apparent antagonism, which developed on the one hand a tenacious devotion to early deities, but on the other an intense eagerness to worship new ones; second, a remarkable aptitude for refining and spiritualizing all forms of thought and life. Now, if in addition to these we remember that this people, so fitted to gather the best elements of new forms of belief, side by side with the venturesome Phœnicians entered the highways of the leading nations of the earth, it is but a natural conclusion that if a knowledge of those marvellous events that form much of Old-Testament history had become at all general, such knowledge must have come within the scope of Grecian thought. Hence the opening question gives place to a broader underlying one: How much of Bible truth existed, either in reliable tradition or in records, in those countries to which the

Greeks had access at the time of the formation of their mythology?

The great subject suggested by this second question can be adequately estimated only in the light of that comprehensive prophecy to which reference has already been made; and in view of God's declaration that races in the line of Shem should preserve His name until the coming of the Messiah, we might expect to find either in the nature or in the circumstances of those races some special adaptation which would ensure the fulfilment of that declaration, and thus preserve centres of religious truth.

The assumption that there was such special adaptation in the moral nature of Semitic peoples has strong confirmation in the testimony of M. Ernest Renan, who, after most careful investigation of the subject, asserts that those peoples always possessed in an unusual degree a tendency to a belief in monotheism; and though the correctness of this statement is doubted by no less a scholar than Max Müller, it is confirmed by so many competent and impartial investigators that we feel justified in grounding thereon an inference that the aptitude in Semitic races to a belief in one eternal, omnipotent God was a miraculous provision for the fulfilment of the "sure word of prophecy."

The nature, degree, and order of the development of this endowment cannot be determined. Possibly it was at times latent while the people possessing it were but spectators of peculiar manifestations of the presence and power of God in His dealings with other races. Be that as it may, however, the unfolding of God's purposes was always in the line indicated by His word.

How far the idea of the God whose name was in Shem became obscured, or how rapidly the terrible deluge of Baal and Astarte-worship devastated the moral world, we cannot know; but this we *do* know—that from the hour in which the abating waters of the Deluge were illumined by the fire of the altar erected to Jehovah, down to the time of the founding of the Jewish nation, the name and worship of Jehovah had been preserved, for the princely Abraham paid tithes in tribute to one who was "king of righteousness and priest of the most high God."

Follow the history of the "chosen people," and we cannot doubt that through the priest-nation other nations heard and recognized the oracles of Jehovah, whether they pronounced the doom of His malignant enemies, or decreed the punishment of Israel's rebellions, or promised untold blessings upon obedience, and when even Nature was commanded to pour destructive hail upon the enemies of God's people, but to prevent the fading of the sun and the waning of the moon if his people needed their light. When Phœnicia's idol fell prostrate in the presence of that ark upon which rested the Shekinah, when the mighty hosts of Assyria "melted like snow in the glance of the Lord," in other lands than in awestruck Egypt was whispered, "It is the finger of Jehovah," the God of the Hebrews.

Another line of inferences may be based upon preserved records. Centuries ago, Chaldæan power and so much as it had of literary zeal· passed from it to Assyria, and in the latter country were gathered vast libraries, not of parchments, but of tablets formed of nearly imperishable clay; and though in time even many of these yielded to the destructive power of earthquake or of fire, enough remains to establish these momentous facts: First, that the inscriptions on many of these tablets were exact copies of similar tablets that had long before existed in Chaldæa, the cradle of the post-diluvian humanity; second, that the original tablets contained accounts of the fall of man, of the Noachian Deluge, and of kindred Old-Testament revelations.

Now, Chaldæan and Assyrian influences so permeated Asia Minor that it is scarcely credible that the traditions, a portion of which formed the subject-matter of the tablets, should not have entered into her religious thought; hence it seems but a natural conclusion that Phrygia, the earliest known home of the primitive Hellenic tribes, was to some extent enlightened by direct revelation. From the Phrygian centre Hellenic tribes passed to either side of the Ægean Sea: "One division peopled the west coast of Asia Minor; the other passed through Thrace into Epirus, and established at Dodona the oldest religion in Greece. Was not this Pelasgic worship of one nameless, omnipotent Deity (afterward called Zeus) a reflection—faint, perhaps, but still a true reflection—of the worship of that God whose awful name no Israelite might mention, but who was adored by them as Jehovah, and was called by surrounding nations 'the God of the Hebrews'?" We know that in time this worship assumed different phases, for from this Epirotic branch of Pelasgians sprang those Dorian tribes that gained such power through the magnificent system of Apollo-worship; but the oracle at Delphi sometimes consulted the oracle of Zeus at Dodona, thus acknowledging its supremacy in sacredness if not in power. Further, in many localities the separate attributes of Zeus received honors as separate deities; but, however rapid the spread of Grecian polytheism, Pelasgic peoples worshipped in "open places" and on mountain-tops Do-

INTRODUCTION. 25

donæan Zeus; therefore, may we not justly conclude that from the time when the sacred oak of Dodona was believed to become oracular through the presence of a great and only god, to the hour when the inspired apostle stood on Mar's Hill, the "unknown God" whom they had ignorantly worshipped was Jehovah, the God of the Hebrews?

> "And still the Athenian altar's glimmering doubt
> On all religions—evermore the same;
> What tears shall wash its sad inscription out?
> What hand shall write thereon His other name?
>
> "His other name? Is it not Love? Be still,
> O piteous lips, or fall and kiss the sod.
> The heavens are His: He writeth what He will—
> Stammering, far off, we spell, ' To the Unknown God.' "

If we ask why Greece sits apart, uncrowned and unhonored by the very nations which wear the priceless jewels that she gave them in her literature and her art, must we not answer, Because, refusing to consult the true oracles, " her wisdom became foolishness," her philosophy " was falsely so called," and her splendid system of mythology was but a tissue of " cunningly-devised fables "?

On entering these illimitable fields that invite our research, we should bring no theory that is dearer to us than truth, and no prejudices that would color or change what is presented for our apprehension. While we allow full value to " half truths," and even to fragments (for fragments may complete a truth that becomes central to a *system* of truth), we ought wisely to recognize their incompleteness, and to remember that in the theories which are continually forming and changing there are many liabilities of mistaking and misplacing materials, thus causing distortion where one would gladly make true presentation.

If in this spirit of fairness we investigate the infinitely varied phases of Mythology, we shall give due weight to the beauty and splendor of the phenomena of earth, sea, and sky, and to the mental creations that they occasioned; but we shall also give due weight to the suggestions, hopes, and beliefs of man's moral nature, whether awakened through indirect or through direct revelation.

SOURCES OF MATERIALS.

M. Pressensé : Early Religions before Christ.
K. O. Müller : Introduction to a Scientific System of Mythology.
" " Ancient Art and its Remains.
" " History and Antiquity of the Dorian Race.
" " Pallas Athene.
Preller : Griechische Mythologie.
Winckelmann : History of Ancient Art.
Lübke : History of Sculpture.
Montfaucon : L'Antiquité, expliquée et representée.
Grote : History of Greece.
Curtius : History of Greece.
Pausanias : Travels in Greece.
Rev. G. W. Cox : Mythology of Aryan Nations.
Gladstone : Juventus Mundi.
M. A. Dwight : Grecian and Roman Mythology.
Murray : Manual of Mythology.
C. Carapanos : Dodone et ses Ruines.
Thomas Taylor : Eleusinian and Bacchic Mysteries.
Pater : The Myth of Demeter.
Gen. di Cesnola : Cyprus ; its Cities, etc.
Athenæum : Researches in Olympia, etc.
Smith : Classical Dictionary.
Anthon : Classical Dictionary.

Tabular Arrangement

OF

Greek Mythology,

BASED UPON

Hesiod's Theogony.

"Classify and conquer."

HESIOD'S THEOGONY.

TABLE A.
COSMOLOGIC PERIOD.

1. CHAOS.   2. DIVINE PRINCIPLE.

3. *Primal Deities*, or *Nature-Powers*.

. Gæa (Earth).   5. Tartarus (Lower World).   6. Nyx (Night).
7. Erebus (Utter Darkness).   8. Eros (Love).

DESCENDANTS OF GÆA AS A NATURE-POWER.
9. Uranus or Cœlus (the Heavens).   10. Oure (Mountains).
11. Pontus (Salt, unproductive Sea).

12. FIRST EPOCH OF THEOGONY.
Eros harmonizes all things in pairs.

13. Marriage of Gæa (4) and Uranus (9).
14. Description of Gæa.   15. Description of Uranus.

DESCENDANTS OF GÆA AND URANUS.
16. Hecatoncheires.
    Briareus, Cottus, Gyges.
17. Cyclopes.
    Arges, Brontes, Steropes.

TABLE A—*continued*.

18. TITANIC GROUPS:

    1st. { 19. Cronus (Time, or Regulator).
            20. Rhea (Succession) ....TABLE B.

    2d. { 21. Oceanus (Source of Fresh Waters).
            22. Tethys (Nourisher).............TABLE C.

    3d. { 23. Cœus (Begetter).
            24. Phœbe (Shining)..............TABLE D.

    4th. { 25. Hyperion (Superiority, or passing over).
            26. Thia (Order)..................TABLE E.

    5th. { 27. Crius (Ruler).
            28. Mnemosyne (Memory) ....TABLE F.

    6th. { 29. Iapetus (Intention).
            30. Themis (Justice)...............TABLE G.

31. REBELLION OF THE CHILDREN OF URANUS.

    DESCENDANTS OF URANUS......TABLE H.

    32. Gigantes (Serpent-legged Giants).

    33. Meliæ (Melian Nymphs).

    34. Erinyes (Furies).

    35. Aphrodite (Venus Urania).

36. MARRIAGE OF THE TITANS AND THEIR SISTERS.

TABLE B.
GROUPS IN THE LINE OF GÆA AND URANUS.

DEVELOPMENT OF FIRST TITANIC GROUP, CRONUS AND RHEA (TABLE A, 19, 20).

1. DESCRIPTION OF CRONUS.   2. DESCRIPTION OF RHEA.
   LEGENDS OF CRONUS AND RHEA.
. Birth of Zeus and other Cronids. 4. Titanic War and overthrow of Cronus. 5. Partition of the universe by Zeus and the other Cronids.

6. SECOND EPOCH OF THEOGONY.
DESCRIPTION OF THE CRONIDS.
. Zeus. 8. Hera. 9. Hades, or Aides. 10. Demeter. 11. Poseidon.
12. Hestia.
DESCENDANTS OF THE CRONIDS.
DESCENDANTS OF ZEUS.
Zeus and Goddesses.

Zeus's Brain (see METIS). 13. Pallas Athena.
Zeus and Demeter. 14. Persephone.
Zeus and Hera. 15. Ares. 16. Ilithyia. 17. Hebe.
Zeus and Leto. 18. Phœbus Apollo. 19. Artemis.
Zeus and Maia. 20. Hermes.
Zeus and Themis. 21. Mœræ (Fates). 22. Horæ (Seasons).
Zeus and Mnemosyne. 23. Musæ (the Muses).
Zeus and Eurynome. 24. Charites (Graces).
Zeus and Thetis. 25. Nymphæ (Nymphs).
Zeus and Selene. 26. Ersa. 26. Nemea. 26. Pandia.
Zeus and Electra. 27. Dardanus.
Zeus and Antiope. 28. Amphion. 28. Zethus.
Zeus and Protogeneia. 28a. Æthlius.

Zeus and Nymphs.

Zeus and Niobe. 29. Argus. 29. Pelasgus.
Zeus and Ægina. 30. Æacus.
Zeus and Pluto. 31. Tantalus.
Zeus and Callisto. 32. Arcas.
Zeus and Calyce. 33. Endymion.
Zeus and Dia. 34. Pirithous.
Zeus and Taygete. 35. Lacedæmon.

Zeus and Human Mothers.

Zeus and Semele. 36. Dionysus.
Zeus and Alcmene. 37. Heracles.
Zeus and Io. 38. Epaphus.
Zeus and Europa. 39. Minos. 39. Rhadamanthus. 39. Sarpedon.
Zeus and Danaë. 40. Perseus.
Zeus and Leda. 41. Pollux. 41. Helen.
Zeus and Laodamia. 42. Sarpedon.

DESCENDANTS OF HERA.

43. Hephæstus. Hephæstus and Gæa. 44. Erichthonius.

DESCENDANTS OF POSEIDON.

Poseidon and Gæa. 45. Antæus.
Poseidon and Amphitrite. 46. Triton. 46. Rhode. 46. Benthesicyme.
Poseidon and Hippea. 47. Polyphemus.
Poseidon and Thoosa. 48. Polyphemus.
Poseidon and Amymone. 49. Nauplius.
Poseidon and Tyro. 50. Neleus. 50. Pelias.
Poseidon and Chione. 51. Eumolpus.
Poseidon and Peribœa. 52. Nausithous.
Poseidon and Celæno. 53. Lycus.
Poseidon and Alcyone. 54. Hyrieus.
Poseidon and ———. 55. Taras.
Poseidon and Euryte. 56. Halirrhothius.
Poseidon and Libya. 57. Agenor (see CADMUS, PHŒNIX, CILIX, a EUROPA). 58. Belus (see DANAUS, ÆGYPTUS, and LELEX).
Poseidon and Canace. 59. Aloeus.
Poseidon and Iphimedia. 60. Otus and Ephialtes.
Poseidon and Bithynis. 61. Amycus.
Poseidon and Lysiannassa. 62. Busiris.
Poseidon and ———. 63. Cycnus.
Poseidon and Pitane. 64. Evadne.
Poseidon and Euycyde. 65. Eleus.

TABLE C.

GROUPS IN THE LINE OF GÆA AND URANUS.

DEVELOPMENT OF SECOND TITANIC GROUP—OCEANUS AND TETHYS (TABLE A, 21 and 22).

1. DESCRIPTION OF OCEANUS.   2. DESCRIPTION OF TETHYS.

River Gods.
3. Achelous.
4. Alpheus.
5. Ardescus.
6. Æsopus.
7. Eridanus.
8. Evenus.
9. Granicus.
10. Hermus.
11. Haliacmon.
12. Heptoporus.
13. Isdrus.
13a. Inachus.
14. Caicus.
15. Ladon.
16. Mæander.
17. Nilus.
18. Nessus.
19. Parthenius.
20. Phasis.
21. Peneus.
22. Rhesus.
23. Rhodius.

24. Sangarius.
25. Scamander.
26. Simois.
27. Strymon.

River Goddesses.
28. Admete.
29. Acaste.
30. Amphiro.
31. Asia.
32. Chryseis.
33. Dione.
34. Doris.
35. Electra.
36. Eudora.
37. Eurynome.
38. Galaxaure.
39. Hippo.
40. Ianthe.
41. Idyia.
42. Ianira.
43. Calypso.
44. Cerceis.

45. Callirrhoë.
46. Clymene.
47. Clytie.
48. Metis.
49. Melobosis.
50. Menestho.
51. Ocyroë.
52. Pasithoë.
53. Plexaure.
54. Polydora.
55. Pluto.
56. Perseïs.
57. Petroie.
58. Rhodia.
59. Styx.
60. Thoë.
61. Tyche.
62. Telestho.
63. Urania.
64. Xantho.
65. Xeuxo.

TABLE D.

DEVELOPMENT OF THIRD TITANIC GROUP, CŒUS AND PHŒBE (TABLE A, 23, 24).

1. DESCRIPTION OF CŒUS.　　2. DESCRIPTION OF PHŒBE.

DESCENDANTS OF CŒUS AND PHŒBE.

3. Leto. See DESCENDANTS OF ZEUS (TABLE B, 18, 19).
4. Asteria (Starry Night). See PERSES (TABLE F, 9).

TABLE E.

DEVELOPMENT OF FOURTH TITANIC GROUP, HYPERION AND THIA (TABLE A, 25, 26).

1. DESCRIPTION OF HYPERION.　　2. DESCRIPTION OF THIA.

DESCENDANTS OF HYPERION AND THIA.

3. Helios (Sun).

   Helios and Perseis.

   　　4. Circe.　5. Æetes.　6. Pasiphaë.　7. Perses.

   Helios and Clymene.

   　　8. Phaëthon.

   　　9. Heliades (Lampetia, Phaëthusa, and Phœbe, or Ægle).

10. Selene (Moon).

    See DESCENDANTS OF ZEUS (TABLE B, 26).

11. Eos (Aurora).

    Eos and Tithonus.

    　　12. Emathion.　13. Memnon.

    Eos and Astræus.

    　　See FIFTH TITANIC GROUP (TABLE F, 3).

TABLE F.

DEVELOPMENT OF FIFTH TITANIC GROUP, CRIUS AND MNEMOSYNE (Table A, 27, 28).

1. Description of Crius.   2. Description of Mnemosyne.

   DESCENDANTS OF MNEMOSYNE (Table B, 23).
   DESCENDANTS OF CRIUS AND EURYBIA.

3. Astræus.
   Astræus and Eos.
       4. Astra (the Stars).   5. Astræa (Constellation Virgo).
       6. Hesperus (Evening Star).   7. Heosphorus (Morning Star).
       8. Anemoi (the Winds).

9. Perses.
   Perses and Asteria.
       10. Hecate.

1. Pallas.
   Pallas and Styx.
       12. Bia (strength), Cratos (power), Zelus (zeal), Nike (victory).

TABLE G.

DEVELOPMENT OF SIXTH TITANIC GROUP, IAPETUS AND THEMIS (Table A, 29, 30).

1. Description of Iapetus.   2. Description of Themis.

DESCENDANTS OF THEMIS (Table B, 21, 22).
DESCENDANTS OF IAPETUS AND CLYMENE.

3. Menœtius.
4. Atlas, or Hyas.
  Atlas and Pleione.
   5. Hyas.   6. Hyades.   7. Pleiades.   8. Hesperides.

9. Prometheus.
  Prometheus and Clymene.
   10. Deucalion.

11. Epimetheus.
  Epimetheus and Pandora.
   12. Pyrrha.

TABLE H.

GROUPS IN THE LINE OF URANUS.

See REBELLION OF THE CHILDREN OF URANUS (TABLE A, 31).

1. Gigantes (Serpent-legged giants):
    Alcyoneus, Enceladus, Porphyrion, Cromedon, Rhœtus.

2. Meliæ (Melian Nymphs, or nymphs of the ash trees).

3. Erinyes (the Furies, or avengers of violated law).
    Alecto, Megæra, Tisiphone.

4. Aphrodite, or Venus Urania.

TABLE I.

GROUPS IN THE LINE OF GÆA AND PONTUS (TABLE A, 4, 11).

DESCRIPTION OF GÆA.   DESCRIPTION OF PONTUS.

1. DESCENDANTS OF GÆA AND PONTUS.
2. Nereus.

DESCENDANTS OF NEREUS AND DORIS, OR NEREIDES.

3. Agave.	20. Galene.	37. Nesaie.
4. Actæa.	21. Glauce.	38. Panope.
5. Amphitrite.	22. Glauconome.	39. Pasithea.
6. Autonoë.	23. Halimede.	40. Pherousa.
7. Doris.	24. Hipponoë.	41. Pontoporeia.
8. Doto.	25. Hippothoë.	42. Polynome.
9. Dunamene.	26. Cymatolege.	43. Pronoë.
10. Ione.	27. Cymo.	44. Proto, 1.
11. Erato.	28. Cymodoce.	45. Proto, 2.
12. Eudora.	29. Cymothoë.	46. Protomedia.
13. Eucrate.	30. Laomedia.	47. Psamathe.
14. Eulimene.	31. Liagore.	48. Sao.
15. Eunice.	32. Lysianassa.	49. Spio.
16. Eupompe.	33. Melite.	50. Thalia.
17. Evagore.	34. Menippe.	51. Themisto.
18. Evarne.	35. Nemertes.	52. Thetis.
19. Galatæa.	36. Neso.	

HESIOD'S THEOGONY. 41

TABLE I—*continued.*

53. Eurybia.

54. Ceto.

55. Thaumas.
    Thaumas and Electra.
        56. Iris.   57. Harpyiæ (Aëllo, Ocypete).

58. Phorcys.
    Phorcys and Hecate.   59. Scylla.
    Phorcys and Sterope.   60. Sirenes.
    Phorcys and Ceto.
        61. Dragon-Guard of Hesperides.
        62. Grææ (Ceto, Enyo, Pephredo).
        63. Gorgones (Medusa, Euryale, Stheno).
            From Medusa: 64. Chrysaor. 65. Pegasus.
            From Chrysaor: 66. Geryon. 67. Echidna.
            From Echidna and Typhaon (see TABLE J).

TABLE J.

GROUPS IN THE LINE OF GÆA AND TARTARUS (TABLE A, 4, 5).

1. Typhœus.
    Typhœus and Hurricane.
        2. Typhaon.   3. Pernicious Winds.
        Typhaon and Echidna.
            4. Cerberus.   5. Hydra.
            6. Orthrus.   7. Chimæra.
        From Chimæra:
            8. Nemean Lion. 9. Sphinx.

TABLE K.
GROUPS IN THE LINE OF NYX AND EREBUS (TABLE A, 6 and 7).

1. DESCRIPTION OF NYX. 2. DESCRIPTION OF EREBUS.

DESCENDANTS OF NYX AND EREBUS.
3. Æther (the sky). 4. Hemera (the day).

GROUPS IN THE LINE OF NYX (TABLE A, 6).
DEITIES OF DESTINY AND RETRIBUTION.
5. Moros (universal, all-controlling destiny). 5. Ker (Fate).
6. Mœræ (the Fates): Clotho, Lachesis, Atropos (see TABLE B, 21).
6. Keres (Fates).
7. Nemesis (conscience).
8. Thanatos (Death).

DEITIES HAVING GENERAL OFFICES.
9. Hypnos (Sleep). 9. Morpheus and Oneiros (dreams). 10. Hesperides (TABLE G, 8). 11. Momus (critic). 12. Apate (deceit). 12. Geras (old age). 12. Oizys (corroding care). 13. Eris (strife).

DESCENDANTS OF ERIS.
Algea (pains), Amphilogeai (disputes), Androktasiai (slaughters), Ate (woe), Dysnomie (lawlessness), Hysminai (battles), Lethe (oblivion), Limos (famine), Logos (fable), Machai (battles), Neikea (quarrels), Ponos (toil), Philotes (desire), Phonoi (murders).

DESCENDANT OF EREBUS.
14. Charon.

KEY TO PRONUNCIATION

OF

GREEK MYTHOLOGIC NAMES IN MOST GENERAL USE.

Greek standard, *The Continental Method;* English standard, *Worcester's Unabridged Dictionary.*

Pronunciation is marked only on such names as are introduced in the tables. Letters unmarked are pronounced as in English.

VOWELS.

A.
ā = *āle*.
ă = *ăt*.
ä = *ärm*.
â = *âll*.

E.
ē = *ēel*.
ĕ = *ĕnd*.
ë = *hër*.
ȩ = *ā*, as in *āle*.

I.
ī = *īce*.
ĭ = *ĭn*.
ï = *ë*, as in *hër*.
î = *ē*, as in *ēel*.

O.
ō = *ōld*.
ŏ = *ŏn*.
ö = *â*, as in *âll*.
ô = *dô*.

U.
ū = *oo*.
û = *pût*.

Y.
ȳ = ī, as in *īce*.
y̆ = ĭ, as in *ĭn*.
ÿ = ë, as in *hër*.
ŷ = ē, as in *ēel*.

DIPHTHONGS.

ai = *ī*, as in *īce*.
au = *ou*, as in *out*.
ei = *ī*, as in *īce*.
eu = *eu*, as in *neuter*.

oi = *oi*, as in *oil*.
ou = *oo*, as in *ooze*.
ui = *we*.
œ = *oi*.

CONSONANTS.

c = *k*.
ch = *k*.

g = *g*, as in *go*.
x at beginning of words = z.

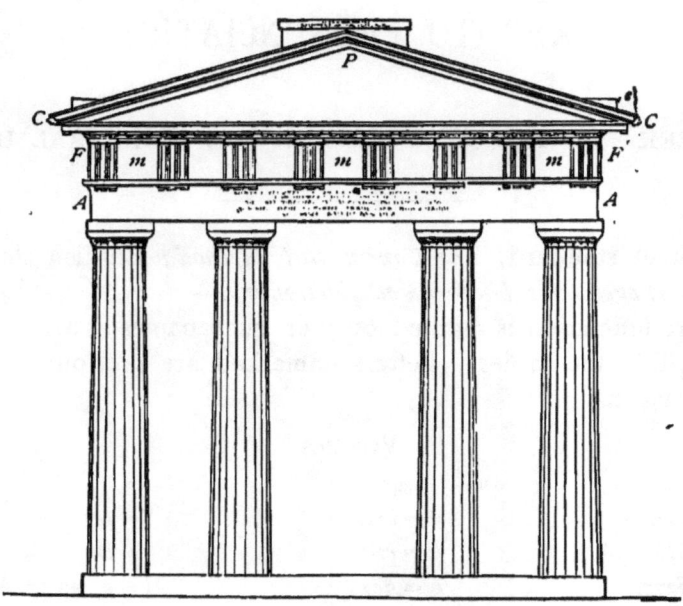

DORIC PORTICO.

ENTABLATURE:
  Architrave (marked *A*, *A*), lower band.
  Frieze (marked *F*, *F*), middle band.
  Square spaces (marked *m*, *m*, etc.), metopes.
  Cornice (marked *C*, *C*), upper band.

PEDIMENT (marked *P*), is the triangular space enclosed by the cornice and roof.

CELLA. The cella (not shown here) is the *body* of the temple. We should distinguish between the frieze of the cella and that of the entablature.

PROGRAMME FOR THE STUDY OF MYTHOLOGIC CHARACTERS.

Central Ideas.—1, Grecian; 2, Foreign.
Offices and Archetypes.—1, Nature; 2, Human Life; 3, Theogony.
Early Legends.—1, Birth; 2, Education, etc.
Abode and Attendants.
Associated Myths.—1, Grecian; 2, Foreign.
Emblems.—1, Nature; 2, Human Life; 3, Theogony.
Representations.—1, Early; 2, Later; 3, Foreign.
Worship.—Location. Oracles and Legends. Temples—1, Sacred Objects; 2, Associated Deities. Priesthood—1, Offices; 2, Attendants. Ceremonies—1, Athletic; 2, Literary and Musical; 3, Religious.
Grecian Comparative Mythology.
Foreign Comparative Mythology and Bible References.
Literature.—1, History; 2, Poetry.
Art.—1, Coins; 2, Ceramics; 3, Statuary; 4, Painting.
Modern Research.—1, Grecian; 2, Foreign.
Survivals.—1, Festivals; 2, Customs; 3, Superstitions, etc.
Descendants.—1, Mythology; 2, History.

ABBREVIATIONS.

Arch., Archetype.
Assoc. Myths, Associated Myths.
Theog., Theogony.
Grecian Comp. Myth., Grecian Comparative Mythology.
Foreign Comp. Myth., Foreign Comparative Mythology.

GREEK MYTHOLOGY.

HESIOD considered that the "great Nature-powers" were primal, and that they sprang from *Chaos* and *Divine Principle*.

CHAOS.
(TABLE A, 1.)

This seems to be a general term for the vague ideas that arise in the mind concerning the beginning of the material universe.

In the early ages the speculations in regard to chaos must have greatly varied. To some it signified merely empty space; to others, darkness or confusion; others thought of it as formless matter that might have always existed; probably to the mass of minds it suggested formless matter, but as containing the germs of all things, thus furnishing the condition of all life, either through its own inherent power or as a passive agent to some power external to itself.

DIVINE PRINCIPLE.
(TABLE A, 2.)

Man's spiritual endowments must have suggested to some, probably to many, minds the "idea of the divine;" perhaps in its feeblest workings it was only a faint apprehension of creative energy. We can never know how gradually or how rapidly dawned and increased in the Greek mind that sublimest thought—"the God-idea."

PRIMAL DEITIES, OR NATURE-POWERS.
(TABLE A, 3.)

A fundamental law of cosmogony is, "from the undefined arises the definite; from darkness, comes brightness." In accordance with this law, by a conception unsettled as to origin, but definite as opposed to Chaos, there stood forth as the first Nature-powers *Gæa* (earth), *Tartarus* (lower world), *Nyx* (night), *Erebus* (utter darkness), *Eros* (love).

GÆA [*Gai'a*], (THE EARTH).
(TABLE A, 4.)

The earliest "earth-idea" was of a mass or disk of aggregated matter, as distinct from surrounding obscurity, and as furnishing a *place* for cosmologic processes. Later, it was thought of as a reservoir of vast *physical forces* and the condition of organisms and growth.

TARTARUS [*Tär'tärŏs*], (SUBTERRANEAN EARTH).
(TABLE A, 5.)

The subterranean portions of earth were distinguished as "Tartarus," and the first application of the term was to the lower invisible regions that held forces or beings that were antagonistic to the operations of the external world. Later, the term was restricted to a portion of that region, and was comprehended under the term "*Erebus*," which had acquired a general signification.

NYX (NIGHT).
(TABLE A, 6.)

Nyx had for its archetype the dark space that closely encompassed the more definitely-conceived earth.

EREBUS [Ĕr′ebŏs], (UTTER DARKNESS).
(TABLE A, 7.)

Distinguished from Nyx more by its greater obscurity than by location, Erebus was spoken of as encompassing the realm of night as a *great* mystery might comprehend a *less* one. We shall find that through the law that "from darkness comes brightness," Nyx, the lower darkness, gave the lower light, Hemera, the day, while Erebus glowed into the glorious ether. By later application of the term, Erebus included subterranean earth, and in this sense comprehended Tartarus as a place of imprisonment, also Nyx in its definite relation to the earth as alternating with day—*i. e.* the darkness that passes over the surface of the earth.

EROS [Ĕ′rŏs], (LOVE).
(TABLE A, 8.)

It is probable that the earliest idea of Eros was that of a mere world-making impulse, which through mysterious attractions combined all things in pairs. Preller thinks that this impulse was soon apprehended as taking more definite form and having more specific work in the organic kingdom; then, as masculine and feminine principles, rising to the higher realm of human relationship, it was recognized as the great world-power, Eros.

We can never know how long a time elapsed before this idea became general, but it is more than probable that in the high, pure regions of the best Grecian thought there floated visions—dim, perhaps, and seen by only a few—but visions of a coming time when the "all-subduing Eros" should reign in a world whence had been banished error, unloveliness, and evil, and where human hearts beat in perfect unison with the divine.

Second Idea of Eros.

It is not easy to mark the time or degrees of the transition from the somewhat cosmologic idea to a succeeding one which has been called the "Eros of the Philosophers and of the Mysteries"—more personal and more potent in the life of man than the one more faintly apprehended. He too was to be an "all-subduing Eros," whose dominion was to extend throughout the universe, and his mission was to infuse with love hearts human and divine; to harmonize all discords; to ensure victory to the True, the Beautiful and the Good, until they should dominate error, unloveliness, and evil, and sit enthroned for ever.

(The relations of Eros and the goddess of Love will be considered under the head of APHRODITE.)

DESCENDANTS OF GÆA AS NATURE-POWER.

By her own inherent power Gæa produced Uranus (the heavens), Oure (the mountains), and Pontus (the barren sea).

URANUS [*Ou'rănŏs*], OR CŒLUS (THE HEAVENS).
(TABLE A, 9.)

It was in accordance with the cosmological law above given that from the earth should arise that which finally became the synonym for brightness and glory—the heavens; and it is in accordance with the laws of man's spiritual development that the heaven-idea should expand into the sublime apprehension of the heavens as pervaded by an all-animating spirit of light, power, and life.

OURE [*Ou'rĕ*], (THE MOUNTAINS).
(TABLE A, 10.)

It is probable that by these are meant the great mountain-chains; perhaps they were thought of as mighty pillars supporting the arch of heaven. We know that in time their caves and streams became instinct with the mystic nymph-life.

PONTUS [*Pŏn'tŏs*], (SALT SEA).
(TABLE A, 11.)

In opposition to Oceanus, the source of all fresh, fertilizing waters, Pontus represents the mass of salt, bitter waters, that were fitted only for the abode of monsters.

FIRST EPOCH OF THEOGONY.
(Table A, 12.)

Through the divine influence of "all-subduing Eros" conflicting elements and antagonistic powers were harmonized, thus laying a foundation for the reign of order and for development.

GÆA.
MARRIAGE OF GÆA AND URANUS.
(Table A, 13.)

This signified a new activity of the great Nature-powers; also the proportioning of matter and force, which resulted in progressive movements. In our study of these movements we must constantly remember that in mythology relationships are personified; so union in operations would be called marriage.

GÆA AS EARTH-GODDESS.
(Table A, 14.)

Central Idea.

Gæa, as earth-goddess, was a personification of productive earth, whether through fertile soil or through moisture.

Offices and Archetypes.

Nature: Mother of all life. *Arch.*, primal productive power of Nature.

Human Life: 1. Producer of minerals for useful arts.
2. Nourisher of the life of the young.
3. Goddess of death, furnishing graves to all mankind.
4. Goddess of oaths and solemn compacts.

Theog.: 1. Furnishing a temporary abode for gods.
2. Mother of Titans.
3. Counsellor of the gods.
4. Prophesied the Titanic War.

Emblems.

Nature: A globe.

Representations.

On ancient monuments, as tending the young.

Worship.

Helice (Ægæ), a temple called "Gaius," dedicated to the "wide-bosomed Earth," and containing a very ancient wooden statue of Gæa.

Athens, a temple to Gæa as "nurse of youths."

Lacedæmonia, a temple called "Gæseptum."

Delphi, a shrine (there *had* been an oracle to Gæa).

Olympia.—In a part of "Altis" called "Gaius" was an altar to Gæa made from ashes.

Grecian Comp. Myth.

1. Dione of Dodona, whose elemental attributes were partially transferred to Hera.
2. Gæa was also called Titania (dust?).

Foreign Comp. Myth.

ROMAN, Gæa, or Tellus, or Terra; INDIA, Prithivi; SAMOTHRACE, Great Goddess.

URANUS.

URANUS AS HEAVEN-FATHER.

(TABLE A, 15.)

Central Idea.

The early idea of an all-pervading heaven-spirit gradually comprehended more and grander attributes, until worship was offered to a Heaven-Father as the source of life and blessings.

Offices and Archetypes.

Nature: To act as a personal divine cause of life and growth. *Arch.*, the earth-embracing heavens.

Human Life: The bestower of blessings on man.

Theog.: 1. To furnish a celestial home for gods
   Arch., ether, far above Mount Olympus.
2. Father of Titans.
3. Prophesied the punishment of his children.

Emblems.
Sun, moon, and stars.

Representation.
Clothed with a starred mantle; with uplifted hands pointing to the sun and the moon.

Grecian Comp. Myth.
Uranus may have been identical with Zeus of Dodona

Foreign Comp. Myth.
ROMAN, Cœlus; INDIA, Varuna; CHINA, Tien; FINNISH, Jumala; MONGOLIC, Tengri; SAMOTHRACE, Universal Mind.

DESCENDANTS OF GÆA AND URANUS.

Remembering that relationships are personified, we shall understand that effects were called "children." The varying, often conflicting, phenomena of the physical world, displayed in earth and sky, suggested powerful or formidable beings who wrought gigantic deeds. Of such nature were the Hecatoncheires (or Centimani) and Cyclopes (TABLE A, 16 and 17). As the apprehension of the order and economy of the universe widened there arose the grand cycle of the Titans (TABLE A, TITANIC GROUPS, 18).

HECATONCHEIRES [*Hĕkătŏnchei'rēs*], OR CENTIMANI.
(TABLE A, 16.)

The violent physical forces of the earth were personified as powerful giants, each having fifty heads and one hundred hands. They were Briareus (hurricane), Gyges (earthquake), and Cottus (volcano). These giants seldom appear in mythology, the chief prominence that is assigned to them being in connection with the Titanic War (see LEGENDS OF CRONUS AND RHEA).

A connection between these forces and the sea is implied in the legend that Briareus married Cymopoleia, a daughter of Poseidon. Briareus, whose Homeric name was Ægeon, seems to have personified the violent heaving of the sea.

CYCLOPES [*Kyklŏ'pĕs*].
(TABLE A, 17.)

Argis (stream of light), Brontes (thunder), Steropes (lightning).

Central Ideas.

From the signification of their names we might infer that the Cyclopes were originally the personified energies of the sky, but their relations greatly varied in different systems of mythology. Hesiod calls them beings having only one eye, in the centre of the forehead.

Early Legends.

At the time of the Titanic War they were thrown into Tartarus by Cronus, but they were liberated by Zeus; in return, they provided Zeus with thunderbolts and lightning, Hades with a helmet, and Poseidon with a trident.

Homer speaks of the Cyclopes as a race of lawless shepherds in Sicily who devoured human beings, and their chief was Polyphemus. A later tradition makes them assistants of Hephæstus, whose workshops were volcanoes. Mount Etna was specially assigned as their abode. As Vulcan's assistants they made metal armor and ornaments for gods and heroes. Ancient walls built of massive stone (probably by Pelasgians), were thought to be the work of the Cyclopes, and were called Cyclopean.

Assoc. Myths (see APOLLO).

TITANIC GROUPS.

(TABLE A, 18.)

K. O. Müller calls the Titans "individual expressions of universal life," and says that it would seem that two orders of beings were included under this head: First, powers that had been active on the earth, but were afterward confined to subterranean regions, and there, as dark and sullen beings, sought to destroy the then existing order of Nature; second, a race of personified mental powers and regulating principles, that perhaps typified the great economy of Nature, which depends on the co-operation of earth and heaven, and is shown in the sacred number of twelve (see TITANIC GROUPS, TABLE A, 18).

Much uncertainty exists in regard to the origin of the word *Titans*. Some derive it from Titaia, an ancient name for the earth. According to this theory, *all* descendants of Gæa and Uranus would be Titans, but the usual application of the word favors Müller's theory.

REBELLION OF THE CHILDREN OF URANUS.

(TABLE A, 31.)

In mythology the instability of any order of things is indicated by anticipated or accomplished rebellion. Uranus is represented as fearing that his powerful children might overthrow him, so he imprisoned the Hecatoncheires and Cyclopes in the earth. At the instigation of Gæa, the Titans, led by Cronus, revolted against their father Uranus.

Gæa produced iron and made a sickle, with which Cronus maimed his father. From the blood that fell upon the earth sprang—

THE DESCENDANTS OF URANUS.

Gigantes (serpent-legged giants, TABLE A, 32); Meliæ (Melian nymphs, TABLE A, 33); Erinyes (Furies, TABLE A, 34).

From what fell into the sea sprang Aphrodite (Venus Urania, TABLE A, 35). At a very early age there was a suggestion (we know not how general) that Aphrodite signified divine concord or universal harmony; and this thought had a grand complement in another—that Eros was her companion in the heavenly labor of blending into sweetness and beauty all harshness and all unloveliness.

MARRIAGE OF THE TITANS AND THEIR SISTERS.

(TABLE A, 36.)

We have found that marriage indicates *union of efforts;* then what a fine system of beliefs may have been comprehended under the marriage of the Titans and their sisters! "Cronus" meant not merely *time* or limited duration, but all interests that have time-relations.

Rhea was more than mere order of sequence or order of events, but signified events as caused and causing—events that form series of progressions. Now, *unite* them and we need not wonder that from such parentage descended a dynasty of the mightiest gods.

If we follow the shining category of the *offices* of the Titans, we shall find that Oceanus and Tethys supplied the nourishing moisture and waters; that Hyperion and Thia came in the splendor of *light-bearers;* and even that the deities of the night, Crius and Phœbe, brought forth " starry Night." It will not be difficult to believe that the noblest Greeks saw the universe as held in the blessed keeping of those beings (the Titans), too mighty to be their brothers, but too royally beneficent to be otherwise than kind. Now, if to this thought we add the apprehension of the united work of Eros and Venus Urania, it seems not impossible that there existed a belief that all human life was to be quickened by divine impulses which were to be manifested in the truly Beautiful and the beautifully True.

GROUPS IN THE LINE OF GÆA AND URANUS.

DEVELOPMENT OF FIRST TITANIC GROUP (TABLE B).

CRONUS [*Krŏ′nŏs*], (TIME).

(TABLE B, I.)

Central Ideas.

In time all things are brought forth; in time all things decay; hence the time-idea was dual, and the offices of Cronus were varied and antagonistic.

CRONUS.

HEAD OF CRONUS, OR SATURN.

Offices and Archetypes.

Nature: 1. To create and to mature all forms of life. *Arch.*, productive, ripening force of Nature.

    2. To destroy and to renew life. *Arch.*, decaying and reviving powers of life.

Human Life: 1. To mark seasons and years. *Arch.*, time in its relations to life.

    2. To bring hidden things to light. *Arch.*, unfolding of events and purposes.

    3. To assist heroes and to establish the Golden Age.

Theog.: 1. Father of the Titans (as ruling deities).

    2. To preside over heroes in Hades.

Emblems.

Nature: Sickle, god of harvests or decaying life; serpent, renewed life of the year.

Human Life: Serpent with its tail in its mouth, the year; scythe, god of death.

Theog.: A globe, encircled by a starry zodiac, ordainer of systematic celestial movements; a sickle, rebellion against Uranus.

Representations.
1. On monuments, bound with cords of wool. (There was a legend that Cronus was thus bound by Zeus, to prevent irregularity in the movements of the heavenly bodies.)
2. With wings (swiftness), feet of wool (noiselessness), leaning on a scythe.
3. Very aged, stooping forward, holding a scythe; near him a serpent with its tail in its mouth.
4. Leaning on a trunk of a tree, round which coils a serpent; near him a sickle.
5. Later, with an hour-glass and scythe.

Worship.
Locations.—Athens, Crete.
Temples.—Athens.
Festivals.—Cronia, to Cronus as god of harvests.

Foreign Comp. Myth.
ROMAN, Saturn, Cronus as god of harvests; INDIAN, Dyu or Dyaus; probably, PHŒNICIAN, Moloch, Cronus as the destroyer; EGYPTIAN, Seb.

Art.
Receiving a stone from Rhea (see LEGENDS OF CRONUS AND RHEA).

Bust with serene countenance, full beard, flowing locks, back of the head veiled (Vatican, Rome).

Survivals.
Carnivals in Rome are survivals of the Saturnalia, which were survivals of the Greek Cronia.

RHEA [*Rhei'a*], OR CYBELE.
(TABLE B, 2.)

The Greek idea of Rhea as earth-goddess was dual, but more in the sense of double than of antagonistic offices. The elemental attributes of Gæa were reproduced in Rhea, and to them was added a new series of attributes and offices, growing out of the mutual relations of earth-products, agriculture, growth of cities, commerce; in short, the general development of material wealth.

In Phrygia and in other countries the elemental or Nature-power idea was made prominent, and it furnished a foundation for the extreme worship referred to under the head of "Animism." (See INTRODUCTION.) Hence the Phrygian Cybele corresponded to Rhea as earth-goddess—*i. e.* "Goddess of Fertility."

Offices and Archetypes.

Nature: 1. All-animating mother. *Arch.*, reproductive power of Nature, often reproducing through destruction of old forms.
2. Ruler of the elements. *Arch.*, harmonious elemental conditions.

Human Life: 1. Giver of mineral wealth in useful arts. *Arch.*, progress through a bronze and iron age, etc.
2. Goddess of earth as peopled and covered with cities. *Arch.*, succession that brings progress.
3. Tamer of wild animals.

Theog.: Mother of Cronids, who ruled in the second dynasty.

Early Legends.

GRECIAN (see LEGENDS OF CRONUS AND RHEA).

RHEA, OR CYBELE.

Assoc. Myths (see LEGEND OF ATYS).

Emblems.
Nature: Sun and moon, as sources of Rhea's power.
Branches of trees, verdure.
Fruits and animals, fertility.
Lions and panthers, Rhea as goddess of uncultivated mountains and plains.
Rhea in a sitting position or with her foot on a stone, stability.
Rhea playing on a tympanon, goddess of the winds.

Human Life: A globe, earth as peopled.
Crown of oak-leaves, times when men fed on acorns.
Spade or pike, or lions with collars, Rhea as causing wild lands to be cultivated.
Antique key, goddess of mineral wealth.
Crown of portions of city-walls or of towers, Rhea as protectress of cities, or of earth as the nourisher of cities.
Serpent, goddess of healing.

Theog.: A sacred stone (Bætylus), the earliest symbol of deity.
A veil, divinity.
Pine tree (see ATYS).

Representations.
GRECIAN.—1. A stone (Bætylus), said to have fallen from heaven.
2. Standing, wearing a mural crown, right foot on a rock, the other on the prow of a ship.
3. Riding on a lion, holding a tympanon, near her the sun and moon.

4. Seated on a chair or throne, under her left arm a dulcimer and pike; with the right hand she presents to a lion the head of a ram; near her is a quiver.

PHRYGIAN.—1. Seated in a chariot, guiding lions or panthers in collars.

2. Square figure with many breasts; many animals on her garments; a lion on each arm. (See DIANA OF THE EPHESIANS.)

3. In company with Atys.

PANTHEISTIC.—A figure combining the attributes of various elemental goddesses.

Worship.

GRECIAN.—*Location.*—Attica, Arcadia.

Temples.—1. Athens (with Cronus).

2. Olympia (see MODERN RESEARCH).

3. Thebes (erected by Pindar to Rhea and Pan).

Priesthood.—Corybantes (see CORYBANTES AND CURETES).

Ceremonies.—Corybantes marched to the mountains; then, to music of fifes and kettle-drums, they rushed through the woods with frantic cries, searching for Atys; when he (an image of him) was found the priests grew frenzied with joy and cut themselves with knives.

PHRYGIAN, AS CYBELE.—*Location.*—Patras (with Atys).

Temple.—Pessinus.

Sacred Objects.—1. Stone image of Cybele; 2. Tomb of Atys.

Priesthood.—1. High priest (archegallus); 2. Priests (galli); 3. Dendrophore, priests who bore branches of trees.

Ceremonies. — *Sacrifices,* tauroboles (bulls), crioboles (rams), ægiboles (goats); baptism of blood (to renew life); offerings, fruits (especially the pineapple), placed on the flame of an altar.

Festivals.—In April the priests crowned a pine tree (see ATYS), and covered it with a veil of Cybele.

Grecian Comp. Myth.

1. Embodying attributes of Dione and Gæa.
2. Crete, "Idæan Mother."

Foreign Comp. Myth.

ROMAN, Rhea, or Ops; CHALDÆAN, Annit; SYRIAN, Universal Mother; EGYPTIAN, Isis (as Earth-Mother), or Mut (Mother of All), or Nutpe (as wife of Seb); ASIA MINOR, Diana of the Ephesians.

Literature.

History.—1. End of Second Punic War; Attalus (Pergamus) gave to the Romans the sacred stone of Pessinus (see WORSHIP): the day of its arrival in Rome (April 10) was ever after sacred.

2. Cities of Greece and Oriental cities were represented by Rhea.

Art.

Statue of Rhea seated on a throne (Vatican).

Modern Research.

1. *Olympia*, temple called Metroön, to Rhea as mother of the gods.
2. Headless statue, with lion crouching at her feet (Cesnola Collection).

Descendants.—(See DESCENDANTS OF CRONUS AND RHEA, Table B.)

LEGEND OF ATYS.

Rhea conceived a deep love for Atys, a young Phrygian shepherd. Atys was about to wed a daughter of the king of Pessinus, when Rhea appeared and broke up the assembly. Atys became frantic, rushed to the mountains, and, maiming himself, died. He was turned into a pine tree, into which his soul passed, while from his blood sprang a wreath of violets. Zeus would not restore him to life, but granted that his body should live for ever, that his hair should always grow, and that his little finger should for ever move.

LEGENDS OF CRONUS AND RHEA.
BIRTH OF ZEUS AND OTHER CRONIDS.
(TABLE B, 3.)

Uranus had prophesied that Cronus should be dethroned by his own son. Fearing this fate, as soon as children were born to him Cronus swallowed them. He had thus disposed of five children when Zeus was born Rhea, having a special desire to preserve this child dressed a stone in his clothing and gave it to Cronus who swallowed it in place of the child.

Zeus was hidden in the island of Crete, where he was attended by the nymphs Ida and Adrastia, and the goat Amalthea furnished him with milk. (This goat was made immortal as the constellation Capricornus.) The divine infant was placed in charge of the Curetes, who kept up a noise with shields and bucklers, that Cronus might not hear the cries of the child. When Zeus matured in knowledge and power, he persuaded Cronus to give back to light the children that he had swallowed also the stone through which Zeus's life had been preserved.

"Cronus swallowing his children represents that conservative force which antagonizes growth, or, more strongly, that disintegrating power that dooms to decay and destruction all new creations. Desiring to check all development of the living world, Cronus united the newly-born with himself, but they tore themselves asunder from him, and introduced a new time—a time of progress."

TITANIC WAR—OVERTHROW OF CRONUS.
(Table B, 4.)

Zeus became a powerful god and rebelled against Cronus.

The Hecatoncheires and Cyclopes were released from Tartarus by Zeus, and they allied themselves to his cause; the former lending their immense muscular strength, and the latter furnishing thunderbolts and lightning. (An early legend says that Zeus nourished his allies with ambrosia and nectar.)

The Titans remained true to their brother Cronus, except Oceanus, Themis, Mnemosyne, and Hyperion, all of whom allied themselves to Zeus or remained neutral. Cronus and his allied Titanic forces were on Mount Othrys, while Zeus and his allies were on Mount Olympus (Thessaly). This war (Titanomachia) lasted ten years, and then resulted in the victory of Zeus. Cronus, with Iapetus and the other allied Titans, was imprisoned in Tartarus; Poseidon built around it a wall of brass, and the Hecatoncheires were placed there as perpetual guards. Menœtius, son of Iapetus, shared his father's imprisonment, while Atlas was condemned to stand for ever at the extreme west, and to support on his shoulder the solid vault of heaven.

"The whole myth of the overthrow of Cronus and the triumph of Zeus covers long transition-periods of earth's history, comprehending—first, a succession of creations and destructions before the world had acquired a permanent constitution; second, the periods after permanent constitution had been secured, in which Time destroyed only inorganic substances (represented by stone), for the new spirit of life, growth, and revolution, as embodied in Zeus, was beyond the reach of devastating Cronus."

Assoc. Myths.

When Zeus rebelled against Cronus, Styx and her four children, Nike (victory), Bia (strength) Cratos (power), and Zelus (zeal), were the first that came to his aid. Zeus conferred on Styx the great distinction of being the oath-sanctioner of the gods (Horkos), while her children were appointed as his personal attendants.

REBELLION OF TYPHŒUS.

Typhœus, a monstrous son of Gæa and Tartarus would have overthrown the new reign, had not Zeus destroyed him with a thunderbolt and then thrust him down to Tartarus.

LEGENDS OF CRONUS.

There is a later legend that, after his overthrow by Zeus, Cronus went to Italy and established a "Golden Age." Another legend assigns to him the office of "protector of the shades of heroes in the lower world."

WAR OF THE GIANTS (GIGANTOMACHIA)

This was a later legend of a rebellion against Zeus on the part of the Giants, but neither Homer nor Hesiod mentions such a contest.

PARTITION OF THE UNIVERSE BY THE CRONIDS.

(TABLE B, 5.)

Zeus, supreme ruler, but sharing the government with the others, and retaining special control of illimitable ether.

Hera (He′ra), queen of heaven, and shared the control of the atmosphere.

Hades (Äides), god of the departed, half-animated spirits in the lower world.

Demeter (Deme′ter), goddess of earth as ministering to mankind.

Poseidon (Pŏsei′dōn), god of the sea as used by man; also of subterranean forces.

Hestia (Hĕs′tĭa), goddess of conserving forces and of life-giving warmth.

SECOND EPOCH OF THEOGONY.

(TABLE B, 6.)

THE second epoch of theogony is marked by striking characteristics: the general becomes special; the impersonal becomes personal; power is recognized as law; gods are endowed with sympathy, so that man is not only governed, but loved.

In the line of Cronus and Rhea descend the most illustrious characters of mythology. Human creations though they were, their influence has been like that of powerful realities; their oracles have appointed historic battle-fields and determined national issues; their ideas have inspired the artist and the poet, and given to philosophy its profoundest problems. We will hope that to the general consciousness there was suggested or revealed a divine one, which said to spirit more than language could utter or art interpret, and that the celestial glory of Uranus and the commanding majesty of Cronus grew dim and feeble in the sublimer splendor of the mighty Zeus.

ZEUS, OR JUPITER.
(Table B, 7.)

However multiform the deities in any polytheistic system, they will be grouped around some controlling deity that embodies the highest thought of the people. We know that the conception of this central, supreme one may be intuitively apprehended as the "first great cause" of all things, or it may be reached through generalization and reasoning; but in whatever way the "Zeus-idea" was obtained, it must needs have been so complex that it was subject to constant and great variations.

Central Ideas.

Pelasgic Zeus-Worship.—Dodona, in Epirus, was the centre of the oldest Zeus-worship, and this had been preceded by the worship of a "nameless deity." Though the fact of the existence of this latter worship is generally admitted, in reference to it a theory and a statement differ from, if they do not contradict, each other. The *theory* is, that the worship of one unnamed God was a survival of Jewish monotheism, a trace of direct revelation; the *statement* is to the effect that the Pelasgians were in the habit of offering prayers and sacrifices to gods to whom they gave no names. Max Müller quotes this statement from Herodotus, and, though he admits that it may be based upon tradition, does not seem to think it improbable.

HEAD OF ZEUS (from Dodona).

It is generally accepted that this "nameless One" was afterward called Zeus, and was worshipped as the chief god at Dodona. Pelasgic cultus was strongly marked by elemental or Nature-worship, and Dodonæan Zeus was enthroned as ruler of all the great forces of the material world, whether manifested in lightnings from mountain-tops or in the blessings of dew, rain, and river, themselves the source of the richer gifts of vegetation. It is probable that he was worshipped as supreme in the regions of upper air and light; for mountain-summits and the sky-parting eagle were sacred to him.

Evidence of an exalted conception of the eternal godhead of Zeus is found in the song of the Peleiades (priestesses) of Dodona:

"Zeus was, Zeus is, Zeus will be, a great Zeus."

The brief résumé given on page 70 of the progressive stages of Dodona-worship is condensed from a work recently published, which contains the results of excavations on the site of the ancient city of Dodona; and, as will be seen by the résumé, while the general tenor of the inscriptions there found lies in the direction of the Pelasgic element, M. Carapanos endorses the views above stated, and connects in a highly suggestive, if not in a demonstrable, manner the Pelasgic and Hellenic systems.

Wherever Pelasgians settled they worshipped Zeus in open places or on mountain-tops; but whenever cities were built, Zeus was supposed to descend from mountains and take up his abode with men as protector of cities. So even in Athens the most ancient and most sacred festival, the Diasia, was in honor of Pelasgic Zeus.

Another phase of this early religion was of a sterner character. When the worshippers of Zeus dwelt upon his purity and justice, there resulted a cultus whose central deity was conceived as demanding sacrifices of human blood, but who could accept instead the blood of animals; hence the "Zeus Lycæus" of Arcadia.

HELLENIC ZEUS.

As different currents flow about a mountain-base, so around the Pelasgic religious centres were formed varied systems bearing the common name of Zeus-worship; but, though they had a common origin in the universal

ZEUS, OR JUPITER.

tendency of the human mind to conceive of a supreme deity, so varying were their component elements that a comparison of their settled stages shows uniformity only in their origin and name.

It is probable that the early idea of Belus, of Baal, and of Zeus Amun was of a god who was the source of all power, life, and light, and whose glory was symbolized by the sun; but as the moral vision of the worshippers became dimmed through increasing ignorance and degradation, the god-idea was obscured and changed. So, through gradations of "astronomic deities" who animated or controlled the heavenly bodies, of rulers over the mysteries of human life and death, and their mystic symbols set forth in the growth and decay of Nature, the god-idea sank into a form of that "animism" which was so fruitful a source of those strange antagonisms that develop on the one hand into sensualism, and on the other into frantic and often cruel orgies.

The Greeks, delighting in new myths, through constant influx of foreign ideas made great changes in their own mythology; and it is not strange that, as Preller asserts, in Crete, side by side with the mountain-worship of the Pelasgic god, existed a Zeus-worship resembling the mystic cave-rites of Demeter and Dionysus.

We must not pass over a strange cultus that was known in the Troad and in Lycia—that of Zeus as "one in himself," but ruling in the threefold form of "Zeus Triopas."

Remembering all these phases of the god-idea, we see how many and varied were the elements that entered into that conception of Zeus that, in distinction from the Pelasgic, we have called the "Hellenic Zeus-worship."

HESIODIC ZEUS-IDEA.

Hesiod seemed to have known and used the Cretan legends of the birth and early life of Zeus. (See LEGENDS OF CRONUS AND RHEA.) When he describes the Titanic War in strains that rise in grandeur until the mighty victor over Titanic foes " walks majestic round the starry frame," we know not how far his eloquence is the glow of genius, or how far it reflects the popular apprehension of Zeus's almighty power; but because the sense of the divine is so deeply implanted in the human nature, when Hesiod reverentially acknowledges Zeus as one who was " to rule the gods and mount the throne of heaven," calling him "almighty Jove, the lord of men below and gods above," it is probable that the poet becomes interpreter to that general belief in a supreme Being which we know as the "god-idea." But, whatever *moral* attributes may have been ascribed to Zeus in the popular worship, Hesiod has not given them prominence in his theogony.

Olympian Zeus.—Whether or not the Olympic system was based upon the Pelasgic (as suggested by Carapanos), they held a certain relationship to each other. Until within a few years it was said that the priests at Dodona were called " Selli." Carapanos says that they were called " Tomouri," from Mount Tomaros, but that they were selected from a people called " Selli " or " Helli."

Now, assuming (what Gladstone asserts) that Pelasgic, Dodonæan Zeus was worshipped by the " Helloi," that these Helloi represent the Hellenic race in its pre-Hellenic form, we have a close connection between the two worships, and we can readily believe, with the same author, that Zeus was transferred from the older to the later system, and that throughout all the expansion and elevation of the Homeric treatment of the great subject there remained traces of the worship in which the nameless one was first called " Zeus."

As political and social relations united more closely different tribes and districts of Greece, the Zeus-idea became Pan-Hellenic, though modified in differing proportions by already-accepted traditions and belief. He ruled over Nature and over man, and yet at no period was the conception of Zeus free from a certain element of weakness. Zeus was supreme when acting in the sphere of the human, yet he was himself subject to the decrees of Fate. Was there not in this vague apprehension of a power that outmeasured that which they had ascribed to their highest god an intimation that there might be a god, as yet unknown, but who would at some time declare himself unto them?

In studying the development of the Zeus-idea we find an increasing tendency to "cast the divine life into human forms" (anthropomorphism); and this tendency may have resulted, in a measure, from the implanted desire on the part of humanity to concrete and embody the abstract that it may be more easily apprehended. Alas that the altar-fires kindled in the worship of the mighty Zeus were not always purifying flame! We think that the inferior, almost degraded, character that was ascribed to the chief god in some minds, and even in localities, can be accounted for upon the generally-accepted principle that, since the conception of Deity is a product of the "moral faculty," it is but natural that those who are morally depraved should endow even their deities with passions like their own. So while, to many, the love-adventures or the fits of anger accredited to Zeus were but allegories full of instruction and truth, to the ignoble and the base they were veritable facts, not at all inconsistent with their low estimate of Deity. To such minds incarnations were degradations that were seized upon as a justification of their own immorality.

Zeus-Idea in History.—In explanation of the fact that so many illustrious Grecian families claimed a direct descent from Zeus, Grote assigns that "pride of birth" that prompted early nations to trace their ancestry to divine origin.

MYTHOLOGY OF DODONA.
Central Ideas.
These will be most readily inferred from a résumé of the theory of M. Carapanos :*

First Stage.—Monotheistic worship of a "nameless deity;" later, worship of this deity as Zeus.

Second Stage.—Associated worship of Dione as "productive earth;" later, associated worship of Aphrodite.

Third Stage.—By a worship of the separate attributes of Zeus, upon the Pelasgic system as a foundation or a cornerstone, there arose the vast superstructure of Hellenic polytheism.

DEITIES OF DODONA.
ZEUS.
Offices.
Supreme *creator* and *organizer* of all things, but, being conceived upon a human model, he was supposed to dwell among men. Mountains, particularly Mount Tomaros, were sacred to him.

Emblems.
The thunderbolt (fulmen).
The eagle.
The oak (as prophetic).
Moisture and rivers (as source of life).

DIONE [*Dīō'ne*].
Offices.
Deification of the feminine productive power of Nature—first, as productive earth; second, nourishing moisture.

---

* *Dodona et ses Ruines*, par Constantine Carapanos.

(Probably) moisture.

APHRODITE, DAUGHTER OF ZEUS AND DIONE.
Offices.
Deification of the "principle of love," by which all things exist.

Emblem.
Doves (called also peleiades).

WORSHIP AT DODONA.

Oracle.—At the time of the worship of the "nameless deity" oaks were held sacred to him, and from one prophetic oak (near which the temple was afterward built) the will of the god was supposed to be made known through the rustling of the leaves.

Temple.—Temple to Zeus in Dodona, to which were brought or sent "votive offerings" from all parts of Greece.

Priesthood.—Priests, Tomouri (chosen from Selli, or Helli). The chief priest was called Naïarque. At first, priests interpreted prophetic signs, but later this was done by priestesses, while the priests attended to sacrifices and other services. Priestesses (called "peleiades"). There were at first *two;* then *three;* at last there was but *one.*

Ceremonies.—Consultation of Oracles: 1. Prophetic oak, gave answer by rustling of leaves.

2. Miraculous spring (at the foot of the sacred oak), gave indications of the will of Deity by the sound of its waters.

3. Near the temple were two columns. On one was a brazen vessel (vase); on the other was the figure of a child holding a whip with three brass chains, each chain having a knob at the end. The constant winds of Do-

:hese chains to frequently strike the brazen
pon the longer or shorter duration of the
riestess based her predictions.
)asins were suspended around the temple,
 one was struck all would resound.
vases and tripods were used in the same
e basins.
sis says that "scrolls or dice were put into
-tuitously drawn." (The replies of oracles
l on plates of lead.)
·In a reply of an oracle that was long pre-
: was made for a " sacrifice to Zeus of nine
companied by two sheep; and to Dione, a
 an ox, and other victims."
f water formed a part of the ceremonies,
 to the river Achelous formed a regular
vorship.
s the religious centre of Greece for so long
study of the results of the excavations of
, whether they were Dodonæan or the ex-
 of other cities, would be of deepest in-
;hest value.

HELLENIC ZEUS:

chetypes.
Source of light and quickening-power of
universe. *Arch.*, illimitable *ether* that per-
s the universe as a condition or cause of
orms of life.
oller of all phenomena of the heavens.
:., earth-embracing *atmosphere*, with its
ifestations of cloud, sunshine, or storm.
d Ruler of the alternations of day and
t and of the change of seasons. *Arch.*,

regular succession of the movements of the earth and the heavens.

Human Life: 1. Father (not the creator) of mankind, bestowing upon them all the blessings of life.
2. Source of all wisdom.
3. Source of law, hence rewarder of right actions, punisher of wrong-doing.
4. Sovereign of mankind, ruler of rulers, and disposer of kingdoms.
5. Judge of mankind, granting expiation for sin.
6. Protector of sanctity of oaths, punishing perjury.
7. Father of heroes, interested in wars and conquests.

Theog.: 1. Supreme god, ruler over all celestial beings; ruler on earth, even over the domains that he entrusted to Hades and Poseidon.
2. Father of gods (see DESCENDANTS OF ZEUS).

Early Legends.

Birth and education (see LEGENDS OF CRONUS AND RHEA, TABLE B, 3).

Marriage (see HERA, page 93).

Abode.

Zeus reigned in person over the regions of ether and the atmosphere, sharing the latter with Hera.

Mount Olympus, in Thessaly, was supposed to be favored with his special presence, and there he held his court.

Attendants.

1. Cyclopes, forgers of thunderbolts; 2. Children of Styx: Nike (victory), Cratos (strength), Zelus (imperiousness), Bia (force); 3. Ganymede, or Hebe, cup-bearer 4. Hermes and Iris as messengers.

Assoc. Myths.

The relations of Zeus in mythology are as great in number as they are in interest. In the history of the Titanic War we find a source of the antagonism between him and the Iapetids that culminated in the sublime story of Prometheus. The jealous dignity of Hera gave rise to a cluster of myths—*e. g.* the wanderings of Io, the labors of Heracles — and formed no feeble motive in the Trojan War. It is but natural that Zeus, as the great centre of Grecian mythology, should sustain to all of its departments intimate and personal relations.

Emblems.

Nature: Ether, light, fire, Zeus as creator of all things.
Fulmen (thunderbolt), Zeus as god of destructive forces.
Mountains, stability.
Mountain-tops, majesty.
Flint-stone, hidden power or lightning.
Wings, Zeus as god of the air.
Water flowing from wings, Zeus as god of fertile showers and parent of streams and rivers.
Eagle, destructive power on earth, Zeus as ruling in the heavens.
Wreath of vernal flowers, Zeus as god of spring.
Letter Alpha, Zeus as creator of all things.
Human Life: Pyramids, pillars, and obelisks, rays of the sun (so represented, Zeus is god of the day).
Fulmen, Zeus as judge of mankind, punishing wrong-doing.
Theog.: The color white, purity and glory.
Olive tree, immortality; oak tree, prophetic power.

Crown of oak, Zeus of Dodona; crown of olive Zeus of Olympia.

Lily, royalty; ram, wisdom; white bull, power and supremacy.

Throne and sceptre, Zeus as sovereign ruler of heaven and earth.

Patera (votive bowl), Zeus as accepting offerings.

Ægis, statue of Victory (Nice), the eagle killing a serpent or a hare — all symbolized Zeus as triumphing over enemies.

Foreign: Animal representations signified wisdom and power: ram's horns in the head of Zeus; heads of bulls on his throne; sphinxes on his throne eagle, etc.

Mountain-summits (single or enclosed by little temples) represented Zeus as god of etherea regions.

Cornucopia, Zeus as the source of the blessings of Nature.

Astronomical representations, as rays of the sun also obelisks, sun, moon, and stars, the zodiac represented Zeus in his relations to the order of the universe.

Representations.

Early (Dodonæan).—The oldest art-remains of Zeus represent him as a god of Nature, and quite marked characteristics distinguish the Zeus of Dodona from Zeus of Crete and from Asiatic locations. The figure on page 71 is a facsimile of a fragment that is supposed to represent Zeus.

Later.—There are traces of the embodiment of the idea of Zeus as youthful before he had assumed full control of the universe.

Zeus of Otricoli (Vatican Museum).

As the Greeks continued to add to the number of the attributes of their chief deity, position, drapery, expression, and indeed every accessory, became significant. The standing position, with fulmen extended, signified Zeus as about to enter into contest with some enemy or to inflict punishment upon evil-doing. The sitting position, with the fulmen depressed or lying in the lap, indicates Zeus as triumphant over opposition or rejoicing in victorious rest. In arranging accessories great attention was given to the hair and flowing beard, also to the chlamys (cloak) and the himation (large robe).

As the ideal of divinity became still more exalted, art became more reverent, and more triumphant in subordinating materials to the expression of divine sentiment, until, through the inspiration of Homer, Phidias wrought that art-miracle, the Olympian Zeus.

Olympian Games.

Institution.—In his *History of Greece*, Grote has given the elements and processes that entered into the institution and expansion of this world-renowned festival:

First, habits of common sacrifices between neighboring families. Second, the feeling of fraternity between two tribes or villages, manifested by sending *theoria* (sacred legations) to take part in each other's festivals. Third, this sentiment of religious sympathy spread from town to town, until one city would invite the attendants of theors from other Hellenic communities. A city holding such festivals was exempt from invasions, and it was under obligation to notify, by heralds, the commencement of the truce to all cities not in avowed hostility to it. Fourth, *Amphictyony*. Sometimes fraternal feeling took a form differing from common festivals. A certain number of towns entered into an exclusive religious partnership for the periodical celebration of sacrifices to a god of some particular temple; all other Greeks were excluded from participation. This element was at first purely religious; then religious and political at once; and lastly mostly the latter. Upon the foregoing principles were established Pan-Hellenic festivals, none of which, if we except the Eleusinian Mysteries, had greater interest or value than the Olympian Games.

The most probable account of the origin of the games, though it is unsatisfactory, is the following: The valley of Olympia lay in a territory of the Pisatid, and the Pisatans celebrated sacred games, said to have been established by Heracles. The Ætolo-Eleans subdued the Pisatans, and, according to the general custom, assumed the responsibility of conducting the religious festivals of the conquered people. The Pisatans endeavored to reclaim control of the games, and invited the assistance of Pheidon (of Argos), who claimed descent from Heracles. The Spartans took the part of the Eleans, the Pisatans were defeated, and the Eleans afterward held control of the games. The festival thus organized derived its expanding importance from Ætolo-Elean settlements in Peloponnesus, combined with Dorians of Laconia and Messina. Lycurgus of Sparta and Iphitus of Elis united in establishing the sanctity of the "Olympian truce" and the inviolability of Elean territory.

Location.—The valley of Olympia, in Elis, has for its southern boundary the river Alpheus. The river Cladeus forms its western boundary, and flows into the Alpheus. Mount Cronius lies in the northern part of the valley, nearer to the western than to the eastern boundary.

Altis.—This was a grove of sacred olive trees lying at the junction of the Cladeus and Alpheus. It was surrounded by a wall and was filled with statues, altars, structures for various purposes, temples to different deities—pre-eminently those to Zeus and to Hera.

The structures connected particularly with the Olympian Games were—

1st, *The Olympium*, temple to Olympian Zeus.

Structure, Doric, surrounded with columns (peristyle). Ornamentation: The roof was adorned at its ends and angles with gilded Victories, vases, and shields. East pediment, statuary—contest between Pelops and Œnomaus. West pediment, statuary—battle between the Centaurs and Lapithæ. Metopes, ornamented with the "Labors of Heracles." Divisions of the temple, three aisles formed by columns. The statue of Olympian Zeus, by Phidias, was one of the "Seven Wonders of the World." Zeus was seated on a throne, and the whole work was sixty feet in height. The materials were ivory, gold, and precious stones. The mantle was golden, embroidered with lilies and other flowers, also with animals (typifying Zeus as god of Nature). The crown represented a wreath of olive-leaves. In the right hand was a statue of Victory; in the other was a sceptre surmounted by an eagle. The throne was adorned with Victories and carvings representing Apollo and Diana slaying the children of Niobe, the children of the Thebans seized by the Sphinxes, contest of Heracles and his comrades with the Amazons, etc.

2d, *Prytaneum*, a building containing a banquet-hall, called Hestiarium (see HESTIA), in which victors at the Olympian Games were honored with banquets.

3d, *Bouleuterion*, a building in which regulations concerning the games were made, and which contained a statue of Zeus Horkos—*i. e.* "god of oaths."

4th, *Thesauri*, treasuries containing choice works of

art, sent as votive offerings from the various states of Greece. They were at the foot of Mount Cronius.

5th, *Zanes*, bronze statues of Zeus, erected from fines for violations of the regulations of the games.

6th, *A Great Altar to Zeus*, made from the ashes of the burnt thighs of the animal sacrifices, wet with the sacred water of the Alpheus.

7th, *Theatre*, place where victors were crowned.

8th, *Pelopium*, sacred enclosure in honor of Pelops.

9th, *Hippodamium*, sacred enclosure in honor of Hippodamia.

Structures not in Altis.—

1st, *Gymnasium*, in which candidates were trained for athletic exercises.

2d, *A smaller enclosure*, for palestræ, or wrestlers. (Both of these were between the river Cladeus and Mount Cronius.)

3d, *Stadium* (east of Mount Cronius), in which athletic games were celebrated.

4th, *Hippodrome*, place for chariot-races.

Ceremonies. (The Olympian Games were celebrated once in four years, and lasted five days.)

*Sacrifices.—*Before engaging in athletic contests the candidates sacrificed first to Vesta (see HESTIA), then to Zeus, then to several deities. The sacrifices were of bulls, rams, etc. Sacrifices were accompanied with offerings of frankincense, wheat, and honey, and with libations of wine.

Athletic Contests.—Foot-races, once the length of the stadium (six hundred feet), were the earliest contests. A list of the victors was preserved, commencing with Corœbus, 776 B. C. Double stadium, up and down the stadium, 14th Olympiad (724 B. C.). Long course, several times up and down the course—15th Olympiad (720 B. C.).

Pentathlon.—1. Jumping; 2. running; 3. quoits; 4. javelin; 5. wrestling—18th Olympiad (708 B. C.).

Boxing-Matches.—Twenty-third Olympiad (688 B. C.).

Chariot-Races.—Chariots and four horses, 25th Olympiad (680 B. C.).

Various races and exercises were gradually introduced, as foot-races in which runners were clad in armor; horseback races, etc.

Rewards.—1. Crowns of olive-leaves. On the last day of the games the victors offered sacrifices, then in a splendid procession proceeded to the theatre (in Altis), where they were crowned with olive-leaves from the sacred tree near the Olympium. Plaudits, praises, and triumphal choruses added to the glory of the occasion. 2. Public banquets in the Prytaneum were given to the victors. 3. Five hundred drachmas in money and free places in the theatre. 4. Free table in the Prytaneum. 5. On their return to the city in whose name they had contended they were received with greatest honors: a breach was made in the wall for their entrance; public banquets were given to them; their praises were sung by poets; and they were exempt from taxes for the rest of their lives. The grateful city erected for the victor a statue in the Altis, which might be a portrait statue for those who had been three times a victor.

Literary Exercises.—Poets read their latest productions and philosophers unfolded new theories and systems.

Results of the Olympic Games. — 1st, Promotion of physical vigor, beauty, and strength; 2d, cultivation of heroic poetry; 3d, deepening of fraternal feeling; 4th, introduction of the ideal of equality of men.

ZEUS.

Grecian Comp. Myth. (see CENTRAL IDEAS).

Foreign Comp. Myth.

ROMAN, Jupiter or Jove; INDIAN, Indra;* EGYPTIAN, Amon-Ra of Thebes; Chnoumis, or Kneph, the ram-headed god of Elephantine and Ethiopia; ASSYRIAN, Jupiter Delus: LIBYAN, Jupiter Ammon; NORSE, Tyr; ANGLO-SAXON, Tiw.

Literature.

History.—Oracles of Zeus and Zeus-worship formed a most important element.

Poetry.—In the Trojan War, Zeus's sympathies were with the Trojans.

Art.

Coins.—1st. Coins of Epirus give the oldest type.

2d. Coins of Elis give the Phidian type.

3d. Coins of different states of Greece give varying types of features and emblems.

4th. Foreign coins are marked with characteristic features of the Zeus-idea.

Statuary.—1. Bust of Zeus (found at Otricoli), now in Vatican.

2. Jupiter Verospi, Vatican.

3. Bronze statue from Epirus, British Museum.

For full list see *Ancient Art and its Remains*, by K. O. Müller.

Modern Research (see OLYMPIUM).

Olympia. — Archæological research has developed treasures of incalculable value in this valley. There have already been discovered thousands of coins and bronzes and hundreds of inscriptions, terra-cottas, and marbles. Prominent among the latter is a mutilated

---

* Later, Dyaus or Dyu.

but noble statue of Zeus and a portion of a colossal Zeus of a magnificent type. A statue of Zeus (without head and feet, but otherwise preserved) that formed the central object of the east pediment has been recovered. This is accompanied by many statues, torsos, and fragments that formed the whole group. A large portion of the statuary of the western pediment has been recovered, and a portion of the adornments of the metopes is in the Louvre; casts of the latest finds are in Berlin, but the art-remains are in Athens or Olympia.

Descendants of Zeus (see TABLE B).

ŒNOMAUS AND PELOPS.

Œnomaus, a son of Ares, was king of Pisa in Elis. He married the Pleiad Sterope and became the father of Hippodamia. An oracle had said that Œnomaus would perish by the hand of a son-in-law; so whenever a suitor for the hand of his daughter presented himself, the king demanded that the suitor should overcome him in a chariot-race. The race-course extended from Pisa to the altar of Poseidon at Corinth. The suitor started with Hippodamia in a chariot, and the king pursued the lovers. Having horses of more than mortal swiftness, Œnomaus was always victorious. Pelops, son of Tantalus and grandson of Zeus, applied for the hand of the princess. Pelops had received from Poseidon a golden chariot and swift horses, and having bribed Myrtilus, the charioteer of Œnomaus, to remove the linch-pins from his master's chariot, the king was thrown from his chariot and was killed. Pelops thus won the race, Hippodamia, and the kingdom of Pisa.

BATTLE OF THE CENTAURS AND THE LAPITHÆ.

Pirithous, son of Zeus, was king of the Lapithæ in Thessaly. Theseus was his devoted friend and companion in military exploits. Pirithous, having obtained the hand of Hippodamia, daughter of Adrastus, king of Argos, invited the Lapithæ, and also the Centaurs (near Peleon), to the wedding. Heated by wine, the Centaurs, led by Eurytion, attempted to carry off Hippodamia. Theseus assisted Pirithous, and there followed the battle so famous in mythology.

HERA, OR JUNO.
(TABLE B, 8.)

Central Ideas.

We have found that the earliest embodiment of the chief goddess-idea was in Gæa (as Dione), as productive matter developing life's lower forms—nursing the young, indeed, but opening to mankind graves that bore no words of resurrection. We have seen the royal Rhea, in the richness of flower and fruit and mural crown, in her stately chariot drawn by conquered lions, ride forth as goddess of the fertile earth peopled, cultivated, and covered with cities. There now entered into Greek theogony a goddess who should preside over the higher relations of human life—Hera, pure in character, grandly true as the wife of Zeus, exerting her queenly power in the general interest of humanity. Like other deities, Hera combined varied characteristics. The Pelasgic tendency was toward elemental or Nature worship, and it is probable that the Greek Hera was identical in nature with the "sovereign lady," the chief goddess that in other countries signified only the deification of the feminine principle of Nature.

Homeric Conception.—Gladstone thinks that Hera was

HEAD OF HERA, OR JUNO.

lifted suddenly from the Pelasgic system and enthroned on the highest pinnacle of the Hellenic or Olympian system; and though he admits that she retained a trace of her Pelasgic origin in her relations to human births, yet he assumes that she was as intensely anti-Pelasgic as she was pro-Hellenic in her nature, sympathies, and operations. (See TROJAN WAR.)

Offices and Archetypes.
Nature: 1. Ethereal, all-pervading, passive productive power—the atmosphere, as containing masses of different materials "in which lie latent the seeds of all things," and which, in conjunction with all-quickening ether, gives rise to series of new productions.
2. Limited control of atmospheric phenomena, showing wifely devotion in a clear sunny atmosphere that resulted in the blessings of Nature, especially in spring; but evincing her coldness or jealousy in retarded growth or devastating storms.

Human Life: 1. Presiding over human births.
2. Protectress of the sacredness of the marriage relations.
3. Presiding over the special interests of woman— *i. e.* employments, dress, and personal ornaments.
4. Limited disposal of gifts of empire.
5. Protectress and champion of the Greeks.

Theog.: Queen of heaven, sharing the power of Zeus and receiving divine honors from gods and men.

Early Legends.

Hera was placed under the care of Oceanus and Tethys. Zeus sought her in marriage; she consented to become his bride, and their marriage was called "the sacred marriage." On this important occasion all of the gods, goddesses, all human beings, and even all animals, were invited, and all accepted save the nymph Chelone, who not only refused to attend, but indulged in raillery. Hermes went in quest of her, and found her in her house, which was upon the bank of a river. He threw the nymph into the river and transformed her into a tortoise, which was condemned to carry its house on its back; as punishment for raillery perpetual silence was enjoined upon her. (See HERMES AND THE LYRE.)

Gæa was a guest at the marriage of Zeus and Hera, and presented to the bride a tree laden with golden apples. One legend places this tree under the charge of the Hesperides, at the foot of the Hyperborean Atlas.

Abode.
1. Plains of ether; 2. Mount Olympus.

Attendants.
1. The Horæ (Seasons), who opened and closed the celestial gates when Hera's chariot passed through them, and who harnessed to, or unharnessed from, her chariot the royal steeds.
2. The Charites (Graces).
3. Iris (rainbow). This daughter of Thaumas (see GÆA AND PONTUS) was born of the vapors that rise from the earth and the sea. Iris ministered only to Hera and Zeus; when a solemn oath was to be administered to the gods, Iris brought water in a golden vase from the Styx; she cut the last thread that bound dying souls to the body.
4. Ilithyiæ, those who presided over births.

Assoc. Myths.
1. Hera, Poseidon, and Athena entered into a conspiracy to put Zeus in chains. Thetis, a sea-nymph, came to the aid of Zeus, bringing as ally Briareus (see HECATONCHEIRES). The plot was thwarted, and as punishment Hera was suspended

from the vault of heaven, with an anvil attached to each foot.
2. Io, a priestess of Hera, excited the jealousy of the goddess. To protect Io, Zeus changed her into a white cow, but gave her into the keeping of Hera at the latter's request. Hera placed Io under the charge of Argus, who had a hundred eyes. At the command of Zeus, Hermes charmed Argus into a sleep, and then slew him. Io wandered through Epirus, over Mount Caucasus, through Asia, and finally into Egypt (see EPAPHUS).
3. Judgment of Paris (see APHRODITE).

Emblems.
Nature: Cuckoo, harbinger of spring.
Human Life: Pomegranate, marriage.
Serpent, health.
Spindle, woman's interests and employments, as spinning, weaving, etc.
Peacock, splendid dress.
Veil, married woman; poppy, or dittany, solacer of pain.
Theog.: Veil, sacredness; peplos, divinity.
Sceptre or spear, royalty; lily, purity.
Votive bowl or patera, goddess who accepts offerings or hears prayers.
Peacock, colors of Iris or eyes of Argus.
Foreign: Deer, golden-horned, of Diana (see ARTEMIS).
Egyptian—vulture, a hawk, or the crescent.

Representations.
1. *Argos*, a long pillar of stone or of wood; 2. *Samos*, a wooden plank; 3. *Dædala*, statue of cypress-wood.

1. Sitting on a throne or on the eagle of Zeus, holding in one hand a sceptre, in the other a starry veil, which falls around her head and form.
2. The statue at Argos (see WORSHIP), seated on a throne, holding in one hand a sceptre on which sat a cuckoo, in the other hand a pomegranate.

Worship.

At Argos, temple, Heræon (forty-five stadia from Argos).

Sacred Objects.—Statue of Hera of gold and ivory (by Polycletus).

Priesthood.—High priestess, called queen; all priestesses greatly honored.

Ceremonies.—Heræa: 1. Procession of men clad in armor; 2. Procession of women, headed by high priestesses seated in a chariot drawn by white heifers (see BITON AND CLEOBIS); 3. Sacrifices in the temple—geese, sows, ewe-lambs, and a hecatomb of white heifers.

A brazen shield was fixed in a nearly inaccessible place in the theatre; he who displaced it received as reward a shield and a garland of myrtle.

At Olympia (in Elis), temple, Heræum (see MODERN RESEARCH).

Sacred Objects.—1. Statue of Hera on a throne; 2. A chest covered with mythic carvings (chest of Cypselus).

Ceremonies.—Heræa: 1. Every fifth year sixteen matrons wove a sacred peplos for the statue of Hera; 2. After sacrificing a pig to Hera they bathed in the sacred well of Peoria; 3. Sacrifices of cows, geese, and ewe-lambs.

1. Races in the stadium, by maidens; the prize was a crown of sacred olive and portions of a cow sacrificed to Hera; they might place their painted likenesses in the temple of Hera. 2. Sixteen matrons performed two sacred dances.

JUNO BARBERINI.

Grecian Comp. Myth.

In some attributes Hera = Dione.

Foreign Comp. Myth.

ROMAN, Juno; EGYPTIAN, Sati.

Literature.

In the Trojan War, Hera was the champion of the Greeks. (See *Iliad*.)

Art.

Coins of Argos.

Statuary.—1. Juno Ludovisi (page 92). Probably this type of Hera represents the Polycletus idea.
2. Head of Hera, in museum at Naples.
3. "Farnese Juno," in same place.
4. "Juno Barberini," in Vatican (page 97), so styled by Cardinal Barberini, who discovered it in the Viminal Baths, near the church of San Lorenzo on Punisperna. It is one of the most perfect specimens of antique sculpture. Thought to be a copy of the statue in her temple at Platæa.

Modern Research.

Olympia.—Recent excavations in this valley, in Elis, have brought to light the temple of Hera (Heræum) which Pausanias mentions as "a Doric temple surrounded by pillars." Full accounts of the results of past and of progressing researches in this valley are given in *The London Athenæum*. One article reports the finding of a colossal head, supposed to be that of Hera.

Mycenæ.—Among the remains of this city, where Hera was especially honored, Dr. Schliemann has found many idols having the head or the horns of a cow. He calls them "Juno idols," and thinks they resemble figures on the brick cylinders of the Babylonian empire; also, that they are closely allied to Egyptian Isis-worship. This theory is doubted by many.

Descendants (see TABLE B).

HADES (AIDES), OR PLUTO.
(TABLE B, 9.)

Central Ideas.

First. Though Zeus had supreme control of the universe, his power was not absolute, for forces antagonistic to his sway were in constant operation. Winter was just as sure in its approach and desolating results as was spring in its promises and summer in its fulfilment. There must be a receptacle for dying bloom—a power that checked or destroyed growth. The mind very

HADES AND PERSEPHONE.

readily inferred a *personal cause*, and very naturally believed that only a deity could rival the mighty Zeus; so there soon prevailed the conception of Hades as one who ruled in gloomy splendor over the regions of the lower world, which was called "Hades." But as the plant-life that came back in the freshness of spring seemed to be nourished by a warmth that had its source in Hades, so the lord of the regions of darkness, decay, and death seemed to pay tribute to the lord of the bright and the living.

Second. The idea of Hades as the abode of departed souls became more prominent, and so the destiny of the soul came to be viewed in wider and wider relations; the shadowy realm of Hades grew first luminous, then radiant, with the hope of immortality.

Offices and Archetypes.

Nature: To assist in the growth of vegetation. *Arch.*, internal warmth of the earth.

Human Life: 1. To furnish mineral wealth for man. *Arch.*, mines of precious metals and gems.

2. God of death of human beings. *Arch.*, that invisible power that removes from earth all mankind.

Theog.: 1. Lord of the lower world (TABLE B, 5). *Arch.*, unseen cause of phenomena that were antagonistic to light, life, and progress.

2. Judge of the departed spirits. *Arch.*, the growing sense of man's moral responsibility.

3. Giver of immortality. *Arch.*, increasing belief in the immortality of the soul.

Early Legends.

A later legend says that at the close of the Titanic War the Cyclopes made for Hades a helmet which rendered the wearer invisible. (See PERSEUS.)

Assoc. Myths.

Rape of Persephone (see DEMETER AND PERSEPHONE).

Abode and Attendants.

Hades.—In the worship at Dodona (Epirus), opposed to Zeus, Dione, and Aphrodite as powers of life, was Hades, the god of destruction and death. The river

Acheron was considered as the entrance to the dominions of Hades, and this river flowed through the Lake Acherusia (see EGYPTIAN MYTHOLOGY). As Epirus was the last country known toward the west, it was considered as the region of darkness; but as the limits of the known world extended on that side, the position of Hades was removed successively to Italy (Avernus), then Iberia—being located wherever the light of day seemed to be extinguished.

Erebus and Hades (TABLE A, 7).—Erebus, a term usually applied to outer darkness, was afterward used to denote the subterranean regions. According to one theory, it was a realm through which souls passed when on their way to Hades; according to another theory, Erebus was a general term, comprehending the palace and domain of Hades; also Tartarus, in which the Titans, Cronus, Iapetus, etc., were imprisoned (TABLE B, 4).

Early.—Hesiod seems to take the latter view, and places in Hades—

1. The palace of Hades and Persephone, guarded by the triple-headed Cerberus.
2. The dwelling of Nyx (night), with her two sons, Death and Sleep.
3. The grotto of Styx, with silver columns and the river Styx (see IRIS).
4. Tartarus, as a prison for Titans (TABLE B, 4).

Elysian Fields.—It is probable that Hesiod located them in the "Isles of the Blessed" in the ocean.

According to Homer, the Elysian Fields were in the Western Ocean: there dwelt heroes under the rule of Rhadamanthus.

Erebus, according to Homer (*Odyssey*), lay in the dreary regions beyond the stream of Oceanus, which, as he supposed, surrounded the earth. The inhabitants were half-animated shades of those who had been on the earth.

Later. — *Hades.* — Entrance, Lake Avernus (Italy); caves near the entrance, where dwelt Old Age, Disease, Hunger, avengers of guilt.

Rivers. — 1, Acheron; 2, Styx (lake?) (one myth said that the Styx encompassed Hades several times); 3, Cocytus; 4, Pyriphlegethon; 5, Lethe.*

Divisions. — 1. Palace of Hades and Persephone.
2. Tartarus, which had been the prison for Titans, now became the prison for wicked men.
3. Elysian Fields. These fields, that had been located in different regions, and had served as a retreat for gods and heroes, were now brought down as a place of reward for good men.
4. Field of Asphodel, where spirits waited for those whose fate had not been decided.
5. Field of Heroes (see CRONUS).
6. Field of Truth, dwelling-place of the judges of souls, as Minos, etc.

Attendants.

Charon, as boatman, conveyed souls of the departed over the waters of the lower world.

Judges of departed spirits: 1, Minos; 2, Æacus; 3, Rhadamanthus.

Hermes, as herald and messenger of Zeus, had constant access to Hades.

Iris came to get the water from the River Styx.

Legends of Hades (see, 1, ORPHEUS; 2, IXION; 3, SISYPHUS; 4, TANTALUS, etc.).

* Acheron (woe), Cocytus (shrieks), Styx (hateful).

Assoc. Myths.
1. Rape of Persephone (see DEMETER).
2. Hades carried Leuce to Erebus. She died, and he caused a white poplar to spring up in the Elysian Fields.
3. Hades loved Mintha, and Persephone changed her into the plant of that name.

Emblems.
Nature: Calathus (basket, or a corn-measure), wealth from vegetation.

Human Life: Staff, as gathering souls of the dead.

Theog.: Helmet, invisibility; veil, secrecy; pointed crown and sceptre, royalty; antique key, no return from Erebus. Cypress and maiden-hair fern were sacred to Hades, as was also the number two (as inauspicious).

Foreign.—Egyptian, pointed crown, Hades as winter sun.

Representation.
1. Sitting on a rock, wearing pointed crown and holding a two-pointed sceptre.
2. Sitting on a throne with Persephone; his head is veiled and he holds his sceptre.

Worship.
One temple at Elis. Few temples, because Hades was inexorable.

Sacrifices.—Black bulls and black sheep, killed at night and the blood allowed to run into the ground. The person offering must turn away his face from the victim. At some time during the ceremony the person offering struck the earth with his hands.

Foreign Comp. Myth.
EGYPTIAN, Serapis; INDIAN, Sama.

Literature.

Sixth book of the *Æneid;* eleventh book of the *Odyssey.*

Art.

Burial-place of Massonian family.

DEMETER, OR CERES.

(TABLE B, 10.)

Central Ideas.

When the universe was divided among the Cronids, Zeus delegated to Demeter a vicegerency over the broad fields that yield the fruits and grain best adapted to the nourishment of man; so Demeter became a great earth-mother. But as the child soon learns that "mother" is the synonym for something more lovely and grand than even sheltering arms and nourishing breast, so the Greeks sought for divine *sympathy.*

We have seen that Hera had guardianship of human births, but she rejoiced in men as subjects rather than as children; Demeter wrought wondrous things for man with a power that was divine, but with a love that was human.

It is not strange that a people who could conceive such a goddess should place in a relation so subtle and so tender that we know not whether to call it divinely human or humanly divine, the daughter Persephone (Table B, 14). Surely, the fascinating myth of Demeter and Persephone, of their sorrow and their rejoicing, must have grander meaning than the life, decay, and new-coming of plant and grain. Though the living, changing hieroglyph of seed-time and harvest may symbolize, it can *only* symbolize, that vaster mystery—life that is human in its conditions, but heavenly in its instincts and destiny.

Persephone, like Demeter, seemed glad to use her

powers in the service of man; so, hand in hand, walked mother and daughter, and wherever human life-ways wended, thither passed the celestial pair, working mir-

DEMETER, OR CERES.

acles of growth and color, bloom and fruitage, until flower and fruit grew fragrant with life-giving nectar. But mysteries of growth ceased and miracles of color paled and vanished, because Persephone's music-waking step was heard no more. Surely she had not deserted her loving worshippers—surely some strong arm held her from them. It could not be that of her father Zeus, for were it so, they well knew that from celestial heights she would pour upon them largesses of blessings in hitherto unknown richness. No, from the sunless, starless depths of the lower world had come the mighty Hades, and not in defiance, but by permission, of Zeus he bore away Persephone.

RAPE OF PERSEPHONE.

The legend says that Persephone was playing with the daughters of Oceanus and Tethys on the Nysian Plain in Asia (later, Enna, Sicily). They were gathering flowers, when Persephone saw a large rich plant covered with blossoms that were strange and beautiful. The flower had been produced by Gæa that it might be a snare to Persephone; so when she reached forth her hand to take it, the earth opened and Hades, in his chariot drawn by four immortal horses, sprang forth, seized her, and bore her to his dark dominions. Hecate, sitting in her cave, "thinking delicate thoughts," heard Persephone's cries, but only Helios saw the sad scene.

For nine days and nine nights the agonized Demeter wandered over the earth (or, as one legend says, rode in a chariot drawn by dragons), refusing to taste of ambrosia or nectar. When the tenth morning came Helios, the watchman of gods and men, told her the whole story. In her grief and anger Demeter forsook the assembly of gods and wandered among men. She came to Eleusis and sat down by a well. The four daughters of Celeus (king of Eleusis), Callidice, Cleisidice, Demo, and Callithœ, came to draw water for their father's household. They did not know Demeter, for "the gods are hard for men to recognize."

Demeter was taken to the palace of King Celeus, and his wife, Metaneira, gave into the care of the goddess her son Demophoön. Triptolemus, a brother of Demophoön, became a great favorite of Demeter, and she instructed him in agriculture and the use of the plough.

During the sorrowful stay of Demeter at Eleusis the whole earth was barren, Demeter refusing to permit a stalk of grain to appear. Zeus sent messengers entreating Demeter's return to Olympus; Iris came; even Rhea besought the sorrowful mother to send forth the needed grain; but she was deaf to all prayers unless she could see her child again. Zeus despatched Hermes to Hades, begging him to restore Persephone to her mother. Hades consented, and Hermes conducted Persephone to her mother at Eleusis. Hecate deeply sympathized in their joy, and became the attendant of Persephone.

Before leaving Hades, Persephone had partaken of a part of a pomegranate, thus placing herself under obligation to return for a portion of the year; so it was decided that she should pass one-third of the year with him, and the remaining portion with her mother, either on earth or on Mount Olympus.

Before leaving Eleusis, Demeter instructed Celeus in the Eleusinian Mysteries, and he erected a magnificent temple in honor of the goddess.

Fine as was the conception of Demeter, it had traces of that ancient worship which was of the earth, earthy; so to her, as to Phrygian Cybele and to Cretan Zeus, caves were sacred, and she was supposed to preside over the streams issuing therefrom, and over the uncultivated vegetation that they produced. It is probable that this phase in the character of the goddess was foreign in origin and quite limited in extent, for a careful analysis of the deepest meaning and of the highest development of the myth of Demeter and Persephone will show a range of elements so wide as to comprehend moral teachings and religious hopes.

Consider the actors in this mystic drama: Hades, bearing from earth a trophy infinitely more precious than its crown of golden grain; Demeter, sublime enough in her sorrow to refuse Olympian nectar and to despise the entreaties of gods; Persephone, bending her lovely brow in seeming submission to the seeming victor, but living, reigning even, in his dominion—nay more, coming forth triumphantly. Such a myth might readily become a hope, a belief, that the land of shades was not one of lasting gloom, but one in which life was held most sacred. The *restored* Persephone came like an angel of hope with a crown of vernal flowers to say that what man calls "death" is only a condition or a phase of life—hidden, indeed, but in the royal keeping of the Lord of life, Zeus.

Gladly and tenderly the returned Persephone wreathed urns and mausoleums with immortelles, while she whispered that unseen ones live, and that those who pass first into the shadows might linger in asphodel meadows until the coming of those they loved; then, if their spirits had gathered only the pure and the lovely elements of the life they had passed on earth, they might enter into that land where purity, sweetness, and joy are immortal.

We know that in the later and higher stages of the Eleusinian Mysteries the myth of Demeter, Hades, and Persephone became a symphony of human life, having pæans of achievement, wails over sorrows and over wan-

DEMETER.

ing powers. the gasp of defeat by the conqueror Death, and the immortal song of resurrection glory.

Assoc. Myths (of Demeter).

Wanderings of Demeter. Ascalabus.—As Demeter was drinking at a fountain this youth annoyed her by his mockery, and she transformed him into a water-newt.

"*Stone of Sorrow.*"—This name was applied to a stone on which the wandering goddess sat down to rest.

"*The Sacred Well.*"—The well and its overhanging olive tree at which the daughters of Celeus found Demeter were held sacred to her.

Demeter at Eleusis.—Demeter refused to nourish herself with wine, but was induced to partake of a preparation of barley and mint. This was commemorated in her worship by the Mystæ.

Demophoön (the son of King Celeus) thrived under the divine nurture of Demeter. She wished to render him immortal, so every night she anointed him with ambrosia and laid him in fire that it might consume his mortal parts. Metaneira watched the goddess, and, being terrified at her strange proceedings, shrieked aloud; the goddess was offended at the mother's want of faith, and the child lost the favor designed for him. Nevertheless, as he had lain in the bosom of a goddess, there was ever about him a nameless charm of manner.

Demeter dwelt for a year in the temple that Celeus had erected to her, and she made Triptolemus (his son) and Eumolpus (son of Poseidon) her priests.

Erysichthon was a youth who cut down some of the trees in a grove sacred to Demeter; in consequence of this he was punished with insatiable hunger.

Triptolemus.—Before leaving Eleusis, Demeter presented to Triptolemus her car and dragons and gave him barley, that he might traverse all lands and sow the grain and teach men agriculture.

Assoc. Myths (of Persephone).

Ascalaphus.—When Persephone partook of the pomegranate offered by Hades, she was seen only by Ascalaphus, who repeated the story, and was therefore changed into a night-owl.

Iacchus.—(For Iacchus and other myths of Demeter, Persephone, and Dionysus, see DIONYSUS.)

Offices and Archetypes (of Demeter).
Nature: 1. Goddess of the life of Nature, as related to the interest of man. *Arch.*, vegetation of fruits and grains as suited to the nourishment of man; also that mystic adaptation of the physical world to the nature of man that makes it possible for the material world to mirror and reflect the varying moods of the human soul.
2. More remotely, goddess of the seashore.

Human Life: 1. Goddess of agriculture. *Arch.*, social order that results from the division, appropriation, and cultivation of lands.
2. Goddess of laws and legal sanctions.
3. Goddess of marriage and of births. *Arch.*, divine sympathy with humanity in its highest interests.

Theog.: 1. Mother of Persephone. *Arch.*, the divinely-human, personal, tender love of a mother for her child.
2. Goddess of sympathy for sorrow. *Arch.*, the sorrow and sympathy for sorrow that result from the loss of loved ones.

3. Goddess of just retribution. *Arch.*, penalty of violated law.
4. Great goddess, resisting even Zeus and compelling him to restore her daughter. *Arch.*, new life springing out of decayed vegetation.
5. Giver of life and of immortality. *Arch.*, life in the fruit that seemed to provide for its own reproduction.

Emblems.
Nature: Crown of wheat-ears, goddess of fruits and grains.
Poppy, by many seeds, productiveness; cornucopia, the same.
Liknon (mystic or fan-shaped basket), goddess of beneficence.
Crane, messenger of the rain that brings fertility.
Human Life: Plough, sickle, etc., goddess of agriculture.
Poppy, goddess who solaced human grief.
Theog.: Rude form with horse's head, ancient earth-goddess or goddess of dark caves.
Dragons and a lighted torch, search for Persephone.

PERSEPHONE.

Offices and Archetypes.
Nature: 1. By concealment of seed in the earth to produce death of old forms and conditions.
2. To preserve the life of the seed given by Demeter to its germ, and to restore it to the earth in a new and living plant, itself endowed with power to produce seed or fruit that again held the life-producing germ.
3. Like Hades, goddess of the life and death of vege-

tation. *Arch.*, internal heat that nourishes or destroys vegetation.

Human Life: 1. As Coré, or universal daughter, child-relation of humanity to divinity.

2. As goddess of death, that all men are mortal, but by reason of the promise from Zeus, the Lord of life (of her return to the earth), the restored Persephone is a crystallization of the universal belief in the immortality of the soul.

Theog.: 1. Queen of the lower world.

2. Associated with Hecate as goddess of magic.

Emblems.

Nature: Wheat-ears, calathus, or the liknon (mystic basket), co-operation with Demeter.

Narcissus, decay that precedes new life.

Veil, mysterious processes of buried seed.

Stars and flames, internal fire or heat that sometimes nourishes life, at others destroys.

Human Life: Poppy with its narcotic juices, sleep of death and dreams that may arise.

Theog.: Key, queen of the lower world.

Pomegranate (bound to Hades), goddess of death. Later, seed sown in the lower world that should live again; hence typified the resurrection.

Apples signified renewed life.

Representations (of Demeter and Persephone).

Early.—1. As the earth-goddess of caves and streams. At Phigalia was a statue of Demeter called "the black Demeter;" the figure was rude and had the head of a horse (see POSEIDON).

2. As earth-goddess, with attributes of grain and fruits.

Later.—1. As mother-goddess (probably the Attic

school—Praxiteles). In this character Demeter is more matronly and mother-like than Hera, is partly veiled and enveloped in drapery.
2. In connection with the story of Persephone, Demeter has distinctive characteristics. She is—1, the sorrowing mother, dumb with grief; 2, the agonized mother, in a chariot drawn by winged dragons, searching the broad earth for her child; and, finally, 3, the enthroned Demeter in the victory of love.
3. Persephone, in co-operation with the earth-goddess, is not always readily distinguished from her mother, but has youth and more exquisite delicacy of outline. As queen of the lower world, Persephone is sedate, even solemn. Even as restored Persephone there is a subtle sadness, as though she were casting secret glances toward the shadows into which she must again enter.

THE ELEUSINIAN MYSTERIES.

Location.—Eleusis, every fifth year.

Priesthood.—Hierophant, one who presided over the ceremonies; assistants, a torch-bearer, a crier, a minister at the altar, a basileus or king, four curators, and ten to offer sacrifices.

Lesser Mysteries (Micra).

The candidates for higher mysteries must first pass through the lesser, which consisted in a series of fastings and purifications. At the end of a year they were called "mystæ," and might then aspire to the *Greater Mysteries*.

Greater Mysteries.

First day, *assembly* (agurmos), for the worshippers convened.

Second day, *purifications*, called "Alade Mystai," from the cry, "To the sea, initiated ones!"

Third day, *sacrifices*, millet and barley from Eleusis (this was for Demeter as the sorrowing one).

Fourth day, *processions*. The calathus, or sacred basket, was borne; also cista, or chests, in which were sesamum, carded wool, salt, pomegranates, poppies, a serpent, thyrsi, cakes, ivy.

Fifth day, *day of torches ;* in the evening a torchlight procession.

Sixth day, statue of Iacchus borne from Athens by Iacchogoroi, who were crowned with myrtle. The image was borne through the sacred gate into Eleusis.

Seventh day, *athletic games ;* prize, a measure of barley.

Eighth day, sacred to Æsculapius as god of health and life.

Initiation or veiling to the outer world (evening of the eighth day). The candidates, crowned with myrtle, entered the vestibule of the temple, and there bathed in holy water. They were then led into the presence of the hierophant, who from two tablets of stone read to them things which must never be revealed.

The mystæ (veiled) took solemn oaths of secrecy.

The *revealing* (epopteia). The goddess revealed herself in vivid light, sealed the solemn instructions that her high priests had uttered, and the enraptured, awestruck worshipper caught visions of the Elysian Fields and heard the chorus of the blessed, "which typified the immortal communion that pure souls should have with divinity." The mystæ had now become the epoptæ, or seers.

Associated Deities (see DIONYSUS and HECATE).

Thermophoria. Festivals participated in only by women.

Grecian Comp. Myth.
Demeter embodied attributes of Rhea; Persephone, Venus Libitina.

Foreign Comp. Myth.
Demeter was identified with PHRYGIAN Cybele, EGYPTIAN, Isis as earth-mother.

Literature.
1, *Homeric Hymns;* 2, *Hymns of Callimachus;* 3, *Rape of Persephone*, by Claudian.

Art.
Coins of Thebes, Demeter as earth-goddess.
Coins of Athens, Demeter with a child (Iacchus or Demophoön).
Vases, scenes connected with Triptolemus.
Sarcophagi, scenes connected with Persephone.
Parthenon.—1, Demeter, Persephone, and Iacchus (posterior tympanum); 2, sending out of Triptolemus (metope).
Statuary.—1, a statue in Capitoline Museum (Rome); 2, mutilated colossal statue from Megara, Greece (in the Academy of Fine Arts, Philadelphia, Pa.); 3, (see MODERN RESEARCH).

Modern Research.
Cnidus, three statues (now in the British Museum):
1. Persephone as goddess of death. The lines and

shadows of the face are delicate; the figure has a tower-like head-dress, from which a veil depends; the corn-basket balanced on the head; in the hand she holds what may be a flower or a pomegranate.

2. Demeter (or a priestess of Demeter) is a tall, veiled, heavily-draped figure; probably represents the goddess wandering in her anguish.

3. Demeter enthroned is a seated figure, representing the goddess enthroned as the "glorified mother of all things."

Cesnola Collection.—" 1. A statue of Demeter, wearing an under-tunic, or chiton; over it a mantle, which falls from the back of her head and is wrapped round the figure, leaving the hands free. The manner of wearing the upper mantle, descending like a veil from the back of the head, is especially characteristic of this goddess, and always distinguishes the mother mourning for the loss of Persephone; for even amid the joy of her presence she could never forget that the period of separation must again arrive.

"2. A statuette group, the central figure of which is probably Demeter. She wears a high crown (stephanos) richly ornamented with rosettes and sphinxes, resembling the figures of the Sphinx in gold found at Curium, and now in the Metropolitan Museum of Art. From the back of the head hangs a veil. She is supported on either side by a female figure, each holding a delabra or toilette-casket. The high crown and the hand raised to the breast would suggest that it meant to represent Demeter, whose worship is known to have existed in this island (Cyprus), and to have been accompanied by a very celebrated festival. This suggestion is confirmed by the discovery, on the same spot where I found this statuette, of two little pedestals with Greek inscriptions in honor of Demeter Paralia—*i. e.* protectress of the seashore—to whom there appears to have been a temple." (These descriptions of the above statues are by General di Cesnola.)

Descendants.

There are legends that Demeter bore to Zeus, Iacchus; to Poseidon, Arion (a black horse gifted with speech); to Iasion, Plutus, a personification of the wealth derived from grain.

POSEIDON, OR NEPTUNE.

(TABLE B, 11.)

Central Ideas.

As god of the sea, Poseidon is to be distinguished from—1, Pontus, the primal mass of salt, unfertilizing waters; 2, Oceanus, the mass of waters considered as the source of fresh, fertilizing streams; 3, Nereus, the subterranean waters. To Poseidon was assigned the control of the sea—first, in its relations to storms and earthquakes; second, in its relations to commerce; third, as the source of vegetation on its shores.

Probably in this duality of Poseidon lies the explanation of the symbolism of the horse, so associated with this deity; for, placing the horse at the head of the animal kingdom, the Pelasgic people would naturally attach great importance to the vegetation of "horse-feeding plains;" to the streams that supplied such vegetation; to Poseidon as supplying the streams and giving general protection to the pursuits connected therewith. The use of the horse in symbolizing the power, freedom, and grace of the moving waves is more Hellenic than Pelasgic.

As the deity having special control of commerce, Poseidon was held in great reverence by the Phœnicians, and his worship prevailed in maritime cities, gradually losing or subordinating the relations to streams, vegetation, and the creating and training of horses.

Offices and Archetypes.

Nature: 1. Lord of the sea (particularly the Mediterranean). *Arch.*, first, the sea as a reservoir of productive forces, which supply moisture, form clouds and streams, extend shores, and form new islands; second, the sea as a reservoir of destructive forces, which produce storms and earthquakes, abrade shores, and destroy foundation-walls of cities.

2. Lord of fertilizing showers and streams *Arch.*, fertility that yields pasturage to animals, particularly the horse.

3. Creator of horses by striking the ground with his trident.

4. Lord of subterranean forces.

Human Life: 1. Protector of shipbuilding, navigation, and commerce.

2. Protector of training of horses and chariot-races.

3. Protector of buildings. *Arch.*, perhaps the depositing of sediment through which shores are extended.

4. Assisting warriors by enveloping their enemies in mists.

5. Inspiring heroes with physical courage by a touch of his trident, but having no power over mind.

Theog.: Position, subordinate to Zeus in the Hellenic system; chief deity in the Phœnician. Character: varied characteristics were assigned to Poseidon. He was haughty (rebelling against Zeus), powerful, vindictive, patient.

Poseidon and Amphitrite.

Early Legends.

Aided Zeus in the Titanic War (TABLE B, 4).

Abode.

1. A splendid palace in the depths of the sea, near Ægæ.
2. Poseidon appeared at the Olympian court, also in the plains of Troy.

Attendants.

Triton (his son), as herald.

Nereides, as attendants of Poseidon and Amphitrite.

Tritons, beings the upper part of whose bodies was human, and the lower part that of a fish.

Proteus, servant of Poseidon, who took sea-calves to graze on the coasts and islands of the Mediterranean.

Assoc. Myths.

1. Poseidon united with Apollo in building the walls of Troy for King Laomedon. Laomedon withheld the promised reward, and thus aroused the anger of Poseidon, who threatened to send a terrible sea-monster to lay waste the country of the king. (See HERACLES.)
2. Amymone (daughter of Danaus) so charmed Poseidon that by blows of his trident he produced for her three springs, one of which formed the Vale of Tempe.
3. Contests (encroachments of the sea).—Poseidon contested with Athena for Attica (see ATHENA); with Hera for Argos; with Helios for Corinth; with Dionysus for Naxos; with Apollo for Delphi; and with Zeus for Ægina.

Emblems.

Nature: Chariot, or large shell, drawn by hippocampi, or by horses, or by Tritons, Poseidon as ruler of the sea.

Dolphin, young fish (Phœnician), productiveness of the sea.
Vase with two handles, god of moisture.
Trident planted on a rock, Poseidon as the earth-shaker.
Water-plants, sometimes grapes and grains, fertility that results from moisture.
Horse—first, Poseidon as god of well-watered pasture-lands; second, the force, motion, and grace of the moving sea.

Human Life: Pine tree, god of shipbuilding.
Horse, Poseidon as protector of chariot-races.
Prow of a ship or a tiller of a ship, god of commerce.
Anchor planted on a rock or a column, god who quiets storms.

Theog.: Trident, ruler of third part of the universe.
Chlamys, divinity.
A band like a diadem, dominion over the sea.

Representations.
1. With Amphitrite in a car or chariot drawn by horses or hippocampi, flying over the sea.
2. Standing on a rock, holding a trident.
3. Holding a dolphin and a trident.
4. Reclining on the shore of a tranquil sea; near him two dolphins and a prow of a ship.
5. Wearing a crown of leaves of water-plants.
6. Sitting on a rock; near him what appear to be monsters having plumeless wings, dragon heads, and webbed feet.

Worship.
Isthmian Games.

Location.—Corinth, Athens, Pilus, etc.; also, islands of Cos, Rhodes, etc.

Ceremonies.—*Sacrifices.* Black bulls, rams, and boars. The gall of victims was also offered. Victims were thrown into the sea.

Athletic Games.—Prize, wreath of pine or ivy. (This prize was originally a wreath of parsley.)

Literature.

In the Trojan War opposed the Trojans (see LAOMEDON).

Art.

A marble statue and a bust in the Vatican Museum.

Descendants (see TABLE B).

HESTIA, OR VESTA.

(TABLE B, 12.)

Central Ideas.

Amid all the changes of time there was observed a perpetuity, a renewal after decay, a triumphing of life over death, that suggested some central, controlling, preserving power which permitted changes, but held all things in the limits of law and safety. By a charming myth this conserving power was embodied in the goddess Hestia.

Early Legends.

At the time of the Titanic War, Hestia lent her gracious influence to the cause of Zeus, and when, in gratitude, he asked her to mention some favor that she would accept from him, she asked the privileges of remaining single, of being always with him, and of having a portion in all the sacrifices and offerings that were made to the other deities. These favors were

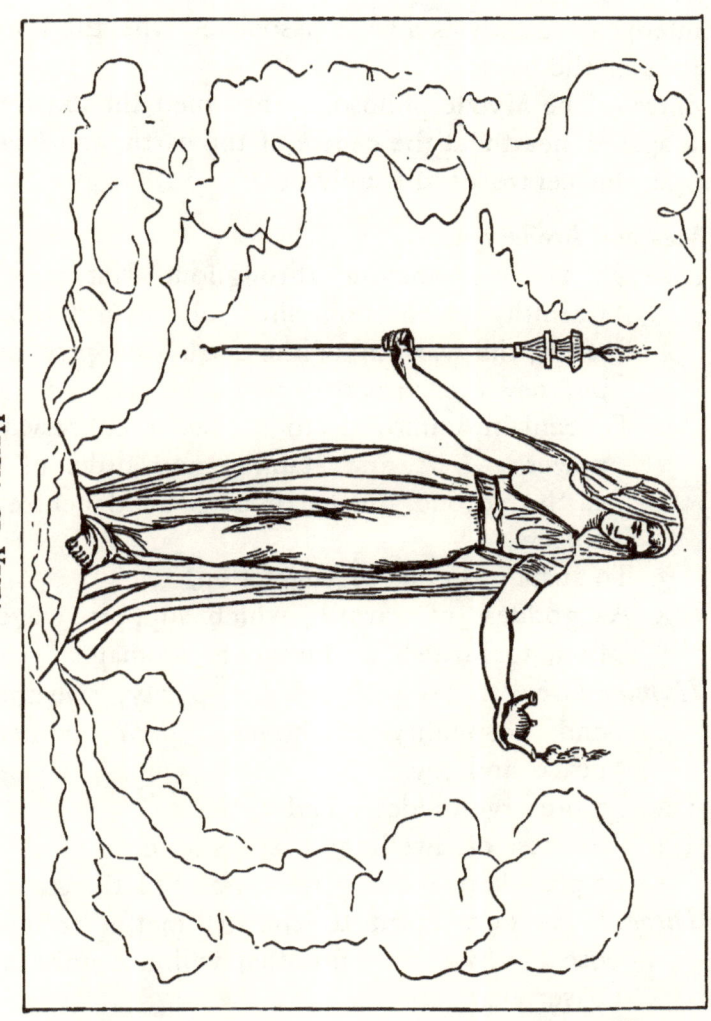

HESTIA, OR VESTA.

granted, so Hestia was always associated with the home-centres of the world.

Later.—The Mystic philosophy assumed the existence of a sacred hearth at the centre of the earth, and finally one at the centre of the universe.

Offices and Archetypes.

Nature: 1. To transfuse throughout Nature that warmth which nourishes all living things. *Arch.*, the warmth of the earth that promotes, but never destroys, growth.

2. To remain unmoved, to act as a conservative power. *Arch.*, first, stability and order of the earth; second, the earth as a solid centre of objects.

3. To sustain the life of vegetation.

4. As goddess of warmth, which supports vegetation, to furnish pasturage to animals.

Human Life: 1. To preserve the purity, sweetness, and hospitality of home. *Arch.*, domestic peace and joy.

2. To preserve modesty and virtue.

3. Patroness of dwellings used as homes.

4. To preside over the general good of the state.

Theog.: As pure spirit to convert matter to noble uses. *Arch.*, pure fire, that will not unite with baser elements

Emblems.

Nature: Fire, source of life-sustaining warmth.

A globe, stability and regularity.

Earth clothed with verdure, fertility and beauty that spring from harmony of forces.

Hestia seated and crowned with flowers signifies the same.

Hestia holding a sickle and grain, near her the head of a horse, may signify that goddess of vegetation which supplies pasturage to animals.

Human Life: Lamps or lighted torch, preserver of human life.

Serpent, fresh or renewed life.

Pure flame (lamp, etc.), preserver of moral purity.

Vestibule, goddess of buildings used for homes.

Propylæa or temple-gates, goddess of cities as public homes.

Hearth-fire; light, love, and hospitality of homes.

Fire in the prytaneum, well-being of the state; also unity of the national life.

The Palladium, in the hand of Hestia, had the same meaning.

Theog.: Altar-fire, preserver of the observance of moral law.

Veil and full drapery, modesty, gentleness, and purity.

Hermæ statue, association with Hermes as the god of sacrifices (because she was goddess of moral law and order).

Representation.

1. With sickle, wheat-ears, and head of a horse.
2. Standing near an altar, holding a lamp or torch.
3. Hermaic statue (see EMBLEMS, IN THEOGONY).
4. Draped and veiled, holding a lamp.

Worship.

Temples to Hestia were very few, as she had the first portion of every sacrifice, and in every prytaneum she had a sacred hearth.

Sacrifices.—The young of animals.

Offerings.—Tender shoots of plants and fruits.
Libations.—Wine, water, and oil.
Priestesses.—Vestal virgins, whose chief office was to preserve the sacred fires used in the worship of Hestia.

Grecian Comp. Myth.

Hestia is often confounded with the earth-goddesses Gæa, Cybele, and Demeter.

Foreign Comp. Myth.

EGYPTIAN, Anouka; ROMAN, Terra, Hestia in her character as earth-goddess.

Art.

1. Hestia and Athena crowning a youth (British Museum).
2. Vesta Giustiniani (Prince Tolmia, Rome).
3. Two statues found at Velleia were believed to be of Hestia.

HESTIA: A SONNET.

BY MARGARET J. PRESTON.

O GENTLE goddess of the Grecian hearth!
  Whose altar was the cheerful table spread,
  Whose sacrifice the pleasant daily bread,
Offered with incense of sweet childhood's mirth,
And parents' priestly ministrations, worth
  More than all other rites that ever shed
  Light on the path that those young feet must tread—
Has thy pure worship ceased from off the earth?
We heap new fires, we overbrim the bowl,
  We pile the board; at our most sacred shrine
    The world holds revel; far and wide we roam
  For better things than household oil and wine;
Yet go unblest. And why? Because the coal
    That kindles comes not from the fire of *Home*.

DESCENDANTS OF ZEUS AND GODDESSES.

PALLAS ATHENA [*Päl'läs Athe'na*], OR MINERVA.

(TABLE B, 13.)

Central Ideas.

One of the grandest individual creations in mythology is that of Pallas Athena, the divine child, illustrating, not the tenderness of the child-relation, as did the story of Demeter and Persephone, but the power, wisdom, and magnificence of her supreme father. She was to accomplish this by pervading every department of the universe with unceasing activity, so that every organization should work—work wisely and under the direction of a noble purpose.

Early Legends.

1. It had been prophesied that Zeus would be dethroned by his own son. He had married Metis, but to prevent the fulfilment of the prophecy he absorbed Metis into his own person, and from his brain sprang Athena, in armor that was terrible to evil-doers, but heavenly in its splendor to those who were entitled to its protection. Then in Athena the Greeks saw a goddess who would inspire, sustain, and direct all wise and grand living—not in a loving way, but still with a gentleness that made right living seem beautiful.

2. It was said that Athena was educated near the marsh Tritonis.

Offices and Archetypes.

Nature: 1. We must always suppose a profound sympathy between the daughter of the Fashioner of Nature and the world that he has

PALLAS ATHENA, OR MINERVA.

fashioned. We remember that the most universally-accepted and the most perfect archetype of Zeus was pure ether, as a force-centre whose manifestations were the mighty forces of light, heat, and life. Then, as Athena was to represent Zeus as having control of the material universe, she was more than queen of the air; and her most worthy archetype would be,

like his, ether, that glows with light and fire
—not the fire that should be utilized to common purposes, nor even kindled on the home-hearth or prytaneum, but that central inspiring force that shone in eternal splendor.

2. To supply moisture and dew to the earth. *Arch.*, dew and mists. The title "all-bedewing" that pertained to Athena indicates that (at least in localities) she was connected with the production of moisture. K. O. Müller asserts in evidence of this that her festivals were held in dew-bearing months, and that in some processions dew-bearing had a place. He explains the whole association of dew with Athena as follows: "The Greeks conceived that the light, the stars, the meteors drew nourishment from the waters, and then returned it to the earth as moisture. This theory is favored by such terms as 'bedewing stars,' 'heaven-producing dew,' etc. If this belief was at all general, it is not improbable that the goddess of light should be esteemed as the bestower of dew and fertilizing moisture."

3. To have a general supervision of vegetation through her offices of giver of light and moisture. The creation of the olive tree was attributed to Athena.

4. Protectress of horses. We have seen that Poseidon became less and less closely identified with streams and vegetation, but more and more closely with maritime interests. Now, whether in her character of the direct representative of the Author of Nature, or through her relations to moisture, or because legends had associated

her with maritime or river deities, there seems to have been quite general the association of Athena with pasturage and protection of horses as they are identified with the service of man.

Human Life: 1. As daughter of the great Artificer of Nature; to preside over inventions, learning, fine arts, and every interest that ennobles mankind. *Arch.*, unity in variety that evinces infinite wisdom and power.

2. To inspire and protect heroes. We have found that Poseidon had no power in the mental world. It was Athena that came to the *mind;* not alone that she might make it wise, but that she might give it such visions of great achievements as should nerve hearts to become heroic in that exalted service in which the strong is ever willing to labor for the weak.

3. To preside over just war. As representative of him who was not only supreme ruler, but "Father of men," and who as the Supreme Good would remove evil from his dominion, Pallas Athena presided over those just wars and contests that had for their exalted aim victory over evil in the interests of right and humanity.

4. Athena protected cities from or during attacks or sieges.

5. *To preserve political order and safety.* As representative of Zeus as maker of laws and maintainer of justice, Athena had special control of the highest and best interests of the state and observance of law. She was said to have formed the court of the Areopagus. A beautiful proof that in their idea of Athena

the Greeks mingled the element of mercy lies in the fact that they believed that when the votes of the judges were equally divided, Athena gave the casting-vote in favor of the accused.

Theog.: " Athena was a divine personification of mind working throughout the universe, carrying out the plans which Zeus as impartial ruler could conceive, but could not absolutely execute." By reason of the complex character of one who was to correct the evil and promote the good, she compelled apparent contradictions into harmony, and enabled mind to subordinate not only matter, but also weaker minds, in furtherance of the highest interests of man.

Assoc. Myths.

1. *Enceladus.*—In the war of the Giants, Athena secured the aid of Heracles, then lent him her counsel, and afterward sustained him in his great labors.

2. Athena protected the Argonauts in their expedition.

3. She gave a shield to Perseus when he slew the Gorgon Medusa, who with Poseidon had profaned her temple; she aided Theseus in his many contests with the enemies of man.

4. Poseidon contended with Athena for possession of the soil of Attica. She produced an olive tree as the best gift to man, whether it symbolized nourishment for his body, wealth that comes from the soil, or the peace that results from national prosperity. Poseidon produced by a blow of his trident, one legend says, a horse, but others say a salt spring, probably claiming supremacy for commerce, the wealth of the seas. Cecrops decided in favor of Athena, who thus became the tutelar deity of Attica.

5. Athena taught men (first Erichthonius) the art of taming horses and of yoking them to chariots.

6. It is said that Athena "wove the robe of the universe"—a charming way of expressing the thought of her as superintending the processes of Nature. Athena is represented as weaving her own robe, as attiring Pandora, and as giving to Jason a mantle wrought by herself.

7. *Arachne* (of Lydia).—Arachne, being proud of her skill in weaving, challenged Athena to a contest of skill. Arachne's work was so perfect that even Athena could find no fault with it, but she tore it in pieces. Arachne, in despair, hung herself; Athena loosened the rope and saved the life of the maiden, but the rope was changed into a cobweb, while Arachne became a spider.

8. Athena adopted Erichthonius, the serpent-legged son of Gæa and Hephæstus. She committed him to the care of the daughters of Cecrops, king of Attica, with injunctions that they refrain from looking at the child. Agraulos and Herse disobeyed, and, frightened at the sight of the strange form, became frantic and threw themselves from a rock of the Acropolis. Pandrosos alone remained true to her trust, and she was therefore made priestess of Athena, and was afterward worshipped in a sanctuary that adjoined Athena's. Erichthonius succeeded Cecrops in the government of Attica, and he instituted Athenæa (sacred festivals in honor of Athena), and after his death he was associated in the worship of Athena (see ERECHTHEUM). King Erichthonius was succeeded by his son Pandion, who was succeeded by his son Erechtheus. The Eumolpodæ (descendants of Poseidon and the priest-family of Demeter at Eleusis) made war upon the descendants of Erichthonius. A reconciliation was effected, and the worship of

Poseidon was associated with that of Athena and Erichthonius.

9. Athena was one of the three goddesses who appealed to the "Judgment of Paris" (see APHRODITE).

Emblems.

Nature: Ether or air, source of light, fire, and power.
    Oil, as feeding lamps and giving light.
    A lamp, an ancient symbol for light.
    Triton, goddess of marshes and pasture-lands.
    Olive tree, creator of the olive.
    Serpent (Erichthonius), abundance of the earth.

War: Ægis, or the scaly belt, power and majesty of Zeus.
    Shield, with the head of Medusa or a lion's head.
    Helmet, whose crest is a cock, a dragon, a griffin.
    A spear, a spike, or a "Victory," a dart or a thunderbolt.
    Laurels, victory.
    Oil, for anointing heroes.

Human Life: Serpent or dragon, that health that comes from right living.
    Chariot and four horses, horses in the service of man.
    Distaff, goddess of employments of women.
    Scroll, goddess of wisdom and arts.
    Vases, called "Athena vases," patroness of ceramics, also physical culture.
    Olive-branch, inventress of olive oil.
    Palladium, protectress of national welfare.

Theog.: Ægis, power and majesty of Zeus.
    Medusa head, victory over evil.
    Cock, as bird of morning light, energy, and courage.
    Owl or the serpent, wisdom.
    Peplum, long tunic, purity of character; also divinity.

Patera, as goddess who accepts worship.

Representations.
1. *Early.*—Olive-wood statue (believed to have fallen from heaven).
2. Goddess of just war—1, as offensive, with shield and brandished spear. 2, as victorious and peacefully ruling, with arm and ægis partially covered with drapery, while the shield rests on the ground.
3. Goddess of battles on the sea, standing on the prow of a ship between a "Victory" and a palm tree, while she launches a dart or a thunderbolt.
4. On horseback or in a chariot drawn by four horses.
5. With distaff or spindle, as the goddess who protected and promoted domestic arts and progress.
6. *Parthenon Representations.*—It would seem that in the pediments of that wonderful temple were suggested the varied, subtle, and important relations of Athena to the departments of soil, moisture, air, and light. The metopes gave splendid prominence to her character as an inspirer of heroes, while in Athena Parthenos she shone in transcendent glory as the champion of eternal justice, truth, and right.

Worship.
Location.—The Acropolis, at Athens, a fortified hill, entered through a magnificent temple-gate called "the Propylæa."

In the Erechtheum, a temple north of the Parthenon, were the following sacred objects:

1. An olive-wood statue of Athena (Athena Polias), said to have fallen from heaven. This statue was the most sacred object in Athens, and was the one that was

invested with the sacred peplos at the time of the Panathenaic Procession.

2. The olive tree created by Athena at the time of her contest with Poseidon.

3. The salt spring produced by Poseidon; also, in a rock, the impress of his trident.

4. A sacred serpent, as symbol of how Erichthonius was nourished in the temple.

5. Altars—1, to Zeus, as supreme; 2, to Poseidon, on which were offered sacrifices to Erichthonius; 3, to Butes; 4, to Hephæstus; 5, an altar of incense.

6. A brazen palm tree, and a golden lamp perpetually lighted.

7. A wooden statue of Hermes, covered with myrtle (a gift of Cecrops).

8. The grave of Erichthonius. The Cecropeum may have commemorated Cecrops.

The Parthenon was a temple to Athena Parthenos, the virgin goddess. Style, Doric, surrounded by columns.

East pediment, Zeus introducing to the Olympic deities the goddess who had sprung from his brain, Pallas Athena.

West pediment, the contest between Athena and Poseidon; the central object, the sacred olive tree.

Metopes, contests between the Centaurs and the Lapithæ.

The ornamentation of the cella, or body of the temple, was the *Panathenaic Procession*. Within the peristyle (surrounding row of columns), at either end, there was an interior range of six columns, standing before the end of the cella and forming a vestibule to its door. The frieze of these vestibules extended around the cella, and gave in low relief a representation of the Panathenaic Procession. This frieze represented the procession as dividing at the south-west angle of the cella, one portion passing around the southern, the other around the northern, portion of the cella, and uniting in the presentation of the sacred peplos to the twelve great deities, who were seated in sublime repose in the eastern front of the cella-frieze.

Sacred Objects.—Athena Parthenos, a statue by Phidias of ivory and gold, with the following emblems: Sphinx as a crest of the helmet; a Medusa on her breast; a Victory; a spear; at her feet a shield, near which is a serpent (Erichthonius). On the base of the statue was carved the nativity of Pandora.

Associated Deities.

Outside of the Acropolis, with the worship of Athena was associated that of Prometheus and Hephæstus; also that of Apollo, Pandora, and Agraulos.

Priesthood.—1. Priestess to Athena, who had the care of the sacred serpent.

2. Priest (descendant of Butes) in the associated worship of Athena, Poseidon, and Erichthonius.

3. Caniphores, maidens who bore the calathus, or basket, containing utensils to be used in worship.

GREATER PANATHENÆA.

Institution.—Theseus gave political unity to the twelve towns of Attica and established the general worship of Athena. The Athenæa (instituted by Erichthonius) were thereafter called Panathenæa—a lesser festival being observed annually, but the Greater Panathenæa being celebrated every fifth year.

Sacrifices.—Citizens from all parts of Attica assembled at Athens, bringing sacrifices consisting of oxen that had never been under the yoke, rams, cows, and lambs.

Athletic Exercises.—In the Stadium and the Hippodrome (outside of the Acropolis) took place the usual athletic contests, the prizes being crowns of olive and painted vases filled with oil made from the sacred olive tree.

Musical and Literary Contests.—In the Odeon (hall for musical contests) were competitive performances on the flute and on the cithara, or by singers accompanied by one of these instruments. In the same place poets contended for fame, and the prizes in the Odeon were like those for athletic victories. Olive crowns were sometimes bestowed on those who had performed heroic actions.

The Panathenaic Procession.—The object of this world-renowned procession was to bear a newly-wrought peplos to the Erechtheum and place it upon the olive-wood statue of Athena Polias. The procession formed on the plains of Eleusis, and it was composed of various classes of people, nearly all crowned with flowers.

1. The older men bore branches of olives.
2. The younger men were clad in fine armor, while youths chanted hymns in honor of the goddess.
3. The young maidens with their hands held upon their heads baskets, which under a rich veil contained sacred utensils to be used in sacrifice, cakes, frankincense, and flowers. These maidens were attended by the daughters of foreigners, who carried umbrellas, folding chairs, etc.
4. The foreigners who joined in the procession bore vases of water and honey, to be used in libations.
5. Eight musicians took part, four of whom played on the flute and four on the cithara. There were rhapsodists who sang the songs of Homer, and dancers who, splendidly armed, represented the heroic deeds of Athena.

6. Deputations from Grecian colonies with offerings of cattle and sheep.

7. The central object of this grand array was a ship (apparently impelled by many rowers and by the wind, but really moving by concealed machinery), which bore as a sail the sacred peplos. Upon this peplos young daughters of the noblest families had embroidered in gold the triumphs of Athena over the giants.

The procession passed through the principal streets of the city, and when it reached the temple of Apollo the peplos was taken from the ship and was carried by persons appointed to the office. The procession ascended the Acropolis and passed through the Propylæa. It then divided at the south-west angle of the Acropolis, one portion passing in a northern direction and the other in a southern; the two divisions joined at the east front of the Erechtheum, and united in placing the new peplos upon the ancient statue of Athena Polias.

Torch-Races.—These took place in the Academy in the evening (see PROMETHEUS).

Banquets.—Banquets in the prytaneum were given by the victors in various contests to their friends, and feasts, furnished from portions of the sacrifices, were spread in many places.

Statue of Athena Promachus.—Near the Erechtheum and the Parthenon was a bronze colossal statue of Athena as champion goddess. Her emblems were shield, spear, and helmet.

Foreign Comp. Myth.

1, ROMAN, Minerva; 2, INDIAN, Ushas; 3, EGYPTIAN, Neith.

History.

1. Palladium in Troy (see TROJAN WAR).

2. Spoils from Marathon formed the statue of Athena Promachus, while spoils from Salamis erected the statue of Athena Parthenos.

Literature.

In the Trojan War, Athena aided the Greeks (see *Iliad*).

Art.

Coins, ceramics, statuary, etc., illustrating the general types mentioned under REPRESENTATIONS, may be found in Athens, Dresden, Rome, London, Paris, and other art-centres.

The "Elgin marbles," now in the British Museum, are portions of the statuary and reliefs of the Parthenon. They are composed of—first, the mutilated statues and fragments of statues from the pediments; second, seventeen metopes (out of ninety-two); third, about four hundred feet of the low relief that formed the frieze of the cella and represented the Panathenaic Procession.

Modern Research.

Dodona.—1, coins, having on one side the head of Athena; on the reverse, Zeus launching a thunderbolt; an owl, an eagle, a bunch of grapes, or a running lion; 2, a relief of Athena in her sterner character.

Olympia.—A metope having a fine figure of Athena.

Mycenæ.—Copies of the primitive Palladium, holding in one hand a spear, in the other a distaff.

ARES [*Ä'res*], OR MARS.

(TABLE B, 15.)

Central Ideas.

Ares is called the "god of war," but in placing him in Greek mythology we must remember that war has a twofold signification. It may be the only alternative of loss of liberty, of honor, or of prosperity; under such conditions its acceptance is heroic. On the other

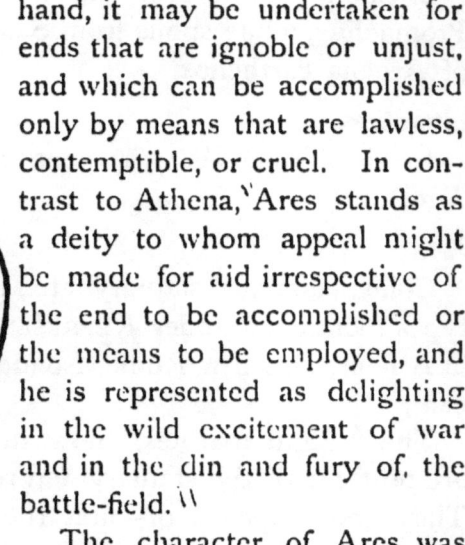

ARES, OR MARS.

hand, it may be undertaken for ends that are ignoble or unjust, and which can be accomplished only by means that are lawless, contemptible, or cruel. In contrast to Athena, Ares stands as a deity to whom appeal might be made for aid irrespective of the end to be accomplished or the means to be employed, and he is represented as delighting in the wild excitement of war and in the din and fury of the battle-field.

The character of Ares was not entirely unattractive, for he was the embodiment of military prowess, and was also endowed with the strength and symmetry of form that constitute the chief charm of manly beauty and presence.

Offices.
1. God of wars that might be just or unjust—that might have victory or defeat.
2. To take part in battles.
3. To preside over manly sports.

Attendants.

Enyo (TABLE I, 62) as goddess of war accompanied Ares to scenes of strife and destruction. She is represented with dishevelled hair, a torch in her left hand, and in her right hand a whip with which she excited the fury of combatants. Other attendants assigned to Ares were—Eris (strife), Deimos (dread), and Phobos (alarm).

Assoc. Myths.

1. *Diomedes.*—In a combat with Diomedes, assisted by Athena, Ares was wounded, and in consequence " roared like ten thousand men." On that occasion he is represented as enveloping himself with clouds, and then appearing to Diomedes as the gloom that precedes a tempest, thus evincing some control over Nature, whether by virtue of his divinity or his descent from Hera, the special goddess of clouds and storms.

2. *Areopagus.*—Halirrhothius (son of Poseidon) offered violence to Alcippe (daughter of Ares). Ares slew him; Poseidon accused Ares in the place where the gods were holding council, and the place was thereafter called the " Areopagus."

3. Ares was captured by Otus and Ephialtes, and imprisoned in a bronze vase for the space of thirteen months.

Emblems.

Helmet, shield, buckler, spear, or burning torch.

Animal Symbols.—Dog and vulture (scourers of battle-fields), the wolf (cunning), the cock (courage and vigilance), the raven (following the line of battle-fields). Dry grass growing on battle-fields.

Representations.

1. Seated in a chariot drawn by furious horses (called by Hesiod Flight and Terror), sometimes accompanied by Enyo and by his other attendants, and sometimes by personifications of anger, clamor, and other abstractions.

2. As a youth of martial bearing, fully armed.

3. As bearded and heavily armed.
4. A poetic representation, as descending from the sky, staying his descent by resting his hand on a mountain-cliff, while the other hand holds a spear and a buckler.

Worship.

The worship of Ares was not general in Greece; its origin was Scythian or Thracian. In Scythia a deity corresponding to Ares was worshipped under the form of a sword, and the worship was marked by cruel rites. It is probable that the Thracian worship was of the same character.

Sacrifices.—Horses, rams, wolves, and dogs. (It is said that the Scythians sacrificed horses, that the Caucasians offered dogs, and that human sacrifices were known in the earliest ages.)

History.

1. Mars' Hill in Athens, named from Ares (see ASSOC. MYTHS).
2. Campus Martius (Field of Mars), field in which the Roman youth practised gymnastics and warlike exercises.

Literature.

In the Trojan War, Ares took part with the Trojans.

Descendants of Ares.

Ares and Agraulos—1, Alcippe.
Ares and Astyoche—2, Ascalaphus, and 3, Ialmenus.
Ares and Aphrodite—4, Eros, and 5, Anteros (see APHRODITE); 6, Harmonia (see CADMUS).

ILITHYIA [*Eileithui'a*], OR LUCINA.

(TABLE B, 16.)

Central Ideas.

The oldest idea of this goddess was as that power

that causes things to come to light after having been prepared or matured. Very naturally there was associated the thought of her as presiding over human births. Hesiod speaks of her as a distinct deity, though she was afterward confounded with Hera, as holding similar offices.

Assoc. Myths.

When Hera, jealous of Leto, delayed the birth of Apollo and Artemis, Ilithyia lent her aid to Leto, and was ever honored by the worshippers of those two deities.

Pausanias relates a curious legend to the effect that when the Arcadians led an army into Elea, Ilithyia produced a child that became a dragon, and it so terrified the Arcadians that the Eleans obtained a victory. The grateful Eleans erected a temple to Ilithyia and to the new god whom she produced, calling the latter Soripolis.

Emblems.

A torch, as bringing to light.

Repesentation.

A wooden statue wrapped from head to foot in a thin veil, one hand extended, and the other holding a torch.

Worship.

The temples to Ilithyia were not numerous. The Delians sacrificed to her, and sang a hymn (by Olen) in her praise.

HEBE [*He'be*].

(TABLE B, 17.)

Central Ideas.

The freshness of Nature, that seems to have inexhaustible sources, suggested the exquisite myth of Hebe, as one who had access to the secret springs of immortal life, and who drew therefrom life-giving nectar for life-giving deities.

Offices.

To preserve youth and freshness, to offer nectar at the Olympian banquets, to minister to Hera when entering or leaving her chariot.

Early Legend.

So closely identified with youth were beauty and gracefulness that it was said that, by an unfortunate fate while handing nectar to the gods, Hebe lost her position and was superseded by Ganymedes. In reference to the promotion of the latter there are, however, three legends — one being that it was the result of the marriage of Hebe to Heracles, and still another to the effect that the honor was conferred on Ganymedes solely because of the friendship of Zeus.

HEBE (from Antonio Canova).

Emblems.
A chaplet of flowers, a goblet, and a vessel of nectar.

Representations.
1. As a modest, beautiful maiden, holding in one hand a goblet, into which, with the other, she pours nectar.
2. Feeding the eagle of Zeus or giving it nectar from a cup.
3. Offering nectar to Heracles.
4. The bridal of Hebe and Heracles.

Worship.
Pausanias mentions occasional temples and altars to Hebe. In Argolis, at the town of Phlius, there was a temple to Hebe situated in a grove. When slaves were set free they hung up their chains among the cypress trees of the grove sacred to the goddess.

Grecian Comp. Myth.
Connected with this worship at Phlius, Pausanias gives a very curious legend, that the Phliusians called the goddess that they worshipped Ganymeda.

Descendants of Hebe (see HERACLES).

PHŒBUS APOLLO [*Phoi'bos Äpŏl'lōn*].
(TABLE B, 18.)

Central Ideas.
The cycle of ideas and myths that have for a centre the Greek Apollo ranges from the physical sphere, whose forces and activities are awakened, sustained, and directed by the sun, to that invisible realm in which spirit is made wise and pure and heroic by the inspiration and help of one who was so glorious, and yet so grandly self-giving, that he typified Him in whom the world finds the way,

APOLLO.

the truth, and the life. Between these widely-distant limits of interpretation, mapped out by minds capable of clearest and calmest thought, there lies a broad mythland in which Apollo reigns as royal representative of the supreme Zeus, reflecting celestial splendor in the sphere of human endeavor and well-being.

In Apollo the loftiest minds recognized a god who, having divine insight into the nature of every spiritual power and faculty, inspired each to its noblest action; he then, in divine wisdom, so harmonized all right-doing that there came into the best lives and organizations a sense of completeness, a sublime repose, that was an earnest of the final and eternal victory over suffering and sin.

Apollo, perfectly-knowing and in harmony with the will of Zeus, became the god of oracles; hence the utterances of his priestesses determined state politics and national movements, and thus made or shaped the materials from which History formed her records. Coming near to human needs as Phœbus, the clear and pure, and as Apollo, the arrester and defender, he became the disperser of evil, whether of ignorance or of wrong; thus leading or lifting human lives into light and joy.

Offices and Archetypes.

Nature: 1. As representing Zeus, the Creator, to animate all forces and light. *Arch.*, light in its eternal splendor and power.
2. To sustain the life of beautiful and healing plants. *Arch.*, the beauty and sustenance that vegetation furnishes to man.
3. To represent Zeus as having the power of death as well as of life. *Arch.*, 1, the decay of plants, affected by the seasons; 2, pestilences, caused by marshes.

Human Life: 1. As protector of human interests in agriculture, Apollo was destroyer of obnoxious animals, as the mouse, lizard, grasshopper.
2. Protector of flocks (remains of Pelasgic worship).
3. Protector of the general and higher interests of homes.

4. Protector of athletic exercises, as promoting health, symmetry of form, and dignity of mien.
5. The god who inspired and assisted heroes.
6. The god of enlivening but tranquillizing music suited for worship.
7. Protector of civil order and prosperity, thus founder of cities and civil constitutions.
8. To gently remove by his arrows men who were appointed to die.
9. As maintainer of the moral law, to punish pride, sin, and blasphemy against the gods.

Theog.: 1. To represent the quickening power of Zeus to the intellectual, to the æsthetical, and to the moral nature of man.
2. To act as leader of the Muses in hymns to the gods.
3. As god of oracles, to declare the order of events which should come to pass according to the will of Zeus.
4. To grant expiation for guilt.

Early Legends.

Leto (darkness) was the mother of the light-deities, Apollo and Artemis. The island of Delos was their birthplace, and it was said that a heavenly radiance illuminated the spot, while swans floated seven times around it, and, growing between a palm and an olive tree, appeared for the first time the sacred laurel. Themis nourished the twin deities with nectar and ambrosia, and as soon as Apollo tasted them he rose to his feet, took upon him the majestic form of a god, and foretold his own great mission.

Apollo ascended Mount Olympus and was welcomed

with songs by the Muses and with dancing by the Horæ and the Graces; but even celestial delights could not chain him to inaction, so he descended to the commencement of his work for man. One tradition said that Apollo went immediately from the island of Delos to Delphi, passing through Attica and Bœotia, while according to another he came to Delphi from the region of the Hyperboreans. All myths unite in placing the first oracle at Delphi, at the foot of Mount Parnassus.

One of the most suggestive myths in connection with this grand character is that of his victory over the Python. At Delphi was an oracular chasm from which the earth-goddess had spoken. This goddess resisted Apollo's occupation of the place, and attempted to throw him down to Tartarus. The guardian of this ancient earth-oracle was the serpent Python, a creature that sprang from the warm clay that was left after the general deluge, and he haunted a dark defile wherein was a fountain supplied from the Styx This serpent, "which personified earthly beings as the shapeless offspring of Nature," was supposed to be connected with the nature of water and of the sea, and was called "Delphine," like the fish of the same name which was sacred to Apollo because subdued by him. The legend generally ran that Python was slain by Apollo, but there is one to the effect that he was conquered by the god, and was then placed by the rocky chasm at the foot of the tripod, and that he was there kept as a memorial of his ancient struggle and defeat. After the victory over the serpent Apollo broke branches from the laurel and wove for himself a crown; and it is said that he sang the first pæan as a strain of triumph. (For another legend of the Delphic oracle, see THEMIS.) Although the destruction of the monster was a triumph of divinity over earthly Nature, Apollo was polluted by the blood of his victim, and was obliged to undergo expiation by wandering upon the earth; and early Delphic legends represent him as subjecting himself as herdsman to Admetus, king of Pheræ (in Thessaly). After eight years the god went to the ancient altar of Tempe, and was purified through sprinkling by laurel-boughs and other expiatory rites. (For the later interpretation of Apollo's servitude to Admetus, see ASSOCIATED MYTHS.)

Tityus, another earth-born monster at Panopæus, offered violence to Leto. Her two children slew him and sent him to Hades, where a vulture perpetually preyed upon his liver, which perpetually grew again. Apollo, triumphant over the hostile powers of Nature, became the oracular deity who proclaimed the decrees of Zeus.

Assoc. Myths.

Apollo having visited the regions of the Hyperboreans, they afterward sent annual offerings to his shrine; these offerings were of fruits and grains, and were called "the golden summer."

Later Legend of Admetus. — Æsculapius (son of Apollo) having offended Zeus by daring to bring back those who had been consigned to Hades, Zeus struck him with his thunderbolts; in return, Apollo shot arrows at the Cyclopes. Zeus then banished Apollo from Olympus, and condemned him to serve as herdsman to King Admetus. (See HERACLES.)

Apollo and Poseidon undertook to assist Laomedon, king of Troy, to rebuild that city. Laomedon having refused the promised reward, Apollo sent a pestilence which depopulated the city and its neighborhood.

Musical Contests.—Apollo is connected with contests in music, and is represented as inflicting severe punishment on the presuming rival; but these fictions are merely mythical embodiments of facts that occurred in the development of music, the lyre or cithara taking precedence over the flute; and the punishment is never inflicted upon mere rivalry, but upon the pride or arrogance that prompted it.

Pan, with a flute, challenged Apollo to compete with him upon the lyre. Midas, king of Lydia, decided for Pan, and Apollo caused the king's ears to grow long like those of an ass. Marsyas having boasted that he could excel Apollo on the flute, he was flayed alive. Linus, the personification of a dirge (said to be the son of Apollo), having presumed to contest musical skill with his father, he was punished with death. Is there not in this myth a suggestion that the tranquillity and yet joyous music that expressed the spirit of Apollo-worship must triumph over that which was depressing and mournful? (For the charming fiction of the gift of the lyre to Apollo, see HERMES.)

A beautiful legend said that Apollo once laid his lyre upon a stone, and the stone at once became musical, like the lyre.

Heracles sought from the priestess at Delphi a remedy for a severe illness with which he was afflicted; she refused to answer, and he sought to carry away the tripod. There followed a struggle between Heracles and Apollo, and they were separated only by a flash of lightning sent by Zeus.

Orestes having murdered his mother Clytemnestra, he was pursued by the Furies. He took refuge in Delphi—was there purified, and then received expiation from Apollo.

Apollo loved Hyacinthus. Zephyrus, jealous of this

affection, blew a quoit, cast by Apollo, against the head of Hyacinthus, and caused his death. Apollo changed the blood of the youth into the flower that bears his name, or, as another myth says, into violets, but still another says into the iris-plant.

Cyparissus, having accidentally killed his pet deer, mourned continually for him, and Apollo changed the youth into a cypress tree; branches of this tree were used at funerals.

Apollo loved Daphne. Fleeing from him, she was changed into a laurel which ever remained pure and living.

Leucothoe having, through Apollo, brought disgrace upon her family, she was by them buried alive, but Apollo transformed her into a tree that dropped frankincense.

Clytie, a sister of Leucothöe, had been beloved by Apollo, but when he deserted her for her sister she pined in grief, and was changed into a sunflower.

(For the story of Niobe and her children, see ARTEMIS.)

Emblems.

Nature: Light, the sun's rays, obelisks (as typifying the sun's rays), all symbolized Apollo's energizing power in Nature.

A cock, coming of light and day.

Dolphin, power over the waters and the sea.

Human Life: Shepherd's crook (rare), protector of herds. (Can it refer to Admetus's "service"?)

Mouse under the foot, Apollo as destroyer of animals that injured grain.

Bow and arrows—first, destroyer of man's foes; second, of men that were appointed to sudden death

A conical pillar, protecting presence of Apollo at the entrance of houses—protector of the higher social relations.

Lyre or cithara, god of tranquillizing and sacred music, also leader of the Muses.

The figure of the Graces borne on his hand, god of elegance and refinement.

Theog.: Ægis, representation of the supreme god.

Hawk, the divine essence.

Tripod, god of oracles.

Helmet, lance, god of just punishment.

Laurel—first, power of purification; second, power of arresting evil; third, oracular power.

Laurel crown, victory over enemies.

Crow and raven, foreknowledge.

Swan, prophecy of happiness after death (by singing at its death).

Rare: 1, a fawn in the hand; 2, lion's skin; 3, a lizard. (The true mythic significance of the lizard is not known. One theory is, that it represents obnoxious animals, and is slain by Apollo, the friend of man; another is, that the lizard represents those animals that pass much time in a torpid state, and it is slain by the god of active life; a third is, that the lizard was used in augury, and was therefore a suitable symbol of the prophetic god.)

Representation.

The conical pillar, that simply indicated the protecting, health-giving presence of a god, was succeeded by rude wooden statues. Statues armed with helmet and lance expressed the power of deity.

Onatas of Ægina, who preceded Phidias, made for

Pergamus a colossal statue that combined great beauty with strength and dignity, but the general characteristic of Apollo made during the period that preceded Alexander was an undraped, strongly-developed physical frame, as though he were to cope with tangible adversaries; the hair was sometimes caught up and pinned together, but was oftener waving down the neck, but in either case it was surmounted by the laurel crown of victory.

Of the Phidian type is an Apollo recently found in Olympia (see MODERN RESEARCH); and though it is the work of Alcamenes, it possesses the combination of simplicity and majesty that characterized the works of the great master.

As the ideal of Apollo became more and more sublime, art grew nobler in its very contemplation, and thus became more worthy to interpret that ideal; so in the schools of Scopas and Praxiteles there was embodied a divinity whose field of action might be a universe, and whose cause was that of truth and purity—a divinity, and yet a leader of heroes, who would lead into all right-doing, assuring to all who would marshal under his guidance the immortal laurels of just triumph.

Worship at Delphi.

The Oracle at Delphi, whose foundation we have given in EARLY LEGENDS, was second only to that of Dodona in authority and influence. The priestess (Pythoness) was seated upon a tripod over a chasm in the earth whence issued a cold vapor, by aid of which, assisted sometimes by chewing leaves of laurel or by draughts of water from a sacred well, she was excited to a frenzy which prepared her to receive the intimations of the will of the deity. Priests trained in the office listened to her utterances and expressed them in ambiguous verse.

Temple.—The Delphic temple was very ancient, its foundation antedating the *Iliad*.

Pythian Games.—The worship of Apollo at Delphi existed from time immemorial, and in its earliest phases represented the events in the life of the deity, particularly those relating to his victory over the Python. At first they occurred every eight years, but were afterward quadrennial. There were at these games sacrifices of cakes and frankincense, expiatory rites, purifications through sprinkling by laurel-boughs, pilgrimages to Tempe, bringing of the "golden summer" by presentation of the first-fruits (thus commemorating Apollo's return from the Hyperboreans). Pæans or sacred hymns were sung in honor of the god, and *hyporcheme*, or sacred dances, were performed by choruses who danced around a blazing altar.

The Pythian Games were under the special protection of the amphictyon, and, like the Olympian Games, became national in their effects. Athletic games and chariot-races were instituted about 585 B. C., and musical and literary competition held a high position in the festival.

Triopia, trials of skill in honor of Apollo Triopus. The prizes, brazen shields, were not taken away by the victors, but were consecrated to the god who had given them the victory.

Grecian Comp. Myth.

In early mythology Apollo was distinct from Helios, but later writers confounded the two deities.

Foreign Comp. Myth.

It is thought that Apollo as the light-deity embodied, at least partially, the attributes of the Oriental Baal and Ra. Late researches identify Apollo as the PHŒNICIAN god Reshiph-Mical; EGYPTIAN, Horus the younger (son of Osiris and Isis.)

Literature.

Though Apollo was honored by the Greeks, his worship had been established in Troy, and he was the protecting deity of the Trojans during the Trojan War. Agamemnon having retained as captive Chryseis, the daughter of a priest of Apollo, the god in punishment of the sacrilege sent a pestilence among the Greeks.

Art.

We have spoken of the earliest types under REPRESENTATION.

Apollo Callinæos, or Victorious God.—This is the celebrated Apollo Belvedere, found at Porto d'Anzio, and placed by Pope Julius II. in the Belvedere of the Vatican. It has been thought to represent that triumphant moment when Apollo has slain the Python, and many recognize such an air of moral grandeur, such a certainty of actual, future, and perpetual triumph, that the Python becomes a hieroglyph for any and all manifestations of error or evil, fated to be overcome by the god of light and truth. A later theory is that Apollo Belvedere is only a copy of a bronze statue that represented Apollo as the succorer or defender of his worshippers; and the advocate of the theory believes that it commemorates the defeat of the Gauls when they attempted to plunder the temple of Apollo at Delphi.* A fearful storm which raged at the time of that event was believed

---
* Sidney Colvin in *Littell's Living Age.*

by the Greeks to be a proof of the miraculous interposition of their protecting deity.

Now, as the ægis of Zeus was a symbol of his power in the heavens, the Greeks may have supposed that the terrible weapon was placed in the hands of Apollo that he might wield it in their behalf; and such a belief would become a sublime *motive* for the highest art. In confirmation of the above interpretation its advocate cites the fact that there is in St. Petersburg a bronze statuette evidently copied from the same original (itself bronze) as was the Belvedere. This statuette bears in its hand, not a *bow*, but a fragment of what looks like an imitation in bronze of a piece of fringed and crumpled leather. Since the ægis was represented as a scarf of fringed or crumpled goatskin, embossed with a Gorgon's head as a symbol of terror, it would be a fitting symbol to be placed in the hands of the god who destroyed or put to flight the sacrilegious Gauls.

Apollo Lycian is the god reposing after conquest, signified by resting one arm on the head, while with the other he holds a lyre. (In Athens.)

Apollo Sauroktonos (*Lizard-slayer*).—The god is shooting an arrow at a lizard creeping up a branch of the tree on which rests his left arm. (Vatican Museum.)

Apollo Cytharœdus (*the Harp-player*) is the god of poetry, the inspired leader of the Muses. (Vatican Museum.)

Modern Research.

Dodona.—Coins (probably offerings from other cities):

1. On one side the head of Apollo; on the reverse—1, an obelisk and laurel wreath; 2, a torch and laurel wreath; 3, an eagle.

2. A diademed head of Apollo; reverse, bow and arrow.

3. Heads of Apollo and Artemis; reverse, prow of a ship.

Olympia.—A colossal statue, not entire, that formed the centre of the group in the western pediment of the temple of Zeus. (See BATTLE OF THE CENTAURS AND THE LAPITHÆ.) Apollo stands as the defender of the Greeks against the Centaurs. The style is archaic, but unites simplicity and majesty. Above the forehead is a row of ringlets, and the hair behind is turned up over the fillet. "The under lip is raised, but only just raised, in scorn; the head is slightly inclined over the shoulders; one arm, to which a drapery hangs, is partly raised, as if for action. The whole conception is governed by the old religious stateliness and high reserve, and is therefore a lofty ancestor to the type of the Belvedere."

Descendants of Apollo.

Apollo and Cyrene—Aristæus. This mortal became a god through his great services for mankind. He was protector of flocks and herds, and taught the care of bees, the olive, and the vine.

Apollo and Coronis—Æsculapius. Æsculapius was the god of the healing art, and is introduced in the early legends of Apollo as one who could even raise from the dead. His symbols are a dish for healing-potions; a serpent, as symbolizing renewed life. It is said that when a cock was offered to Æsculapius it signified that death was welcomed as a cure for evil or as a convalescence. May it not be that, as the cock is the harbinger of the morning light, it typified the new, the immortal day, or life?

Apollo and Chione—Philammon; Apollo and Evadne—Iamus; Apollo and Creusa—Ion and the Ionians.

ARTEMIS [Är′tĕmis], OR DIANA.

(TABLE B, 19.)

Central Ideas.

In Artemis, the twin-sister of Apollo, was reflected at least a part of the attributes of that deity. Like Apollo, Artemis was especially honored by the Dorians, and it is not strange that a people who held women in such honor

ARTEMIS, OR DIANA (Museum Capitolinum).

as did that race should conceive of a goddess who embodied feminine beauty, purity, strength, and eternal youth.

The association of light and the life-principle is universal; hence Artemis, as light-goddess, had energizing power in Nature and care over births; at the same time, the apprehension of the possible duality of any nature made it very easy to attribute to the same goddess the sterner qualities of a death-dealing or of an avenging deity.

It is possible that the character of Artemis as twin sister of Apollo, the god of light, connected her with nocturnal phenomena, the moon being the central force and symbol; then there would exist a natural relation between night, dew, moisture, and rivers. So Artemis as had other deities, might have emblems as varied as are the departments of Nature and human life.

ARCADIAN ARTEMIS.

The association of a night-goddess with moisture and rivers was made prominent by the Arcadians, and they worshipped under the name of Hymnia a goddess who was afterward called Artemis. This same deity had been introduced into the genealogies as Callisto, who was the mother of Arcas, as representing the Arcadian people. K. O. Müller gives an interesting group of myths growing out of this conception of Artemis; one of which is that she was loved by the river-god Alpheus; that to protect herself from him she sank into the land of Elis; that Alpheus followed her under the sea to the island of Ortygia. There was no river in Ortygia, so when a grand temple was erected to Artemis a fountain near by was supposed to contain the sacred water of the Alpheus. After a time the origin and meaning of the fable were lost, and the fountain-nymph Arethusa was associated with Alpheus.

This same Arcadian Artemis is considered by some to have been a mountain-goddess and the protectress of the chase.

ARTEMIS AS IPHIGENIA.

Even the simplest outline that the complex nature of this subject permits involves facts connected with the Trojan War and with the comparative mythologies of Troy, Tauria, Attica, and Sparta. Artemis, like Apollo, was worshipped at Troy.

Agamemnon, the commander of the Grecian fleet that was proceeding against Troy, recklessly destroyed a stag that was sacred to Artemis. As a punishment for this sacrilege the offended goddess detained the fleet in Aulis until Agamemnon should appease her by sacrificing to her his daughter Iphigenia. Patriotism moved him to obey this terrible summons, but after the goddess found that he would obey her, she appeared in person and provided an animal for the sacrifice; she then bore Iphigenia away in a cloud, and placed her as priestess in her temple at Tauris.

Among the Tauri was worshipped a goddess (identified with Artemis) who was appeased by human sacrifices, particularly strangers that were thrown upon the coast. Iphigenia and her brother Orestes carried the image of this goddess to Brauron in Attica; hence she was called 'Brauronia," and her worship was received at Athens and at Sparta.

Iphigenia, who was to have been sacrificed, but who became the sacrificing priestess of Artemis, was soon identified with the goddess and worshipped as Artemis. The scourging of boys at the festivals of this goddess, cruel as it was, had been substituted for human sacrifices.

In different localities ancient goddesses were considered as identical with Artemis; so, many subjects for careful analysis are suggested by the worship of Artemis Orthia and Artemis Tauropolus.

EPHESIAN ARTEMIS, OR DIANA OF THE EPHESIANS.

There prevailed in Asia Minor an ancient form of that elementary religion whose rites were at the same time wild, sensual, and cruel. The dual character of Artemis, as possessed of destructive as well as of life-giving powers, fitted her for easy adoption by Asiatic peoples, and as "Diana of the Ephesians" she was a goddess of extended influence.

Offices and Archetypes (of Artemis).

Nature: 1. As goddess of nocturnal influences, to give light and quickening energy, hence goddess of productiveness.
2. To furnish dew and moisture, hence goddess of rivers, and therefore of horses.
3. To nurture the young of animals.
4. To destroy wild beasts, but to protect favorite animals.

Human Life: 1. As feminine productive power, having limited care over human births.
2. As protectress of herds from beasts of prey, goddess of hunting.
3. As goddess of waters and the tides, protectress of fishermen.
4. To bestow physical strength and beauty and to preserve freshness and youth.
5. To preserve pure morals and to punish impurity of life.
6. To remove by death women, as men were removed by Apollo.
7. Associated with Apollo as goddess of music.

Theog.: 1. In a limited sense to represent Zeus.
2. To inflict severe punishment for sacrilege.
3. To share with Apollo divine honors.

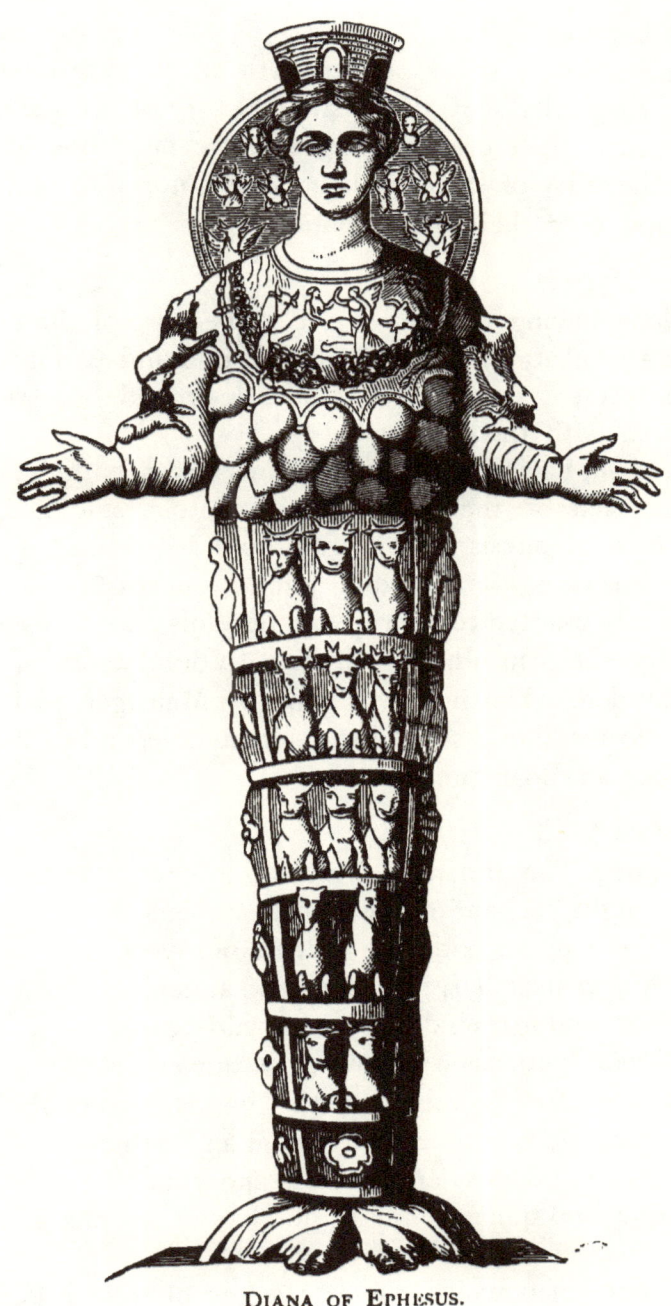
DIANA OF EPHESUS.

Early Legends.

The sister is so associated with the twin-brother in their early life that their early history is like a coin stamped with a double image; so we need not repeat here the story of their birth at Delos, nor that of their triumph over their first enemies.

Assoc. Myths.

Niobe having boasted over Leto because of the number and beauty of her children, Apollo and Artemis, as a punishment for her arrogance, destroyed her twelve children with their arrows.

Actæon, having surprised Artemis when bathing, was transformed by the angry goddess into a stag, and he was torn in pieces by his own hounds.

Œneus, king of Calydon, after a successful vintage purposely omitted to sacrifice to Artemis; to punish his impiety she sent a huge wild-boar to desolate the fields of Calydon. The boar was slain by Meleager, and this myth forms the basis of the celebrated legend of "The Calydonian Boar-hunt."

Emblems.

Nature: The moon, a crescent, torches, goddess of light, life, and nocturnal phenomena.

Water-plants and fish, goddess of rivers.

A deer near her, protectress of animals.

Bow and arrow, destroyer of wild beasts.

Moon, goddess who sways the tides.

Human Life: Torches in the hands, giver of life, therefore protectress of human births.

Laurel, goddess of freshness and youth.

Bow and quiver, hounds, goddess of the chase, protectress of herds.

Lance or bow and quiver, avenger of wrong-doing.

Theog.: Lyre, one who receives pæans.

Laurel, one who purifies.

The symbol of the Arcadian Artemis was a bear; that of the Ephesian was a bee, as the type of nourishment.

Representations.

1. As life-giving goddess, holding torches in her hands. The bow bent and quiver open indicated activity, while the reverse signified repose or victory.
2. As night-goddess, floating drapery, a starry veil, and a crescent about her brow.
3. As virgin goddess, clothed in long, elegant drapery.
4. As huntress, the dress was short (*chiton*), buskins, bow and quiver, and she was attended by nymphs; otherwise, riding in a chariot drawn by four stags with golden antlers.
5. As goddess of rivers, reeds in the hair and fish surrounding her.
6. As goddess of horses, in a chariot with four horses.
7. As sea-goddess, standing on a pedestal, with a moon on her head, in her hand the carved stern of a ship (*aplustre*), and near her a stag.

Foreign Representations.—1. As Taurian Artemis, or Iphigenia, an antique idol which could be carried in the hand.
2. As Diana of the Ephesians, in the general outline and the emblems greatly resembling the Phrygian Cybele (page 163).

Worship.

The worship of Artemis and that of Apollo were so closely associated that the former needs no separate consideration.

Literature.

Artemis is identified with the interests of the Trojans in the Trojan War.

Comparative Mythology.

This topic was included under the head of CENTRAL IDEAS, with the exception of the supposed identity of Artemis with Hecate, who, as the deity of darkness and magic, not unnaturally suggested the night-goddess. EGYPTIAN, Bubastis.

Art.

The statue at Versailles embodies the idea of the protectress of animals. Illustrations of the different types given under the head of REPRESENTATIONS are furnished by all the art-centres—Athens, Rome, Berlin, etc.

Modern Research.

Examinations at Ephesus by Mr. Wood have revealed interesting relics of the worship of Diana of the Ephesians.

HERMES [*Hĕr'mĕs*], OR MERCURY.
(TABLE B, 20.)

Central Ideas.

The conception of the god Hermes passed through varied stages of belief, and it incorporated so many of the distinctive features of each that it presents an exceedingly complex subject for mythologic study.

There are unmistakable evidences that Hermes originally belonged to a Pelasgic elemental worship, in which he was regarded as an embodiment of the productiveness of Nature, and to him was assigned special protection of flocks and herds. In this system special importance was attached to the influence of this god in his relation to human births.

It was but natural that with the protection of herds and flocks Hermes should be considered as special patron of the wealth that came through the possession of them. It was just as natural to extend that patron-

HERMES, OR MERCURY.

age until it comprehended all systems of human effort whose end is wealth; and since Hermes was not supposed to possess high moral qualities, his devotees implored his aid less in choice of right methods than in the success of undertakings. Hermes seems to be a personified practical wisdom that is entirely independent of moral considerations; and there may have been, in this creation of Greek mythology, a foreshadowing of that policy that allows the end to justify any means.

Hermes was not, like Athena and Apollo, a deity who energized and directed intellectual power, but rather one whose object was to utilize by expressing it.; hence he was the god of speech and oratory. The communication of the thoughts and will of the gods to man offered a most important office to some deity; and no one could so well fill it as the clear-sighted, self-contained, eloquent Hermes; so he was made messenger to the gods, and his mighty circuit embraced Olympus, earth, and Hades.

With his practical shrewdness there was mingled a kindly spirit that made him guide to the traveller and companion to the weary; and his whole nature was so filled with humor and drollery that even when he cheated he charmed.

Offices and Archetypes (see EMBLEMS).

Nature: To preside over the fertility of Nature.

Human Life: 1. Presiding over the productiveness of human life.
2. God of physical strength and athletic sports.
3. Guide, messenger, companion.
4. Protector of roads and travellers.
5. Inventor of speech, eloquence, alphabet.
6. Inventor of weights, measures, numbers.
7. Inventor of music, the lyre, syrinx, etc.
8. Protector of traffic, prudence, skill, and even knavery.
9. Protector of commerce.
10. God of good-luck and of wealth.

11. Guide of souls to and from Hades.

Theog.: 1. Herald, messenger of the gods.
2. One who persuaded men to listen to the gods.
3. Protector of animals that were used in sacrifices, particularly sheep.

Early Legends.

Hermes was born in a cave of Mount Cyllene in Arcadia; like Apollo, he became at once a mature god. A few hours after his birth he stole some oxen belonging to Apollo, and, developing at once his dishonesty and shrewdness, drove them into a cave, but drove them backward, so that it might appear that they had left the cave. He killed two of the animals, part of which was cooked and eaten; the rest was burned, while the skins were fastened to a rock. The god then returned to his own cave, at whose entrance he found a tortoise, to whom he prophesied that it should sing for ages. He killed the animal, and, putting strings to its shell, he thereby invented the lyre.

Meanwhile, Apollo had traced the author of the theft of his oxen, and, accusing Hermes, was asked by the latter how he, a child only a few hours old, could have done such a deed. The case was presented to Zeus. Hermes at first denied the theft, but afterward restored the oxen to Apollo, at the same time so charming the latter with his lyre that he willingly gave the oxen back to Hermes, receiving in exchange the wonderful lyre. Hermes is said to have then invented the syrinx, and he and Apollo became firm friends. Apollo gave to Hermes his golden shepherd's staff and taught him to prophesy by dice and by signs, but forbade him to use speech in prophesying.

The caduceus of Hermes has several interpretations, one being to this effect: Hermes saw two serpents fighting; he placed between them the staff received from Apollo, and they entwined around it in lasting concord. The staff of the caduceus was simply a herald's staff, and the two serpents had been the white ribbon that always belonged to such a staff. The staff had once been an olive-branch, and the serpents were formed from the wreaths or from the fillets of wool which had adorned the branch.

Hera placed Io, of whom she was jealous, under the care of Argus, a person who had a hundred eyes, of which only fifty were closed at once. Zeus commissioned Hermes to kill Argus and set Io free. Hermes told so many charming tales, and produced such exquisite music upon the shepherd's pipe, that every one of the hundred eyes closed; Argus was slain, and Io was released.

Emblems.

Nature: A corn-basket (calathus), fertility in vegetation.

A goat, productiveness in animal life.

Human Life: Hermæ (square columns with head of Hermes) at the entrance of houses, god of productiveness in human life.

Hermæ in gymnasiums, protector of athletes.

Palm tree, giver of physical strength.

Hermæ at cross-roads, protector of roads and travellers.

Olive-wreath on a milestone, preserver of order.

Alphabet and language, inventor of speeches and god of eloquence and oratory.

Number 4, inventor of numbers, weights, and measures.

Tortoise and lyre, inventor of the lyre.

Syrinx, inventor of the syrinx (see PAN).

As god of traffic, Hermes's symbols were—first, a column, firmness; second, a club, force; third, olive-branch, peace (these three elements being necessary to success).

Fish, power over the sea.

Stern of a ship (*aplustre*), protector of commerce.

Purse, god of wealth.

Dice, god of luck.

A globe (Hermes standing upon it), universal power.

Caduceus, empire over animal nature and god of wealth.

Theog.: A ram, protector of sacrifices.

A patera, one who received sacrifices.

As messenger of the gods the symbols of Hermes were—first, winged shoes (*talaria*); second, winged hat (*petarus*); third, chlamys (short mantle); fourth, caduceus (staff and serpents); fifth, a cock, vigilance; sixth, a crow, good omen.

Caduceus, Hermes as conductor of souls to Hades.

Representations.

First Type.—As the god of bounty, represented by a Hermes pillar (Hermæ).

Second Type (early).—Strongly-formed man with pointed beard and long tresses. He wears a travelling hat, his chlamys is thrown back, and he carries the caduceus, which is sometimes like a sceptre.

Third Type.—Like an athlete in form, but wearing a short chlamys, which is sometimes wrapped around the left arm; near him a palm tree.

Fourth Type.—Messenger of the gods, with winged hat and winged shoes, wearing the chlamys and carrying the caduceus. In this form he appears at one time flying through the air, at another delivering his message or resting after his journey.

Worship.
Locations.—Attica, Arcadia, Samothrace, Lemnos, etc.
Sacred Festivals.—Hermæa.
Sacrifices.—Incense, honey, cakes, and tongues of animals, pigs, lambs, young goats.

Foreign Comp. Myth.
ROMAN, Mercury; INDIAN, Sarameya; EGYPTIAN, Thoth (as god of letters and wisdom), Anubis (as Psychopompus).

Literature.
In the Trojan War, Hermes was identified with the Greeks.

Art.
The lovely figures called "Hermaphrodite" are combinations of the strong features of Hermes and the gentle graces of Aphrodite.

Upon the square statues called "Hermæ" were sometimes placed the heads of other deities, thus forming Hermæathena (Hermes and Athena), Hermacles (Hermes and Heracles), etc.

Modern Research.
One of the most important discoveries in Olympia is that of a statue (by Praxiteles) of Hermes carrying the infant Bacchus.

Ephesus.—A statue of Hermes as Psychopompus, conductor of souls to Hades. The soul that he is conducting is represented under the figure of a beautifully-draped woman, and she turns half toward the guide, who precedes her and looks back and beckons. Hermes is nude, winged, with a sword slung round his shoulder, and he bears throughout that beautiful but indefinite androgynous aspect and character that personifies the Genius of Death. His sword is not for slaughter, but for the severing of a lock of hair which devotes the victim to the gods below:

> " I go with sword to initiate the rite,
> For consecrate is he to the gods below
> Whose locks this knife has severed from his head."—
> *Alcestis.*

Descendants of Hermes.

Hermes and Chione—Autolycus; Hermes and Herse—Cephalus; Hermes and Cleobula—Myrtilus; Hermes and Libyus—Libys; Hermes and Aphrodite—Hermaphroditus.

HORÆ [*Hō'rai*], OR SEASONS
(TABLE B, 22.)

Central Ideas.

These lovely beings were the daughters of Themis, who herself represented the balance and order of the universe. The regularity with which the changes of the seasons occurred, and the unfailing supplies with which they met human needs, suggested the existence of those whose service was to assist in preserving throughout space that obedience to law whose general result was order and harmony, and whose specific result on earth was, in the physical world, seed-time, growth, and harvest.

By easy transition, the Horæ were supposed to shed sweet influences, equally quieting and uplifting, throughout every department of human interest. To the Horæ were committed the opening and the closing of the gates of the Olympian court, and they lent assistance to Hera and to Aphrodite.

Offices and Archetypes.

Nature: Under the control of Zeus and Hera to have charge of the regions of space, to preserve the regular succession of the yearly changes, thus ensuring the variety and abundance of Nature's gifts.

Human Life: 1. To protect and nourish all young persons.
2. To secure obedience to law, especially to social requirements.

Theog.: 1. To aid everywhere order and harmony.
2. To open and shut the gates of Olympus.
3. To assist in yoking the horses to the chariot of Hera.
4. To perform kindly offices for other deities.

Early Legends.

At Athens only two Horæ were originally recognized —Thallo, or "blossoming," answering to the spring, and Carpo, or "fruit-ripening," corresponding to harvest. Thallo was supposed to accompany Persephone on her ascent from Hades.

As men marked more and more clearly the distinct phenomena of the year, the seasons were more definitely divided and assigned to a greater number of controlling deities, so that in time the Horæ were three, then four, and finally the twelve months were personified as Horæ.

THREE HORÆ.

Early Idea.

At the first period Winter was not numbered among the Horæ, because it was only a time of death or torpor. The Horæ were then spring, summer, and autumn.

Representation.

1. Three maidens fully draped, with joined hands;

the hand that is left free holding a bud, a blossom, or a fruit.
2. Three maidens dancing, their garments tucked to their knees; crowns of upright palm-leaves.
3. Three maidens seated—Spring with lap filled with flowers; Summer holding a bundle of grain and a sickle; Autumn with emblems of fruits.

Later Idea.

Winter took its place as a season; then the Horæ were Spring, Autumn, and Winter; and as moral supervision over human affairs was attributed to them, they may be grouped as follows: Spring (Eunomia), wise legislation; Autumn (Dice), justice; Winter (Irene), peace.

Representation.

Spring, as a maiden before whose feet a flower has just sprung; Autumn, with fruits in her hands, standing near an altar; Winter, standing near a pile of stones on which burns a feeble flame.

FOUR HORÆ.

In later times the year was divided into four seasons.

Representation.

Long garments; Spring as a young maiden; the others in the gradations of ripening or ripened age.

MUSÆ [*Mou'sai*], OR THE MUSES.
(TABLE B, 23.)
THE DESCENT OF THE MUSES.

NINE sisters, beautiful in form and face,
  Came from their convent on the shining heights
  Of Pierus, the mountain of delights,
To dwell among the people at its base.

> Then seemed the world to change. All time and space,
>   Splendor of cloudless days and starry nights,
>   And men and manners, and all sounds and sights,
> Had a new meaning, a diviner grace.
> Proud were these sisters, but were not too proud
>   To teach in schools of little country towns
>   Science and song, and all the arts that please;
> So that, while housewives span and farmers ploughed,
>   Their comely daughters, clad in homespun gowns,
>   Learned the sweet songs of the Pierides.

Central Ideas.

We have found that the Greeks placed a deity at the centre of every place of influence, and we know that owing to the many modifications of place and time there was a wide difference between the early legends and the highest ideals of any deity.

We believe that man looks upon human life as a border-land, uniting a sphere that is visible and tangible with one which, though now invisible and mysterious, is yet one in which the best and grandest interests of life shall "put on immortality." From that other sphere man hopes for messages and for messengers—messengers who shall bring him heavenly food and break it with him in blest companionship.

What are the early legends? and what is the highest ideal of the Muses? According to the former, they were spirits of the springs, but we know that they did not linger there, for, daughters of Zeus, they were at home in the presence of the assembled gods of Olympus. They were at home, but they came down to human homes with messages to those whose home was not always to be human. They told man of celestial splendors, that he might never rest satisfied with that which is only earthly.

The Muses came often to the earth, and they so filled

the air with music that it welled forth in human choruses and marriage-songs as well as in pæans to the gods.

Because of their coming language had a higher meaning, and this meaning became an inspiration to higher living. Then Clio so emblazoned, and Calliope so sang, heroic deeds that life was everywhere uplifted. It is not impossible that Urania, whose name signifies "the heavenly," was thought to prophesy of a time when throughout the universe there should appear fairer proportions than those that the beautiful exactness of mathematics had revealed, and sublimer harmonies than those of the morning stars, for in that time, which should then be worthy to be eternal, all souls should shine out symmetrical and complete, and all soul-life should move in harmony with the will of the gods.

Early Legends.

The number of the Muses originally worshipped at Mount Helicon was three: 1, Aoide (song); 2, Melete (meditation); 3, Mneme (memory).

By another tradition the Muses were said to be the daughters of Zeus and Plusia, and then were four in number: 1, Arche (beginning); 2, Aoide (song); 3, Melete (meditation); 4, Thelxinoe (heart-delighter).

At Athens eight Muses were worshipped. Homer makes one mention of nine Muses, but nowhere gives their names; so Hesiod was the first writer who gave the names of those that are now generally known as the "Nine Muses."

Abode.

First, Mount Olympus, in Thessaly; second, Mount Parnassus, in Phocis, with its Castalian spring; third, Mount Helicon, in Bœotia, with its springs, Aganippe and Hippocrene. About the latter spring was a grove sacred to the Muses, and it was filled with choice works of art.

Offices and Archetypes.

Nature: According to an early myth, the Muses presided over the seasons and the stars.

Human Life: 1. To preside over music, song, poetry, and the fine arts.
2. To enliven scenes of human joy, to alleviate human sorrow.

Theog.: 1. To join with Apollo in sacred song and dance.
2. To give prophetic inspiration to the priestess at Delphi.
3. To sing at the banquets of the Olympian gods.
4. To sing the praises of the gods.

Assoc. Myths.

Thamyris received from the Muses the gift of musical skill, but as he used it in competition with themselves, they deprived him of the gift and punished him with blindness.

The Sirens challenged the Muses to a trial of musical excellence, and the Muses being victorious, they took the plumes of the Sirens and wore them as trophies.

The nine daughters of Pierus presumed to enter into a contest with the Muses for musical supremacy, and, being defeated, they were changed into birds.

A. DIVISION.

1. EUTERPE [*Eutër′pe*].

Special office—1, music; 2, lyric poetry.

Representation.

1. Standing, tresses floating, playing on a double pipe or a flute.

Euterpe (Vatican).   Terpischore.   Erato (Vatican).

Polymnia (Louvre).   Thalia (Vatican).

MELPOMENE (Vatican).

CLIO (Sweden).

CALLIOPE (Vatican).

URANIA (Sweden).

MUSÆ.

  2. Standing, leaning against a pillar, holding a double pipe.
  3. Standing, right hand extended and holding a pipe; left hand holds another pipe.
  4. Seated on a rock; right hand rests on the rock; left hand holds a pipe.

2. TERPSICHORE [*Tĕrpsĭ'chōrḝ*].

Special office—choral dance and song (sacred odes).

Representation.
  1. Sitting on a rock, holding a lyre.
  2. Standing, playing on a lyre.
  3. Standing; left foot rests on a slight elevation; left hand holds a lyre, right hand plectrum; head bent toward lyre.
  4. In the attitude of dancing to the music of cymbals or a tympanum, which she is playing.

3. ERATO [*Ĕ'rätō*].

Special office—poetry pertaining to love, marriage (mimic imitations).

Representation.
  1. Standing, playing on a psaltery; wreath.
  2. Standing, holding a lyre by her side; in the other hand an arrow or a wreath of myrtle and roses.

B. DIVISION.

4. POLYMNIA [*Pŏlў̆m'nĭa*].

Special office—1, sacred poetry; 2, oratory; 3, myths, and fables.

Representation.
1. Standing, lost in meditation, one finger on her lips; crown of laurels.
2. Standing, left hand by her side holding a mass of drapery; right hand rests on her left shoulder.
3. Standing, leaning forward on the top of a short pillar; arms concealed under her drapery; sometimes wearing a veil, in deep contemplation.

C. DIVISION.

5. THALIA [*Thălei'a*].

Special office—1, comedy; 2, burlesque; 3, pastoral poetry.

Representation.
1. Standing; fringed mantle thrown over left shoulder; right arm, free, holds a shepherd's crook; right hand holds a comic mask.
2. Sitting on a rock, comic mask on the rock near her; right hand holds a shepherd's crook, which rests on the rock near her; ivy crown.

6. MELPOMENE [*Mĕlpŏm'ĕnĕ*].

Special office—tragedy.

Representation.
1. Standing on a rock (against its base rests a lyre); right hand on the hip; left hand at her side, lost in drapery; right foot in cothurnus, slightly showing; face looking upward, as if communing with Zeus.
2. Standing; right hand holds tragic mask; left hand extended, as if in declamation.

3. Standing, holding a dagger or a club; crown of cypress.
4. Standing, left foot on a rock; right hand, a mask; left hand, a roll (part of a play); crown of vine-leaves.

D. DIVISION.

7. CLIO [*Clī'ō*].

Special office—history.

Representation.
1. Seated on a rock, holding with both hands a partly-unrolled parchment; near her a cylindrical box of manuscript rolls and an open chest of volumes.
2. Seated on a rock; left hand holds a partly-unrolled manuscript; right hand extended toward it.
3. Standing; in left hand a manuscript; right hand, a stylus.

8. CALLIOPE [*Cällī'ŏpę*].

Special office—1, heroic poetry; 2, eloquence; 3, rhetoric.

Representation.
1. Standing; holds manuscript roll or a pipe twined with laurel; crown of laurel.
2. Seated; holds a tablet and stylus or a roll of parchment.

E. DIVISION.

9. URANIA [*Ourä'nia*].

Special office—1, mathematics; 2, astronomy; 3, astrology.

Representation.
1. Standing; right hand holds pointer; left hand, a globe.

2. Standing; crown of stars; looking toward the heavens; one hand holds a lyre, the other points to a globe beside her.
3. As Hope, standing; crowned with flowers; right hand rests on a column; left hand holds poppies and wheat-ears.

CHARITES [*Chä'ritēs*], OR THE GRACES.
(TABLE B, 24.)

Central Ideas.

The name of these deities was derived from the word *Charis*, a term originally applied to a personification of grace and beauty, but in time the term was changed in form, as it was applied to a plurality of deities.

In the Graces were embodied those sweet, refining influences that came into social life as does the light into Nature, transforming from beauty to beauty. Their presence was invoked at the festal board, that they might inspire the guests with pure thoughts and manners, yet restrain every pleasure within limits of self-control and elegance. Wherever loveliness and gentleness were sought the Graces bestowed their benediction; even Aphrodite and Pandora accepted their exquisite suggestions. These pure, tender beings were associated with Eros and with the Muses in their gracious ministrations to man.

Early Legends.

The Spartans worshipped two graces—1, Cleta (sound); 2, Phaenna (brightness). The Athenians worshipped the same number, but under different names: 1, Auxo (increaser); 2, Hegemone (leader). In other places were worshipped—1, Aglaia; 2, Pasithea; 3, Peitho (persuasion). Homer in the *Iliad* speaks of Charis as the wife of Hephæstus, though in other places he uses Charites in a plural sense.

When the use of the term became quite general it comprehended the three deities Aglaia, Euphrosyne, and Thalia.

Offices and Archetypes.
1. To preside over social enjoyments and promote temperance, gentleness, and good manners.
2. To inspire all men with kindness and courtesy.
3. To favor poetic inspiration.
4. To lend the charms of refinement and beauty to every mode of life.

Emblems.
Roses and other flowers.
Poppy-heads, boughs of myrtle.
Wheat-ears, perfume vases.
Musical instruments, as the lyre and cithara.

Representation.
Early.—Clothed in long garments, the hands joined.
The Eleans represented the Graces in golden robes—one holding a rose; another, dice; and the third, a bough of myrtle.
There is a curious group of three figures, generally called the Graces, one of which wears a helmet, another holds an apple, and the third a lily. It has been suggested that this group may indicate Athena, Venus, and Hera.
On a curious vase the Graces appear under new names: 1, Gelasia (sweet-smiling); 2, Comasia (amiability); 3, Lecoris (brilliant beauty).
Later.—As young maidens, undraped, with linked arms, joining in dancing, or in talking, or in adorning themselves or each other with flowers.

Worship.

The Graces were generally associated with other deities, particularly with Eros, Aphrodite, and the Muses.

Charitesia were festivals in their honor, in which athletic games, music, and dancing held prominent places. At banquets the first cup of wine was offered them.

NYMPHÆ, OR THE NYMPHS.
(TABLE B, 25.)

Central Ideas.

The Nymphs were semi-divine, semi-human beings, who had supervision over those operations of Nature that had special relation to man's personal comfort and pleasure. In their nature, sympathies, and occupations they were entirely superior to the Fauns and Satyrs, for, whether they lingered in grotto or on mountain, near fountain or in forest, they created and preserved freshness and beauty.

The Nymphs were to some extent connected with Greek genealogy. It was a noble ambition, in those who fully believed in the existence of gods, that prompted them to claim relationship to the deities that they honored, and through a modification of the same feeling many families and tribes traced their origin to one of these supernatural beings, who were of the earth, but were not earthy.

Offices and Archetypes.

Nature: 1. To preserve the freshness of Nature.
    2. To renew the freshness of the waters and of vegetation, and to care for the well-being of flocks and herds.

Human Life: 1. To care for the objects and processes

in Nature that furnish for man sources of beauty and pure pleasure.
2. To awaken in human hearts a love for Nature's charms.
3. To have charge of heroes in their infancy.

Theog.: 1. To have the charge of infant gods.
2. To lend kindly offices to gods and goddesses.
3. On some occasions to attend the assembly of the gods.
4. To give prophetic inspiration to priestesses.

Representation.

Young maidens of wonderful beauty, as engaged in dancing, singing, bathing, hunting with Artemis, etc. Their emblems were appropriate to the occasion represented, the water-nymphs holding shells or pouring water from vases; the meadow-nymphs gathering flowers, etc.

Worship.

Grottos, caves where water dripped or flowed, and where bees hummed, were sacred to them. Sanctuaries called Nymphæa were erected to their honor in valleys, caves, and even towns; those in towns were sacred to marriage-rites.

Sacrifices.—Goats, lambs, milk, oil; but wine was forbidden.

CLASSES OF THE NYMPHS.

TERRESTRIAL NYMPHS.

Land-Nymphs.—Dryades, wood-nymphs in general.

Hamadryades, those that lived in and died with the trees.

Meliades, nymphs of fruit trees.

Leimoniades, nymphs of meadows and flowers.

Oreades, nymphs of mountains (Peliades, nymphs of Mount Pelion; Idæan, nymphs of Mount Ida, etc.).

Napææ, nymphs of mountain-valleys, where herds graze.

Epimelian, nymphs of the flocks and herds.

Water-Nymphs.—Naiades, nymphs of fresh waters in general.

Limniades, nymphs of lakes and marshes.

Potameides, nymphs of rivers (Acheloides, nymphs of the river Achelous, etc.).

Oceanides, children of Oceanus and Tethys (TABLE C).

SEA-NYMPHS.

Nereides, children of Nereus and Doris (TABLE I).

NYMPHS OF THE AIR.

Auræ, or Sylphs.

CELESTIAL NYMPHS.

Atlantides, children of Atlas and Pleione (TABLE G), Pleiades, Hyades, Hesperides.

NYMPHS OF THE LOWER WORLD.

Avernales, nymphs of the rivers of Hades.

NYMPHS HAVING SPECIFIC OFFICES.

Bacidæ, nymphs that inspired the priestess of Apollo.

Bacchæ and Mænades, nymphs that inspired or were themselves priestesses of Bacchus.

Melian, nymphs who sprang from the blood of Uranus.

Local, nymphs that belonged to certain places, as Dodonæids of Dodona, etc.

Genealogical, nymphs from whom families claimed descent.

ECHO.

This nymph was an Oread. It was said that if Zeus turned his attention to any one but Hera, Echo would prevent Hera from being suspicious by incessantly talking, and thus diverting the mind of the goddess. When this came to the knowledge of Hera she inflicted this punishment: Echo was never to speak until some one had spoken, and after any one spoke she must repeat what had been said. While in this condition Echo fell in love with Narcissus, but as her love was not returned, she pined away until there was nothing left of her save her voice.

NARCISSUS.

Narcissus was a beautiful son of the river-god Cephisus and the nymph Liriope. Narcissus was incapable of the feeling of love, and one of those whose love for him he had slighted besought Nemesis to punish his heartlessness. Nemesis caused Narcissus to see his own image in a fountain and to fall in love with it. He pined away in unrequited love, and was transformed into the flower that was called by his name.

A group of statuary often called "Castor and Pollux" is supposed by art-critics to represent Narcissus leaning on the Genius of Death. The latter holds an inverted torch (the torch of life), which he is just placing on a tomb, as though to quite extinguish it. In the background, but approaching, is a goddess who holds in her hand an apple. Some critics consider this to be Persephone; others think it is Venus Libitina, not only as

death-goddess, but as one who avenges despised love
and possibly as one who brings to life again (see
APHRODITE).

ORPHEUS AND EURYDICE.

Orpheus is one of the characters that is involved in
great mystery. Neither Homer nor Hesiod refers to
him, and yet Greek poetry and philosophy give him
a prominent place. One tradition says that he lived
in Thrace—that he accompanied the Argonautic expedition. Through the music-power of his lyre the
Argo moved down to the sea, the Argonauts were enabled to tear themselves from the pleasures of Lemnos, the moving rocks (Symplegades) which threatened to crush the ship were kept in their places, and
the Colchian dragon, which guarded the Golden Fleece,
was lulled to sleep.

Orpheus married Eurydice; she died and went to
Hades. Orpheus entered the dreary regions, and by
playing on his lyre so charmed and moved even Hades
that he consented to permit the return of Eurydice to
earth, provided Orpheus would not look back as they
were journeying out of Hades. But, overcome by his
deep love, he looked back, and saw only the vanishing
form of his beloved wife.

(The relation of Orpheus to philosophy will be given
under the subject of DIONYSUS.)

DARDANUS [*Där′dänŏs*].
(TABLE B, 27.)

It has been said that Dardanus was of the Pelasgic
race. In whatever country he had his birth, Samothrace
was the first centre of importance as regards his connection with mythology and history. Dardanus left Samo-

race, passed over to Asia, and dwelt among the Teucrians, whose king, Teucer, gave him his daughter Batea in marriage; also part of his territory, in which Dardanus built the city of Dardania at the foot of Mount Ida.

Descendants of Dardanus.
Ilus, Erichthonius. Ilus died without children, and left his kingdom to his brother, Erichthonius. This son of Dardanus and Batea was the most wealthy of mortals; three thousand mares grazed in his fields.

Descendant of Erichthonius and Astyoche.
Tros, king of the Teucrians.

GANYMEDES AND THE EAGLE (from Thorwaldsen).

Descendants of Tros and Callirrhoe.
Ilus II., Assaracus, Ganymedes.

Descendants of Ilus II. and Assaracus (see TROJAN GENEALOGIES).

GANYMEDES.

Writers do not agree as to the parentage of Ganymedes but many unite in the one above given. He was the most beautiful of mortals, and as Zeus desired him as his cup-bearer, in the form of an eagle Zeus, or a god sent by him, carried the beautiful youth to minister to the gods of Olympus. (See HEBE.) Tros received from Zeus, in compensation for the loss of Ganymedes, a pair of horses of great value.

AMPHION [*Ämphi'ŏn*] AND ZETHUS [*Zĕ'thŏs*].
(TABLE B, 28.)

Antiope, the mother of Amphion and Zethus, was the daughter of Nycteus, who was regent of Thebes during the minority of Labdacus. Owing to her relations with Zeus, Antiope was banished from her father's house, and having fled to Sicyon, the king, Epopheus, received her kindly and made her his wife. In time Nycteus died, leaving to his brother Lycus all of his power and privileges in Thebes, and also the sacred duty of avenging the wrong done him by Epopheus.

Lycus made war on Epopheus, slew him, and carried Antiope back to Thebes, and on the return she gave birth to Amphion and Zethus. The children were exposed to death on Mount Cithæron, but were removed and brought up by a shepherd. Antiope was kept a prisoner in the house of Lycus at Thebes, and received most cruel treatment from the latter's wife, Dirce. The sons grew to manhood; Antiope escaped from Dirce's cruelty, and, making her way to Mount Cithæron, discovered her children. Dirce pursued her escaped servant, and would have punished her by binding her to the horns of a bull, but the sons rescued Antiope and inflicted upon Dirce the terrible punishment designed for their mother.

According to another story, when the brothers reached manhood they made war upon Lycus of Thebes, slew him, and inflicted upon Dirce the death above related.

Amphion had received from Apollo a lyre of wonderful power and sweetness, and his whole nature was filled with love of poetry and music; Zethus excelled in physical strength. The brothers resolved to build the walls of Thebes. Zethus by vast labor would pile the huge stones, but Amphion would touch his lyre and the stones would move of their own accord and arrange themselves in appropriate places.

AMPHION AND NIOBE.

Amphion married Niobe, daughter of Tantalus and sister of Pelops. Their children were many and beautiful, and in her maternal pride she boasted over Leto, who had only two. Apollo and Artemis avenged this injury done to their mother, and their arrows left the wretched Niobe childless. Amphion slew himself, and Niobe, paralyzed by agony, was changed to a rock that never ceased to weep. (Fig. on page 194.)

ARGUS.

(TABLE B, 29.)

Niobe, the mother of Argus, must not be confounded with the daughter of Tantalus. Argus's mother was the daughter of Phoroneus (son of Inachus and Melia), who was ruler of Argos. He was the third king of Argos, and gave to the town its name.

Descendants of Argos and Evadne.

Ecbasus, Epidaurus, Criasus, Peiras.

Descendants of Ecbasus.

Agenor. The son of Agenor was Argus Panoptes. In this line Io had her descent, some calling her the daughter of Iason, though others place her in the line of Peiras.

NIOBE (Florence).

DESCENDANTS OF ZEUS AND NYMPHS.
ÆACUS [*Aï'äkŏs*].
(TABLE B, 30.)

Æacus was born on the island of Œnone, whither his mother Ægina had been carried by Zeus; the island was afterward called Ægina. There is a curious tradition that Zeus changed some ants into men (Myrmidones), that Æacus might have subjects over which to rule. Æacus was noted for piety, and it was believed that after a severe drought rain was sent in answer to his prayers.

TANTALUS.

On the island of Ægina was once a magnificent temple to Zeus which was said to have been built by Æacus, who was considered as the tutelary deity of Ægina, and after his death became one of the three judges of Hades.

(The statuary from the pediment of the temple of Zeus was discovered in 1811, and is now in Munich.)

TANTALUS [*Tăn'tălŏs*].
(TABLE B, 31.)

The name of Tantalus is suggestive of a punishment as peculiar as it was dreadful. In the midst of waters,

SISYPHUS, IXION, AND TANTALUS.

but they always receding, he was always tormented by thirst; delicious fruits continually tempted him to put forth his hand to take them, but they just as continually eluded his grasp; always near and above him was a huge rock that seemed just ready to fall upon him. The cause of this punishment has been attributed to various crimes on the part of Tantalus. The one most generally assigned is this: Tantalus, wishing to test the omniscience of the gods, cut his son Pelops in pieces and placed these before the gods as a repast. (The word *tantalize* originated in this myth.)

PELOPS.

After the horrible crime of Tantalus, Hermes restored Pelops to life, and, as Demeter had unwittingly eaten a piece of his shoulder, the gods replaced it with ivory. Pelops remained for a time in Olympus, but came to the earth, went to Elis, and became a suitor for the hand of Hippodamia; his contest with Œnomaus has been related. (See ŒNOMAUS.)

Descendants of Tantalus.

Pelops (see PELOPIDÆ); Niobe (see AMPHION).

ARCAS [Är′käs].
(TABLE B, 32.)

Arcas, who gave a name to the Arcadians, was also their king. Connected with the youth of Arcas is a story similar to the one told of Tantalus. Lycaon, the grandfather of Arcas, wishing to test the divine character of Zeus, placed before him the flesh of his grandson. Zeus destroyed the house of Lycaon by lightning, but restored Arcas to life.

Zeus having changed Callisto into a she-bear, her son Arcas pursued her in the chase, and when just on the point of killing her Zeus changed them into constellations, Callisto becoming the "Great Bear," and Arcas the "Little Bear," or Boötes.

ENDYMION [Ĕndy̆′mĭōn].
(TABLE B, 33.)

Various legends cluster about this beautiful youth. One says he was a celebrated sportsman of Caria; that one night, wearied with the chase, he lay sleeping on Mount Latmos, when Selene, the moon-goddess, riding through the sky, saw the youth, and, charmed with his beauty, descended to kiss him. Then, again, it was said that Selene threw him into the sleep that she might kiss him. It was also said that Selene bore to Endymion fifty daughters. The physical origin of this myth may lie in the mutual influences and charms of sleeping Nature and the moonlight.

(In the British Museum there is a fine statue of the "Sleeping Endymion.")

PIRITHOUS [*Peiri'thŏŏs*].
(TABLE B, 34.)

Pirithous was king of Thessaly. He invaded Attica, but when its king, Theseus, came out to meet him, he was struck with admiration, and the two kings became the most faithful friends.

His marriage with Hippodamia, and the battle which resulted between the Centaurs and the Lapithæ, have been related (page 91). Hippodamia died, and both Pirithous and Theseus aspired to marriage with a daughter of Zeus. Theseus carried off Helen from Sparta, and placed her under the care of Æthea at Aphidnæ. Pirithous aspired to marry Persephone, queen of Hades. Theseus remained true to his friend, even in the rash enterprise. They were unsuccessful, and Hades fastened them to a rock in his dominions. Theseus was rescued by Heracles, but Pirithous for ever remained in Hades, and with Theseus was afterward worshipped as a hero at Athens.

LACEDÆMON [*Lăkĕdai'mōn*].
(TABLE B, 35.)

Lacedæmon was the king of the country that bore his name. He married Sparta, the daughter of Eurotas, and he gave to the capital of the country her name.

Descendants of Lacedæmon.

Amyclas, Asine, Eurydice.

DIONYSUS [*Diŏnỹ'sŏs*], OR THE THEBAN BACCHUS.
(TABLE B, 36.)

Central Ideas.

The title usually given to this deity is "the god of wine," but this title very imperfectly suggests the wide circle of operations that were supposed to be under his control. Dionysus should be considered as the god not merely of the juices that quicken the blood with new vigor, but of those influences that come to the immaterial part of man's nature and act upon it as an inspiration to a new activity that may be noble. The simpler and material side of this myth has to do with the culture of the vine and the festivals connected therewith. The other and profounder side looks toward solemn themes—the power of the material over the immaterial Nature, and man's influence over man.

Perhaps no one has stated more finely than has K. O. Müller what might be called the relations of the wine-god to Nature. That author says that Dionysus is a personification of earth-life as producing fruits whose juices are potent for inspiration or for intoxication according to the use made of them. The vine was not the only, but the most perfect, expression of this earth-life; and as the new force that appeared in the grape resulted from the combined effects of earth-moisture and sun-heat, it waxed more and more potent from spring to vintage; but since it shared in the general torpor of winter, we may think of the growth, fruitage, and decay of the vine as expressing the life of Nature

Dionysus, or Bacchus.

in what might be called "the rejoicing and the sorrowing of vegetation."

We shall find that in the first stage of the Greek development of the idea and worship of Dionysus he was received not alone as the giver of the enlivening wine, but the gift of the wine was considered as a pledge of the presence and the companionship of the god himself; and as the wine gave physical animation and strength, so the belief in the nearness and the gentleness of the god infused into the hearts of his worshippers a noble ambition and courage as well as genial, kindly feelings toward each other. Had the Greeks retained this ideal, it might have been a refining power; but, failing to embody in daily life its better teachings, those teachings grew dim; so the ceremonies of the vintage-festival, like the pleasures of the banquet-hall, sank to the level of mere gratification of sense. On the other hand, instead of the ambition and courage that would have directed to right living, there gradually came into the whole cultus of Dionysus an excitement whose effect was as disorderly as its cause was unnatural.

Then Dionysus should be considered as the god of wine in its double power to quicken the pulse of the physical life into generous activity and to stupefy the better tendencies, while at the same time it rouses those that should be controlled; and the wine becomes a most expressive symbol of all those influences which are physical in their origin and nature, but which, having access to man's immaterial nature, through it largely affect his social and moral life.

We have made frequent reference to the form of animism that combined the worship of the productive with that of the destructive forces of Nature, and then appeared in sensual or in cruel rites. The association of the vine with the waxing and the waning of the earth-life was a preparation for the acceptance of that Oriental animism which in the autumn mourned the death of Adonis or of Osiris, and in the spring rejoiced in the resurrection of their beauty and brightness; and since around these central ideas were grouped those that were degrading, the whole moral tone of the Greek worship was lowered. An increasing tendency toward unrestrained expression of religious feeling made the followers of what had been a simple form of this worship ready to accept any system that could minister to this growing love for excitement; hence there was willing adoption of the wild orgies of Phrygia and Crete.

Through the Orphic Philosophy there was an attempt to lift the worship of Dionysus to a higher plane, not only in its own doctrines, but by incorporating it in the Eleusinian Mysteries (see DIONYSUS ZAGREUS); but it yielded in time to Oriental or to other corrupting influences, and became at last powerless for good; and the great truth that the inevitable consequence of disobeying ennobling impulses in any department of man's nature is degrading to the whole of that nature has had no stronger demonstration than in the various phases of the ideal and the worship of Dionysus.

Offices and Archetypes.

Nature: 1. To preside over the fruitfulness of the year.
2. To create the vine, and care for the growth of trees.

Human Life: 1. To instruct men in the cultivation of the vine.
2. Inventor of the wine-press.
3. To exercise the gift of healing diseases.

4. To give pleasure and joy and to soothe sorrows.
5. To exercise oracular power.
6. To promote civilization and refinement.
7. The inventor of dithyrambic choruses, tragedy, dramatic dances, and lively music.

Early Legends.

Birth of Dionysus.—Semele, the mother of Dionysus, was a daughter of Cadmus of Thebes. Hera incited Semele to demand that Zeus should appear to her in the glory of his divine presence and power. Zeus besought her to withdraw her rash request, but, as she still insisted, he appeared in the splendor and terror of lightning. Semele was consumed, but gave birth to a child. Zeus placed the child in his own thigh, where he was nourished for a time, and was then born as Dionysus—the very name commemorating the fact that he was twice born.

Education.—Traditions vary as to the person who was honored with the care of the infant god—one assigning it to Ino and to Athamas, who were thrown into a state of madness by Hera. By another tradition the infant was changed into a ram, and was then taken to Mount Nysa, and he was there cared for by nymphs, who were after honored by a place among the stars as the Hyades. Silenus is said to have been the foster-father of this god, and it was said that Hermes had the important trust. There is a story that at one time the infant would have been destroyed by Hera had not an ivy-vine sprung up and concealed the child. When Dionysus reached maturity Hera caused him to become mad, and he wandered through many lands, introducing the vine and principles of civilization and refinement.

The most noted legend connected with his wanderings is that which pertains to his journey to India, his introduction in that country of the cultivation of the vine and the principles above referred to, and his triumphal return. Equally prominent with the cultivating, refining influences ascribed to Dionysus are exhibitions of vindictive and ferocious anger at all who refused to receive from him the vine and his teachings, madness or terrible death being sent in punishment for such refusal.

On a voyage from Icaria to Naxos he hired a vessel from some Tyrrhenian pirates, but they determined to sell him as a slave, and sailed toward Asia for that purpose. Then the divine power and splendor of the god was manifested: the music of flutes floated around them, rivers of sweet wine flowed through the vessel;

> " On the topsail there ran, here and there,
> A vine that grapes did in abundance bear;
> And in an instant was the ship's mainmast
> With an obscure green ivy's arms embraced,
> That flourished straight, and were with berries graced;
> Of which did garlands circle every brow
> Of all the pirates, and no one knew how."

Furthermore, there appeared a lion, "horribly roaring," and "a male bear with a huge mane." The captain of the pirates and the crew all plunged into the sea, and were changed into dolphins. The master of the vessel had befriended Dionysus, so his mind was kept sane, and through the gratitude of Dionysus he was made " the blessedest man that ever plied his trade."

Ariadne was a daughter of Minos of Crete. Theseus was sent to convey the tribute of the Athenians to Minotaurus, and Ariadne gave him the clew by which he found his way out of the Labyrinth. Theseus promising to make Ariadne his wife, she left Crete in company with him, but when they reached the island of

ARIADNE (from the statue by Danneker at Frankfort-on-the-Main).

Naxos, Theseus deserted her. Here Dionysus found her and made her his wife.

Attendants.

In early times the Graces were said to be the companions of Dionysus, but as the tone of his worship was lowered he was supposed to be surrounded by lower orders of beings, as centaurs, fauns, and satyrs.

Emblems.

Vine-leaves and grapes; pine tree and cone; ivy and its berries (corymbs).

The asphodel, goats, tigers, panthers, dolphins.

Thyrsus, a staff ending in a pine-cone and twined with ivy.

A cloak made of the skin of an animal.
A cup or bowl for wine.
Two-handled vase.
A mirror. (In Orphic Philosophy this signified a search for the " hidden one.")

Representations.

As god of Nature, Dionysus was represented by a Hermes.

First Type.—Full, majestic figure; curling hair and beard; full drapery; holding the drinking-horn (*carchesion*) and vine-shoot in his hands.

Second Type (Praxiteles).—Youthful manliness, combined with soft and delicate outlines of feminine beauty; sometimes fully robed in feminine fashion; sometimes undraped, bearing as a sceptre the thyrsus.

Third Type.—Accompanied by satyrs, fauns, bacchantes in some scene appropriate to his worship.

Fourth Type (called Sardanapalus).—As returning in triumph from his conquest in India.

Fifth Type.—His marriage with Ariadne.

Worship.

Locations.—In all places where the vine was cultivated.
Sacrifices.—Rams.
Offerings.—Grapes, vine-branches, figs.
Festivals (*Athens*).—1. *Anthesteria* (February, awakening of Nature in spring).—The new wine was first broached; banquets and ceremonies were celebrated in splendor. In connection with this worship there were sacrifices of boiled vegetables to Hermes (as conductor of souls to Hades), also to the spirits of the dead. Persephone was now supposed to return to earth, and to

express their joy the guests crowned each other with flowers.

2. *Greater Dionysia* (March, true spring festival).—An ancient wooden statue of the god was carried through the streets by people dressed as satyrs, in commemoration of the removal of this statue from Lenæon to Ceramicus, which, according to an old legend, was once done by satyrs. In addition to banquets, the festival was gay with musical and theatrical representations.

3. *Linæa* (feast of the wine-press).—They drank unfermented wine, called "ambrosia;" procession of people wearing ivy-crowns.

The forms of this worship that were attended with wild revels and extravagant demonstrations were results of the Asiatic influences; some of the expressions of its fury were loud music, frantic gestures, cutting of the flesh, and tearing in pieces of the young of animals.

Grecian Comp. Myth. (see IACCHUS).

Foreign Comp. Myth.

ROMAN, Bacchus; EGYPTIAN, Osiris.

Literature.

From the "dithyrambic chorus" of this worship developed comedy and dramatic dances.

Art (see p. 199).

Modern Research.

At Olympia the statue of Hermes, recently found and known to be by Praxiteles, bears in its arms the infant Bacchus.

DIONYSUS ZAGREUS.

In the account of the Eleusinian Mysteries we found that one of the ceremonies was the carrying in procession the statue of Iacchus. In the Attic faith this Iacchus was called a son of Demeter and Zeus, but in the Orphic Philosophy there was recognized a strange being, having a serpent's form, who was called Zagreus, "the horned one," and who was supposed to be the son of Zeus and Persephone. It was said that Hera incited the Titans to kill this child. They, having covered their faces with earth, approached the child when he was seated on the throne of Zeus, and while he was contemplating his face in a mirror they slew him They then cut the body in seven pieces, and with the exception of the heart they boiled the body in a caldron. Athena carried the heart to Zeus, and in his anger he struck the Titans down to Tartarus. The heart was swallowed by Zeus, and then Zagreus was born again. The mission of this new divinity was to have universal dominion, to establish the reign of happiness, and to release all souls from the dominion of death.

ORPHIC PHILOSOPHY.

The legend of Dionysus Zagreus was a stranger, but only another typical expression of human death and resurrection, that had long been symbolized by the yearly changes in the life of vegetation, and had been used in the Eleusinian Mysteries as the basis of a system of pure moral teaching—a belief in the immortality of the soul and in its future punishment or reward. But the Orphic combined with these beliefs one far more mystical in its character, though equally pure in its aims. It was believed that before its embodiment in human form spirit exists free and pure; that the body is but a prison-house for the soul; that there is, and should be, a constant conflict between the two natures; that spirit should keep itself pure and unenslaved by the entire

ments of the body; that all who follow only true, right ways of living shall be rewarded by eternal companionship with divine beings.

The whole keynote of this worship of Dionysus Zagreus, as taught in the Orphic Philosophy, was as different from that of which the Theban Dionysus was the centre as is a heavenly note from an earthly one. When this system was incorporated with the Eleusinian, it was of this elevated nature, and until it was corrupted by foreign influence it was a source of great moral power.

HERACLES [*Hę'räklęs*], OR HERCULES.
(TABLE B, 37.)

The sons of Perseus, king of Mycenæ, were Electryon, Sthenelus, Alcæus, and Mestor. Alcmene, the mother of Heracles, was the daughter of Electryon, who succeeded his father in the government of Mycenæ. A branch of the descendants of Perseus had founded a colony in the island of Taphos. The people of this colony laid claim to a share of Mycenæ, but, as Electryon resisted it, a war followed. Electryon determined to go in person to Taphos, but before leaving Mycenæ he promised that if he returned victorious Alcmene should become the bride of her cousin Amphitryon, son of Alcæus.

Electryon was victorious, and returned, bringing the herds of which the Taphrians had deprived him. As he approached his home Amphitryon went forth to meet him, but a cow having wandered from the herd, Amphitryon threw a club at her, but unfortunately the club hit and killed Electryon. This dreadful accident quenched all hope in the heart of Amphitryon, who fled to Thebes, where he was joined by Alcmene, who became his wife.

The legend now runs that the great beauty of Alcmene attracted even Zeus as her lover. On the day on which

Heracles was to be born Zeus announced that there should be born a hero, of a race of men descended from himself, who should rule over neighboring states. Hera cunningly pretended to doubt this statement, and thus incited Zeus to take a solemn oath that the event should take place as he had foretold and on that day. Hera then went to Argos and hastened the birth of Eurystheus, a son of Sthenelus, while she delayed the birth of Heracles. Eurystheus, being in the line of the descendants of Zeus, and preceding Heracles in birth, was entitled to the honor that Zeus had intended for Heracles.

Alcmene became the mother of Heracles and Iphicles, the son of Amphitryon. Heracles soon gave evidence of his high parentage. Hera sent two serpents to destroy the babe, but he strangled them both. Heracles was now committed to the care of those who were to instruct him. Castor and Eurytus taught him warlike accomplishments; Linus, son of Apollo, taught him to play on the lyre; while Chiron, the wise centaur, gave him constant instruction.

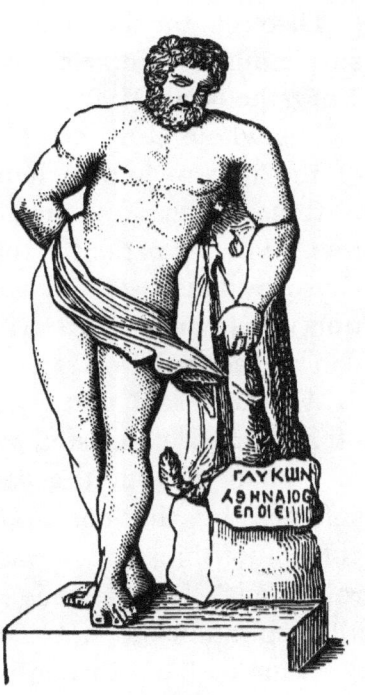

HERACLES, OR HERCULES.

There is a beautiful though probably not a very early legend to the effect that when Heracles reached manhood he was visiting in a lonely spot when Luxury and Virtue appeared to him. The former promised that if he would choose her as the guide of his life he should have ease and pleasure, but she could offer no lasting good; Virtue told him that if he became her follower he must expect a life of toil and self-sacrifice, but that the reward should be immortal fame. It is needless to say that he who afterward became the prince of heroes chose the guidance of Virtue.

Through the influence of Hera, Amphitryon became suspicious of Heracles, who was sent to the court of Eurystheus at Mycenæ.

The whole story of Heracles is a grand embodiment of the idea of loftiest heroism. By a mere accident of birth he was made subordinate to the contemptible Eurystheus, yet he patiently submitted to the humiliation, because by reason of the solemn oath of Zeus the condition was in accordance with the decrees of Fate and the will of the gods.

We have said that Apollo came as the representative of Zeus, and manifested a divine splendor in the sphere of human life, but the conception of Apollo was never softened by the charm of sympathy. Dionysus had companionship, but it was never used in self-giving, heroic deeds. But glorious Heracles so caught and obeyed all inspirations to noble action that they became to him a "wine of life" through which he had companionship with gods.

Eurystheus, too weak to comprehend the magnitude of the tasks that he imposed, but base enough to desire them to be overwhelming, now demanded of Heracles those "Labors" that became the synonym for stupendous efforts. The uncomplaining spirit in which Heracles undertook them was as sublime as were his triumphs. No victory nor series of victories awakened in his heart pride or rebellion, but each endeavor and success refined and exalted, until the human portion of his nature was transmuted into the divine and his life was crowned with apotheosis.

THE TWELVE LABORS OF HERACLES.

The gods, appreciating the magnitude of the tasks assigned him, lent him their aid in his preparation. He received from Zeus a shield; from Apollo, a bow and arrows; from Athena, a coat-of-arms and a helmet; from Hermes, a sword; from Hephæstus (Vulcan), a golden cuirass and brazen buskins; while Poseidon furnished him with a horse.

First.—The Nemean Lion.

The forest of Nemea was haunted by a lion whose attacks upon the herds of the surrounding country threatened their universal destruction. Heracles found the monster and attempted to shoot him, but finding the creature invulnerable against his arrows, he seized him by the neck and strangled him. Heracles carried the lion to Mycenæ, in order to present it to Eurystheus, but that cowardly spirit not only refused to see the hero and his trophy, but demanded that thereafter the reports of the results of his labors should be delivered at the gates of the city. The skin of this lion was worn by Heracles as a cloak, while a club that was cut from a wild olive tree became the symbol of his power.

Second.—The Lernæan Hydra.

Hydra, a monster with many heads, was one of the dreadful line of Phorcys and Ceto (TABLE I), and its home was in the morass of Lernæ in Argos. Heracles made the attack with a sickle-shaped sword, but as soon as a head was severed there appeared in its place a new one. Heracles commanded Iolaus (son of Iphicles) to burn with a hot iron the root of the head just removed. As Heracles was now on the road to certain victory, Hera interfered and sent a crab to gnaw at his heels. This enemy was despatched, and the hero drove the last head of the Hydra into the ground and placed upon it a huge stone; he then dipped his arrows in the poisonous blood of the monster. Hera commemorated the annoyance that the crab had given to Heracles by placing it among the constellations (Cancer).

Third.—The Erymanthian Boar.

The fields of Arcadia were wasted by a huge wild-boar whose lurking-places were in the Erymanthian Mountains. Heracles was commanded to catch this dreadful creature and bring it alive to Eurystheus. He obeyed, but when Eurystheus caught sight of the animal he was overcome with fear and hid himself in a brazen cask.

Fourth.—The Stag of Artemis.

This stag had golden horns and brazen feet, and was famous for its swiftness. The task assigned was that he should present it alive at the gates of Mycenæ. The hero pursued the animal for a whole year, and finally captured it. As he was carrying his prize to Mycenæ he met Artemis, who took the stag from him, severely reproving him for thus using an animal sacred to her. Upon learning the whole circumstance she returned the stag, and Heracles bore it to the city.

Fifth.—The Stymphalides.

In Arcadia was the Stymphalian Lake, which was inhabited by birds of most terrible appearance. With their claws and bills of brass they could pierce the strongest armor, and it was said that they were armed with darts. Even Heracles would have been unable to cope with these enemies had not Athena given to him a brazen rattle that frightened the birds and caused them to rise into the air, where they were pierced with arrows.

Sixth.—The Cleansing of Augeas's Stables.

Augeas, a king of Elis, had kept three thousand oxen in his stables for thirty years without having had the stables cleansed. Eurystheus demanded that Heracles should thoroughly cleanse these stables in a few days. Augeas, thinking such a task impossible, promised a reward of one-tenth of all his herds if it should be accomplished. Heracles turned the course of the river Alpheus into the stables, and thus completed the stupendous work in one day. Augeas, on the pretext that Heracles had cheated him, refused the promised reward. Heracles made war upon the faithless king, killed him, and placed Phyleus upon the throne.

It is said that Heracles built three temples to Zeus and that he renewed the Olympian Games.

Seventh.—The Cretan Bull.

The inhabitants of the island of Crete had shown indifference in the worship of Poseidon, and that deity expressed his displeasure by sending among them a bull that exhaled fire from his nostrils. Heracles captured this terrible creature, and carried him on his shoulders to Mycenæ.

Eighth.—The Horses of Diomedes.

Diomedes, son of Ares, had four fire-vomiting horses that he fed on the flesh of strangers who landed on his inhospitable shores. Heracles was ordered to bring these horses to Eurystheus. Heracles first threw the cruel Diomedes to be devoured by his horses, and then carried them to Eurystheus.

Ninth.—The Girdle of the Queen of the Amazons.

The queen of the Amazons had secured from Ares a girdle which could be retained only by the constant possession of inviolable courage. This was one of the most difficult of the "Labors," but by the assistance of Theseus the queen was taken prisoner, the girdle secured, and carried in triumph to Eurystheus.

Tenth.—The Triple-Bodied Geryones or Geryon.

This triple-bodied monster was in the line of Phorcys and Ceto (TABLE I, 63). He ruled over three islands in the dusky regions of the West, and on these islands grazed oxen of so fine a breed that they had made their possessor famous throughout the world. They were guarded by a fierce two-headed dog, and were kept by the herdsman Eurytion. In obedience to the order of Eurystheus, Heracles undertook the capture of these herds. By slaying the guards and the king, Geryon, the task assigned was accomplished.

Eleventh.—The Apples of the Hesperides.

It will be remembered that at the marriage of Zeus and Hera, Gæa presented to them some golden apples. It was said that this precious fruit was placed in the keeping of the Hesperides, daughters of Atlas (TABLE I), who lived in gardens that lay near the great river Oceanus. They were assisted by Ladon, a serpent-guard. Heracles was requested to bring these apples to Eurystheus. One tradition says that he compelled Nereus, the sea-god, to tell him where he might find the gardens, and that when he found them he gave to Ladon a stupefying potion, and then brought away the apples. Another story is that, after many long journeys, Heracles reached Mount Atlas, where Atlas was sustaining on his shoulders the solid vault of heaven. He promised to bring the apples to Heracles if the latter would relieve him of his burden. This proposition was accepted, and the apples were taken to Eurystheus, but Athena finally returned them to the keeping of the Hesperides.

Twelfth.—The Capture of Cerberus.

The command now came to Heracles to bring from Hades the triple-headed Cerberus. Heracles was solemnly initiated into the Eleusinian Mysteries, and then descended to his mighty contest. On his way he saw Theseus and Pirithous, who had been chained to a rock (see page 197). Heracles had to measure his strength with Hades, but the hero triumphed, brought away Cerberus, and liberated Theseus, though he failed to set Pirithous free. When Cerberus was shown to the cowardly Eurystheus he shrank from even looking at the dreadful creature. Heracles kept him for a time, tamed, between his knees, and then permitted his return to Hades.

CERBERUS (from a bronze statue).

We have presented the famous "Twelve Labors" in one group, but connected with them, as in addition to them, were many others even more brilliant and noble.

Some interpreters of mythology see in these "Twelve Labors" only astronomical phenomena; but if we consider the myth of Heracles as embodying the Greek idea of a hero, we find it outlining a character whose victories over the wild beasts typify that victory and control that higher natures may have over the lower.

As we now consider other adventures and exploits, we shall find the hero, grown strong by mastering the lower, using that strength in helping those who needed aid or rescue, or with almost divine majesty inflicting deserved punishment for crimes and sacrilege.

EXPLOITS AND ENTERPRISES OF HERACLES.

The Giant Antæus.

This giant, the son of Gæa and Poseidon, lived in Libya. When Heracles was passing through that country Antæus challenged him to a trial of strength. Heracles accepted the challenge, and the struggle began. Observing that whenever his opponent touched the earth he received new strength, the wise hero lifted the giant in the air and crushed him with his arms.

Busiris, king of Egypt.

When in the course of his journey Heracles reached Egypt, he found that Busiris, son of Poseidon (TABLE B, 62), sacrificed all foreigners to Zeus. As a punishment for his cruelty, Heracles offered him as a sacrifice on one of the altars that he had so profaned.

Cacus.

When Heracles was returning with spoils that he had taken from Geryon he met this son of Hephæstus and Medusa, who was a three-headed monster that vomited flames. Cacus stole some cows from Heracles, but was detected and punished with death.

The Rescue of Hesione.

The versions of this myth vary, one saying that the rescue occurred when Heracles was returning from his contest with the queen of the Amazons; another, that it took place in connection with the Argonautic Expedition. According to the latter, as the Argonauts approached Troy, Hylas, the friend of Heracles, went on shore for water, but not returning, Heracles sought for him, calling up and down the shore for Hylas, but the Naiads had drawn the youth into a well. Heracles then went to Troy, and the leading circumstances of the rescue are quite generally given as follows: It will be remembered that Apollo and Poseidon had assisted King Laomedon in building the walls of Troy; that the king refused to give them the promised reward; and that, in punishment, Apollo sent among the Trojans a devastating pestilence (see APOLLO), and Poseidon threatened to send a sea-monster to ravage the coasts. About the time of Heracles' arrival at Troy, through the advice of an oracle, in order to appease Poseidon, Laomedon had exposed his daughter Hesione to the sea-monster by fastening her to a rock on the shore. Heracles offered to slay the sea-monster that Poseidon would send, and restore Hesione to her father, provided the king would give him six of the fine horses that Zeus had given in recompense for the loss of Ganymedes (see GANYMEDES). Priam, brother of Hesione, urged the king to promise the reward. This was done; Heracles' rescued Hesione from a monster that was about to devour her, and restored her to her father. Laomedon refused to give the promised reward, and Heracles, indignant at his treachery, slew him and his family with the exception of Hesione and Priam. Hesione was given in marriage to Telamon, the friend of Heracles, and Priam, whose life was granted at the request of his sister, was placed on the throne of Troy. Afterward, Priam, offended that his sister had been sent to Greece, demanded her return; and it is said that the refusal on the part of the Greeks to yield to his demand was one of the causes of the Trojan War.

The Pillars of Heracles.

After many wanderings the hero reached the frontiers of Libya and Europe, and there he erected two pillars (Calpe and Abyla) on the two sides of the Straits of Gibraltar, and these pillars were called by his name.

The Service to Omphale, queen of Libya.

Having caused the death of Iphitus while in a fit of madness, Heracles made expiation by entering into the service of the Lydian queen. All traditions unite in attributing to him the performance of many noble deeds while in that servitude, but those of Lydian origin represented him as leading an effeminate life, permitting himself to be attired in a woman's dress, while Omphale wore the lion-skin that was the symbol of his power. This Lydian tradition is not at all consistent with the lofty character of the Greek hero.

The Rescue of Prometheus. (For this beautiful legend see PROMETHEUS.)

The Rescue of Alcestis from Hades.

If we take into consideration all the circumstances of this legend, this rescue might be called the crowning act of heroism. The first descent to Hades, the struggle with its stern monarch, and the capture of Cerberus were all accomplished in obedience to the command of Eurystheus. But the second time he entered into a contest with the king of Hades it was for a more noble purpose. Admetus, king of Pheræ, became very ill; upon consulting an oracle he was told that his illness would prove fatal unless some one would voluntarily die in his stead. Alcestis, his wife, willingly offered to do this, and she was about to carry into execution her grand design when Heracles came to her rescue. One form of the legend is that Heracles saved Alcestis from entering Hades by compelling Hades to promise that she should remain with her husband; while the other is that Alcestis actually performed her heroic sacrifice, and that the prince of heroes went down to Hades and brought her in triumph to the light and life of the earth. (Read Browning's *Balaustion's Adventure*.)

HERACLES IN WARS, EXPEDITIONS, ETC.

Wherever help was needed thither went the "helper." He took part in the first Trojan War, the Calydonian Hunt, the Argonautic Expedition, the war of the Giants, and in many less famous enterprises.

THE PRIVATE LIFE AND APOTHEOSIS OF HERACLES.

Megara, daughter of Creon, king of Thebes, was the first wife of Heracles. He destroyed their children in a fit of madness sent upon him by Hera, and then, thinking that his marriage must be obnoxious to the gods, he gave Megara to be the wife of Iolaus. Heracles afterward demanded the hand of Iole, the daughter of Eurytus, king of Ochalia; it was promised to him if he would accomplish certain feats. He did so, but the king refused to keep his promise. The hero married Deianira, daughter of Œneus, king of Calydon.

The centaur Nessus having offered harm to Deianira, Heracles shot him with one of the arrows that he had dipped in the poisonous blood of the Hydra. Nessus told Deianira that his blood would always secure the return of her husband's love if it should ever leave her.

Meanwhile, in punishment for the treachery of Eurytus, Heracles had made war upon him, had slain him and carried away Iole, and had gone with her to a promontory in Eubœa for the purpose of offering sacrifice. His wife, hearing of this and fearing Iole's power, took the white robe in which he was accustomed to offer sacrifices, steeped it in the preparation given her by Nessus, and sent it to her husband. Scarcely had he put on the fatal garment when the poison began to take effect. Seeing that his death was approaching, Heracles gave his bow and arrows to his friend Philoctetes, erected a funeral-pyre on Mount Œta and placed himself upon it, and prevailed upon the shepherd Pœas to set it on fire. His shade descended to Hades, but a cloud was sent from Olympus to receive his spirit, and Hermes and Iris conducted the new deity to celestial glory. Even Hera did him honor, and he married Hebe, the goddess of immortal youth and beauty.

Representations.
1. Inexhaustible strength characterized the embodiments of Heracles before his apotheosis.
2. His first opponents being of the animal kingdom, representations of the earliest portions of his history exhibit strength steeled and proved by exertion.
3. The increase in power that came through nobly using it, and the ease that results from conscious possession of the guarantee of sure victory, soon blended with the stronger outlines softness and dignity; and as moral grandeur more and more characterized the ideal hero, it gave elevation to the embodiments, until the mind is prepared to recognize Heracles in glorious apotheosis.

Worship.

Location.—Doris was the chief centre, but his worship was general throughout Greece.

Sacrifices.—The animals thus used were those that typified power, as bulls, boars, and rams, but the lambs used seemed to symbolize the gentler elements of his nature.

Festivals.—Sacred festivals were observed every fourth year.

Foreign Comp. Myth.

ROMAN, Hercules; EGYPTIAN, Dsom; INDIAN, Dorsanes; PHŒNICIAN, Melicertes, or Melkart.

Literature.

The Heraclidæ, or those who claim descent from Heracles, form an important group in Grecian history. In union with the Dorians they conquered the Peloponnesus.

Art.

The "Farnese Heracles" represents those phases of the hero's life during which the nature of his labors demanded vast strength wisely applied, as well as invincible courage (Naples Museum).

In the Naples Museum is also a marble group of Heracles and Omphale, a painting of the adventure with Nessus, and a painting of a scene in the life of Telephus.

The celebrated "Torso of Heracles" in the Vatican Museum is supposed to represent him as resting after some great achievement.

In the same museum is a statue of Heracles holding the child Telephus in his arms.

The "Twelve Labors of Heracles" formed a favorite subject for the adornment of temples; they adorned the Theseum at Athens, and also other temples, such as that to Zeus in Olympia.

The "Mastai Heracles" (or Heracles victorious) is an antique statue in gilt bronze. It represents Heracles in great strength, leaning on a club; a lion's skin is thrown over his left arm; in one hand he holds the apples of Hesperides (Vatican).

Modern Research.

The colossal figure of Heracles in the Cesnola Collection wears the skin of the Nemean lion, the head of which rests upon his, while its fore paws are knotted on his breast; his left hand holds the club; at his side hangs a quiver, while at his right are what appear to be the remains of a bow. Cesnola suggests that it is strange that he is not represented as wearing the skins of other animals that he had slain, and says that Heracles is sometimes represented as wearing a lion's skin while only a boy.

A fact of peculiar interest attaches to this statue. It is probably the only one in which the base of the statue is ornamented with a design that bears reference to the main figure. The scene depicted on the base is the capture of cattle belonging to Geryon. The cattle are guarded by a herdsman, Eurytion, and a two-headed dog, Orthrus.

Olympia.—Here was found a statue of Heracles and Atlas. On his neck Heracles has a cushion as a support for the heavens, which he endeavors to raise with his arms. Atlas is distinguished as king by the plain band round his flowing locks. Behind Heracles stands a woman in a long robe, who helps him, with one hand, to bear the heavens. This may be one of the Hesperides.

On a bronze plate is a figure of Heracles as a kneeling archer shooting a flying centaur, without the later emblems of the lion's skin and club.

A portion of the metopes of the Zeus temple at Olympia were found several years since, and were placed in the Louvre. Further excavations have recovered nearly the whole of the remaining metopes, and they are now in the possession of Greece.

Dodona.—1, Apollo and Heracles disputing for the tripod; 2, Heracles throwing the Cretan bull; 3, Omphale (with an emblem like a head).

Descendants of Heracles (Heraclidæ).

Heracles and Deianeira—Hyllus, Leichas; Heracles and Auge—Telephus; Heracles and Hebe—Alexiares, Anticetus.

TELEPHUS.

Auge was a daughter of Aleus, king of Tegea. When Telephus was born he was exposed, but was saved and educated in Arcadia by Corythus. He became king of Mysia, and married Laodice, daughter of Priam, and at the time of the Trojan War he opposed the landing of the Greeks on the coast of Mysia. Dionysus caused Telephus to stumble over a vine, and he was then wounded by an arrow from the bow of Achilles. An oracle having informed him that the wound could be healed only by the one who caused it, he went to the Grecian camp, and Achilles cured the wound by the rust of the arrow that caused it. Meanwhile, the Greeks had found that they could learn from no one but Telephus the route that they must take to reach Troy, and he gave them the information.

EPAPHUS [Ĕ'păphŏs].

(TABLE B, 38.)

Io, the mother of Epaphus, was the daughter of Inachus, king of Argos (or of Iason). The story of the jealousy of Hera, and of its sad consequences, was given in the myth of Hera (page 95). After long wanderings, Io arrived in Egypt. There she assumed her proper form and became the mother of Epaphus. The metamorphosis of Io into a cow is supposed to be associated with the idea of a moon-goddess, and then Argus's hundred eyes may symbolize the stars. Io is considered by some identical with Isis, considered as the moon-goddess; then Osiris represents the sun. It is thought that figures of a woman having the horns of a cow are intended to represent Io.

Shortly after the birth of Epaphus, Hera incited the Curetes to conceal the infant; after a long search Io found him in Syria. He became king of Egypt, married Memphis, a daughter of Nilus, and built a city which he called after her name. His daughter, Libya, gave her name to Africa, and, marrying Poseidon, became the mother of Agenor and Belus (TABLE B, 57 and 58).

MINOS [Mī'nŏs], RHADAMANTHUS [Rhădămăn'thŏs], AND SARPEDON [Särpĕ'dōn].

(TABLE B, 39.)

Europa was the daughter of Belus or of Agenor. Zeus was charmed with her beauty, and in the form of a white bull conveyed her to Crete, where she became the mother of the three brothers whose names are above given. Asterion, king of Crete, married her and adopted her sons.

MINOS.

When Asterion died, Minos asserted that the gods desired him to ascend the throne of Crete, and when he was sacrificing to Poseidon prayed that as an evidence of the favor of the gods a bull might come from the sea, promising that he would offer it in sacrifice. Poseidon sent a bull in answer to the prayer of Minos, but the latter substituted an inferior animal in sacrifice. In punishment of this impiety Poseidon caused Pasiphaë, the wife of Minos, to fall in love with the bull that came from the sea, and she became the mother of Minotaurus (the Minotaur), a monster having the body of a bull and the head of a man.

Dædalus, the great artist, constructed as the abode of this Minotaur the "Labyrinth."

Dædalus displeased Minos in some manner, and the latter imprisoned both Dædalus and his son Icarus in the Labyrinth, but the ingenious artist made for them wings with which to escape. Icarus flew too near the sun, his wings melted, and he fell into the sea (Icarian Sea).

The Athenians having slain Androgeos, son of Minos, the king made war upon them, and demanded an annual tribute of seven maidens and seven youths, who were all devoured by the Minotaur. The Minotaur was finally slain by Theseus.

When Dædalus escaped from Crete he went to Sicily. Minos pursued him, but the daughters of King Cocalus, wishing to retain Dædalus, had the water of a bath so heated as to cause the death of Minos. After his death Minos was made one of the judges of departed spirits in Hades.

Descendants of Minos.

Acalle, Androgeos, Ariadne, Deucalion, Glaucus, Catreus, Phædra, Xenodice.

RHADAMANTHUS.

This brother of Minos married Alcmene of Ocalea in Bœotia. Noted for his justice throughout life, he was made one of the judges in Hades.

SARPEDON.

This brother of Minos must be distinguished from the Lycian prince of the same name. Sarpedon, having difficulty with Minos, united his fortunes with Cilix, whom he assisted against the Lycians.

TALUS.

While Europa was on the island of Crete the island was watched by a wonderful being made by Hephæstus. Talus was made of bronze, but he had life-blood running in a vein from heel to neck. When any one attempted to land on the island, Talus became heated like red-hot iron, clasped the victim in his arms, and held him until he died; Talus meanwhile laughing in fiendish glee. This creature opposed the landing of the Argonauts, but Pœas, the father of Philoctetes, pierced the vein of Talus with an arrow from the bow of Heracles.

PERSEUS [*Për'seus*].
(TABLE B, 40.)

Acrisius, the grandson of Danaus, was the father of Danaë. An oracle having declared that Acrisius would lose his life through a son of Danaë, her father imprisoned her in a tower. Zeus visited her as a shower of gold, and she became the mother of Perseus. Acrisius enclosed both mother and son in a chest and threw them into the sea. The chest was cared for by Zeus, who caused it to land on the island of Scriphos, whose king was Polydectes.

When Perseus reached manhood, he resolved to bring away the head of the Gorgon Medusa. The Grææ, three strange beings having in common one tooth and one eye, told Perseus where he could find the nymphs who could furnish him with needed equipments. They provided him with winged sandals, a magic wallet, and the helmet of Hades which rendered the wearer invisible. Hermes added a curved sword, and Athena gave him a mirror.

The Gorgons lived near Tartessus. They had heads that were covered with scales, large tusks, golden wings, and brazen hands, and they had the power of turning into stone all things upon which their gaze might fall. Perseus looked at the figure of Medusa in the mirror, and then slew her, put her head into the magic wallet, made himself invisible by his helmet, and departed for home; but then occurred—

HEAD OF MEDUSA.

THE RESCUE OF ANDROMEDA.

Andromeda was the daughter of Cepheus and Cassiopea (of Ethiopia). Her mother had awakened the displeasure of the Nereides by boasting of the superior beauty of her daughter. Poseidon, in order to punish this proud mother, sent an inundation and a sea-monster to lay waste the country. To preserve his people, King Cepheus fastened Andromeda to a rock by the shore as a sacrifice to the sea-monster. Perseus found her, slew the monster, and obtained her as his wife. At the marriage Perseus was obliged to fight with Phineus, a former suitor, who was thus slain.

Perseus then went to the region of the Hyperboreans, and it is said that he changed Atlas into the mountain of that name by the power of the Gorgon's head. He then returned to Seriphos, and found that Polydectes was treating his mother with great unkindness; so he turned Polydectes and his friends into stone. Perseus now returned his equipments to their owners, and he gave the Gorgon's head to Athena, who placed it on her shield or breastplate.

It is said that while Acrisius was the guest of Tentamidus, king of Larissa, games were celebrated in honor of the royal guest. Perseus took part, and accidentally killed Acrisius, thus fulfilling the prediction of the oracle.

Perseus is said to have founded Midea and Mycenæ. He was worshipped as a hero.

A fine representation of the procuring of the head of the Gorgon was made in bronze by the celebrated Cellini. This is now in the Vatican.

Descendants of Perseus and Andromeda.

Autochthe, Alcæus, Electryon, Gorgophone, Heleus, Mestor, Sthenelus.

DIOSCURI [*Diŏskou'roi*], OR CASTOR AND POLLUX.

(TABLE B, 41.)

Central Ideas.

Those who limit mythic meaning to physical phenomena give these interpretations to the Dioscuri:

1. They were the evening star and the morning star.
2. They were the dusk and the dawn.

3. They were day and night, or the sun and the moon.

A study of the references to these fine conceptions will prove that as persons they were soon endowed with noblest qualities of soul, and were considered brave, heroic, magnanimous, and helpful to man, and their fraternal affection is almost without parallel. Their offices were therefore helpful and inspiring. They were supposed to preside over manly sports, and to have special interest in martial music and the war-dance.

Early Legends.

1. Homer calls them sons of Tyndareus and Leda, and brothers of Helen, so noted in the Trojan War. He said of them that they were buried, and then they rose again on alternate days.

2. Another tradition says that both brothers, and also Helen, were the children of Zeus and Leda, and that they were produced from an egg.

3. The tradition most generally accepted is, that Pollux and Helen were the children of Zeus and Leda, while Castor and Clytemnestra were the children of Leda and Tyndareus.

Assoc. Myths.

1. Helen, the sister of the Dioscuri, lived with King Tyndareus at Sparta. Theseus carried her to Aphidna, and placed her under the strict supervision of Æthra, his mother. In the absence of Theseus from Attica, the Dioscuri entered and ravaged the country, rescued their sister Helen, and brought away Æthra as a prisoner.

2. In the country of the Bebryces, Pollux met in single contest and conquered Amycus, the giant son of Poseidon.

3. The Dioscuri took part in the Calydonian Hunt, also in the Argonautic Expedition. A pretty story is told of

the brothers while they were with the latter. During a violent storm the Samothracian deities were invoked, the storm subsided, and stars appeared on the head of the Dioscuri. During this expedition they founded the city Dioscurias.

4. These brothers joined Idas and Lynceus (sons of Aphareus) in carrying away a herd from Arcadia. Idas took possession of the herd; a war between the two parties followed, and was conducted in Laconia. Castor, being mortal, was slain by Idas, who was himself destroyed by a flash of lightning sent by Zeus. Pollux killed Lynceus. Out of this story grows one of the finest illustrations of fraternal love that the mind has conceived. Pollux prayed that Zeus would permit him to die, that he might be with his brother, who, being mortal, must needs descend to the land of shades. As Pollux was immortal (by reason of his divine descent), Zeus would not grant his request, but permitted him to relinquish the celestial joys of Olympus on alternate days, that he might spend them with his brother in Hades.

It is believed by some that as a reward for this superhuman love the Dioscuri were placed among the stars as Gemini, while others said that Poseidon did reverence to their devotion by giving them control of the winds and waves, and that ever after, when shipwrecked mariners addressed their prayers to the Dioscuri, they came on golden wings to quiet the storm and to lend all needed aid. It was believed that "St. Elmo's Fire" was a bright signal of the presence of Castor and Pollux.

Emblems.

Stars.
St. Elmo's fire.
Burning fire.

Two parallel bars, joined by cross-pieces (each bar representing a plank of wood as a symbol of deity).
Long lances.
Conical helmets. (Some say that these were sailors' caps; others, that they commemorated their birth from an egg.)

Representation.
1. Two noble youths riding on splendid white horses, each bearing a spear and wearing a conical helmet surmounted by a star.
2. In the palæstra (places for wrestling), as patrons of athletic games.
3. The colossal statues called the "Colossi of Monte Cavallo" represent the Dioscuri (Quirinal in Rome).

Worship.
Location.—Sparta was the centre of this worship, but it spread over Greece, Italy, and Sicily, and even the Olympic Games were under their special protection.

SARPEDON [*Särpe'dŏn*].
(TABLE B, 42.)

The Lycian Sarpedon was the son of Zeus and Laodamia, the daughter of Bellerophon. (By some he is called the son of Evander and Deidamia.) Sarpedon was prince of Lycia, and at the time of the Trojan War was allied with the Trojans. In a contest with Patroclus he was slain. So beloved was he of Zeus that Apollo himself was commissioned to care for the remains of Sarpedon. The body was then tenderly cleansed and perfumed with ambrosia, and given to the angels of Sleep and Death, that they might carry it to Lycia for honorable burial.

DESCENDANTS OF HERA.

HEPHÆSTUS [*Hēphais'tŏs*], OR VULCAN.

(TABLE B, 43.)

Central Ideas.

It is in accordance with the theogony of Hesiod and with the traditionary character of Hera to attribute to her the sole parentage of Hephæstus, though many consider him the son of Hera and Zeus.

Since into all mythic creations there enter largely personifications of the forces of the physical world, we would expect to find in every system what might be termed in a general sense a "god of fire." In order, however, to express the Greek idea as embodied in Hephæstus, we must use the term in a peculiar sense.

The fire that shone on hearths, sending warmth and joy through homes, was specially under the care of the gentle Hestia; fire used as a symbol of Apollo, Athena, and Hades was as varied in its meaning as were the departments of action and influence under the control of the respective deities. As the god who mastered the mighty element and compelled it to do grand service for man, the Greeks worshipped Hephæstus.

There is a curious legend that Hephæstus was lame from his birth, and that when Hera saw that he was deformed she threw him from Olympus—that he fell to the earth and reached the island of Lemnos. It is thought that this may be a mythical form of saying that fire is so great a gift that it must be of celestial origin. Be that as it may, whether his forges made volcanoes heave, joined substances unlike save in unloveliness, freed from their dross the gold and silver, or, in power as marvellous as at other times mighty, it made the faintest tracings on the vases and enamels shine out in beauty as imperishable as brilliant, over all the workings of the mysterious, mighty, glorious fire ruled Hephæstus.

The early legends say that for nine years the god dwelt in a grotto under Oceanus, that Thetis and Eury-

HEPHÆSTUS, OR VULCAN.

nome were his companions, and that he there wrought many lovely things. When we take into consideration the facts of the joint action of fire and water, whether we observe them in Nature or in Art, we shall not be surprised that what may be called compound myths grew out of phenomena resulting from the sea and volcanic islands.

Mr. Gladstone sees in this last legend an ethical compound. Assuming that Hephæstus may have been a Pelasgic Nature-power, that his later character, as presiding over arts, is of Eastern (say Phœnician) origin, he thinks that Thetis in her friendliness represented the Pelasgic element, while the Eastern idea allied him with Eurynome. Another legend connects Hephæstus with Dionysus in this manner: the grapes that grow near volcanoes are of finer flavor than those that grow elsewhere, hence the god of volcanoes and the god of the vine are friends.

With Hephæstus as artist-deity were naturally associated the Cyclopes, Curetes, etc., and other strange mythical beings who wrought in metals; and as the practical arts expanded more and more perfectly into the fine and imaginative, the ideal of the artist-god grew finer until Hephæstus was associated in worship with Athena and Prometheus.

Hephæstus was restored to Olympus, built there magnificent palaces for the gods, and in his own was his workshop wherein he wrought wonderful things. He furnished the banquet-hall of the gods with most curious tripods or tables that moved at his bidding to and from the hall; he made the armor of the gods and the heroes; he seemed to have power to bestow motion and speech, for at the request of Zeus he made the bronze sentinel Talus; and he made for his own assistance in walking two golden maidens gifted with motion and speech.

It was a fine thought on the part of early writers to associate with Hephæstus in marriage a goddess who was very beautiful. In the *Iliad* it is Charis; in Hesiod his wife was Aglaia (splendor), one of the Three Graces; while in the *Odyssey* and according to popular belief it was Aphrodite, the very goddess of beauty. There seemed to be a subtle suggestion that the province of true Art is to lift materials from the beauty of the Useful to the high utility of the Beautiful, and that he who wrought loveliness for others deserved great reward.

Hephæstus is identical with the Egyptian Pthah, the creating deity.

Assoc. Myths.

1. (For the charming story of Pandora see PROMETHEUS.)

2. In order to punish Hera for her unnatural treatment of him, Hephæstus made for her a golden throne from which, when once seated, she could not rise without his aid. Ares endeavored to force Hephæstus to free Hera from the throne, but only by the kindly efforts of Dionysus was she released and a reconciliation effected. Other phases of the character of Hephæstus present him as dignified and gentle, even taking the part of his mother when she and Zeus were engaged in controversy.

3. At the time of the Trojan War the river-god Scamander was pursuing Achilles, and Hera sent Hephæstus to the aid of Achilles.

4. At the command of Zeus, Hephæstus was compelled to fasten Prometheus to the rock, but he obeyed with remonstrances, and even with tears.

Representations.

First Type.—As a dwarfish form, as it was an ancient idea that whatever had great innate power had a diminutive form.

Second Type.—As a strong laboring man, at first youthful; later, more mature.

Third Type.—Mature, bearded man, with short garment (chiton), so arranged as to leave the right arm and shoulder free; he wears a pointed cap (*pilos*), which is the badge of an artisan (or fisherman); he holds a hammer, and he stands near an anvil or a forge. Sometimes he appears just ready to strike with a hammer; at others, turning a thunderbolt with pincers.

Fourth Type.—As artificer of the gods, seated at work in his palatial workshop.

Worship.

Location.—Lemnos and Athens were the chief centres.

Sacrifices.—Animals—calves and boar-pigs—were offered entire.

Festivals.—1. *Chalceia*, a festival to Hephæstus and Athena as protecting potters and workers in metal.

2. *Apaturia*, to Zeus, Athena, and Hephæstus as deities of the hearth. On this occasion sacrifices were offered at the hearth, and men carrying lighted torches sang songs in his praise.

Art.

In the Ceramicus (Athens) was a temple to Hephæstus that contained the sanctuary of the Dædalidæ, a guild of potters in the line of the famous Dædalus. Near the statue of Hephæstus was one to Athena Ergane (industry).

Descendants of Hephæstus.

Hephæstus and Gæa (or Hephæstus and Atthis)—1, Erichthonius (Erechtheus I.).

Descendants of Erichthonius and Pasithea.

2, Pandion.

Descendants of Pandion and Zeuxippe.

3, Erechtheus (Erechtheus II.); 4, Butes; 5, Procne; 6, Philomela.

Descendants of Erechtheus II. and Praxithea.

7, Cecrops II., Creusa, Chthonia, Metion, Orneus, Orithyia, Pandorus, Procris.

Descendants of Butes.

Butes was a priest of the associated worship of Athena and Poseidon (see ATHENA).

8, The Attic family of the Butadæ were descended from Butes.

PROCNE AND PHILOMELA.

Procne married Tereus, a son of Ares, and became the mother of Itys. Tereus desired to marry Philomela; so he concealed Procne in a wood, first cruelly removing her tongue. He then told Philomela that her sister was dead, and so obtained her for his wife. The unhappy Procne wrought the terrible account of her treatment into a piece of tapestry and sent it to her sister Philomela, who sought and found her sister. They then planned a dreadful punishment for Tereus; they killed Itys, and served his flesh to his father. When Tereus knew the facts he drew his sword and pursued the sisters. Tereus was changed into a hoopoe, Procne into a swallow, and Philomela into a nightingale.

DESCENDANTS OF POSEIDON.
ANTÆUS [*Ăntai'ŏs*].
(TABLE B, 45.)

This giant lived in Libya. He was a noted wrestler, and was invincible, provided he was in contact with the earth. He challenged every foreigner to a trial of strength, killed those that he overcame, and with the skulls of his victims built a temple to Poseidon. He was slain by Heracles.

TRITON [*Trī'tŏn*].

(TABLE B, 46.)

Triton was the son and herald of Poseidon (see POSEIDON).

POLYPHEMUS [*Pŏlȳphę'mŏs*].

(TABLE B, 47.)

Polyphemus was one of the Lapithæ (Thessaly), and was married to Laonome, a sister of Heracles. He accompanied the Argonauts, but being left behind them he founded Chios.

POLYPHEMUS [*Pŏlȳphę'mŏs*].

(TABLE B, 48.)

Thoosa, mother of Polyphemus, was a daughter of Phorcys. Her son was one of the Cyclopes that lived in Sicily, and his home was in a cave of Mount Etna. This giant was a monster, having but one eye, which was placed in the middle of his forehead, and he lived on the flocks of the mountain, but also devoured human flesh. Polyphemus loved the nymph Galatea, but finding that Acis was his successful rival, he crushed the youth beneath a rock. Ulysses was thrown into the power of this monster, and would have lost his life had he not put out the single eye and then made his escape.

NAUPLIUS [*Nau'plĭŏs*].

(TABLE B, 49.)

Amymone was a daughter of Danaus. When they arrived in Argos the country was suffering from a drought, and Amymone was sent to search for water. She was attacked by a satyr, but rescued by Poseidon, who supplied the required water—according to some, by showing her the wells of Lerna; but others say that he asked her to draw his trident from a rock, and that as she did so a threefold spring gushed forth, one of the streams forming the Vale of Tempe.

Of Nauplius, the son of Amymone, very little is told. He was famous as a navigator, and founded the town of Nauplia.

NELEUS [*Ne'leus*].
(TABLE B, 50.)

Poseidon visited Tyro as the river-god Enipeus, and she became the mother of Neleus and Pelias. She exposed her children, but they were saved and reared by some countrymen. Cretheus, king of Iolcos, married Tyro, who bore a son, Æson. At the death of Cretheus, Neleus and Pelias usurped the throne; then Pelias expelled his brother Neleus, who went to Pylos (Triphylia). Neleus married Chloris (daughter of Amphione). When Heracles had slain Iphitus in a fit of madness, he went to Neleus to be purified, but as the latter was a friend of Eurytus, the father of Iphitus, he refused to grant the request. Heracles then made war on Neleus, and slew all his sons but Nestor.

Descendants of Neleus and Chloris.
Nestor, Chromius, Pero, Periclymenus.

PELIAS [*Pe'liäs*].
(TABLE B, 50.)

In the account of Neleus we learned that he and Pelias had usurped the throne of Iolcos, to the exclusion of Æson; also, that Pelias then usurped sole authority. After Pelias had reigned many years, Jason, son of Æson, came to Iolcos and claimed the throne. Instead of forcibly resisting this claim, Pelias sought to divert Jason from his purpose by proposing that he bring from Colchis the Golden Fleece, and thus originated that expedition so well known in literature and in art as the Argonautic Expedition.

Jason returned from that expedition, and Pelias met with a terrible fate. His daughters had been told by Medea that if they would cut their father in pieces and boil them, they would thus ensure his restoration to youth, and they acted upon the horrible suggestion. Acastus, his son, expelled Jason, and Medea instituted funeral games in honor of Pelias. Alcestis, so nobly distinguished for her heroic devotion to Admetus, was a daughter of Pelias.

EUMOLPUS [*Eumŏl'pŏs*].

(TABLE B, 51.)

Chione was a daughter of Boreas. When Eumolpus was born she threw him into the sea, but Poseidon saved the child. Eumolpus was placed in the care of Benthesicyma (of Ethiopia), whose daughter he afterward married. In the course of time, for ill-behavior, Eumolpus, with his son Ismarus, was expelled from Ethiopia, then from Thrace, and finally took up his abode in Eleusis. He assisted the Eleusinians in their war against Athens, and was slain by Erechtheus. He is called the founder of the Eleusinian Mysteries, and was the first priest of Demeter.

NAUSITHOUS [*Nausī'thŏŏs*].
(TABLE B, 52.)

Nausithous was king of the Phæacians. He led his people to the island of Scheria to escape from the Cyclopes. His sons were Alcinous and Rhexenor.

LYCUS [*Lў'kŏs*].
(TABLE B, 53.)

Lycus, the son of Poseidon and Celæno, must not be confounded with a grandson of the same name. Lycus the son was transferred to the Islands of the Blessed.

HYRIEUS [*Hў'rĭcus*].
(TABLE B, 54.)

Hyrieus was king of Hyria in Bœotia. Agamedes and Trophonius, two architects who built a temple of Apollo at Delphi, also built a treasury for Hyrieus. They, however, left a stone so that it could be removed at their pleasure, and by that means they removed vast stores of wealth. Hyrieus detected them. Trophonius cut off his own head, and was immediately swallowed up by the earth. Afterward on the spot was an oracle; in a grove of Lebadea was the cave of Agamedes, with a column by the side of it.

Descendants of Hyrieus and Clonia.
Lycus, Nycteus, Orion.

TARAS [*Tä'räs*].
(TABLE B, 55.)

This character is mentioned in connection with Tarentum, a Greek city in Italy, as the city is said to have derived its name from him.

HALIRRHOTHIUS [*Hălĭrrhŏ'thĭŏs*].
(TABLE B, 56.)

Halirrhothius was in love with Alcippe, daughter of Ares, but offering her violence was killed by Ares. Poseidon demanded that Ares be tried for the murder of his son. The trial took place on a hill at Athens, thereafter called the Areopagus.

AGENOR [*Āgē'nŏr*].
(TABLE B, 57.)

Libya, the mother of Agenor, was the daughter of Epaphus (TABLE B, 38). One legend makes Agenor and Belus the sons of Epaphus and Libya.

Descendants of Agenor.
Cadmus, Phœnix, Cilix, Thasus, Phineus, Europa.

CADMUS.
(TABLE B, 57.)

Europa, sister of Cadmus, Phœnix, and Cilix, was carried off by Zeus, who had transformed himself into a white bull for that purpose. After a fruitless search for their sister, Phœnix settled in the country that afterward received his name; Cilix settled in Cilicia; while Cadmus was instructed by an oracle to follow a cow until it should lie down, and there to found a city.

Leaving Delphi, he saw a cow, and followed it through Bœotia, until it lay down upon the spot where Thebes was afterward built. Intending to sacrifice the cow to Athena, Cadmus sent an attendant to a fountain to bring water; the fountain was watched by a dragon under the protection of Ares. Athena assisted Cadmus to slay the monster, and at her command he planted its teeth in the ground; there sprang up a number of giants called Sparti. Cadmus threw a stone among them, and so infuriated them that they commenced killing each other, and did not cease until five only survived; from these five noble Theban families claim descent. To appease Ares for having slain his dragon, Cadmus was compelled to serve that god for eight years. He then became king of Thebes, and married Harmonia, daughter of Ares. The Olympian deities honored the bridal with their presence, and the Muses sang a marriage-song. The gift of Cadmus to his bride was a splendid peplos worn by Athena and a necklace wrought by Hephæstus. Cadmus and Harmonia went to the Enchelians, who chose Cadmus for their king.

Cadmus is accredited with introducing into Greece the use of an alphabet of sixteen letters. Cadmus and Harmonia were transferred to the Elysian Fields in the form of serpents.

Descendants of Harmonia and Cadmus.

Agave, Autonoë (see ACTÆON), Ino (Leucothea), Polydorus, Semele (see DIONYSUS).

INO (LEUCOTHEA).

Ino married Athamas, who, becoming frantic, would have done violence to his wife. She eluded him by jumping into the sea, and was afterward worshipped as a marine goddess under the name of Leucothea.

Agave was the mother of Pentheus, who resisted the introduction of Dionysian festivals on Mount Cithæron. His mother in a frenzy mistook him for a wild beast and tore him in pieces.

Autonoë, married the pastoral deity Aristæus, and was the mother of Actæon (see ARTEMIS).

Ino and Athamas (son of Æolus) were parents of Learchus and Melicertes.

Polydorus, king of Thebes, was father of Labdacus. Semele was the mother of Dionysus. Her son finally took her from the lower world, led her to Olympus, and as an immortal she was called Thyone.

PHŒNIX.
(Table B, 57.)

Phœnix joined in the search for his sister Europa, and eventually settled in the country that bore his name, and Phœnicia has had great importance in history.

CILIX.
(Table B, 57.)

Cilix accompanied his brothers in the search for Europa, and settled the country called Cilicia.

THASUS.
(Table B, 57.)

This character is of little importance, and is sometimes called a son of Poseidon. It is said that he joined in the search for Europa, and that he gave his name to an island near Thrace.

PHINEUS.
(Table B, 57.)

Phineus married Cleopatra (daughter of Boreas). Their two sons are called by some Oryithus and Crambis; by others, Polydectus and Polydorus. He afterward married Idæa, and their sons were Thynus and Mariandynus. Idæa accused his eldest sons of improper conduct, and Phineus put out their eyes.

For his cruelty he was tormented by the Harpies, who spoiled or carried away his food. When the Argonauts asked for information they obtained it from Phineus upon the condition of freeing him from the Harpies.

EUROPA.

The story of Europa has been related in connection with that of MINOS.

BELUS [*Bē'lŏs*].
(TABLE B, 58.)

Belus seems to be a general term applied to a personage of high rank and great power, and it was of wide application among Eastern nations. The legends of his Grecian connections vary—one making him (like Agenor) the son of Epaphus and Libya; another, of Poseidon and Eurynome; and still another, of Poseidon and Libya.

Descendants of Belus.
Danaus, Ægyptus, Lelex.

DANAUS.

Danaus received from Belus the kingdom of Libya, but, fearing to take possession of it, he fled to Argos, taking with him his fifty daughters. He became king of Argos. These daughters, called Danaides, married the fifty sons of Ægyptus, but at command of Danaus they murdered their husbands. Hypermnestra spared Lynceus, her husband, and he avenged the death of his brothers by killing Danaus. The Danaides were punished in Hades by being compelled to fill with water jars whose bottoms were like sieves.

The Argives, and finally the Greeks collectively, were called Danai.

ÆGYPTUS.
(TABLE B, 58.)

The histories of Ægyptus and Danaus were so interwoven that they scarcely need separate consideration.

Descendant of Lynceus and Hypermnestra.

Abas (his sons were Acrisius and Prœtus). Acrisius was father of Danaë, the mother of Perseus.

LELEX.
(TABLE B, 58.)

Lelex is said to have given his name to the Leleges, a people whose origin and early history are lost in obscurity.

ALOEUS [*Ălō'eus*].
(TABLE B, 59.)

Aloeus, "the Planter," is of little importance in mythology, but he gave his name to two sons that his wife Iphimedia bore to his father Poseidon. (See ALOIDÆ.)

ALOIDÆ, OTUS [*O'tŏs*], AND EPHIALTES [*Ĕphĭăl'tĕs*].
(TABLE B, 60.)

Though the Aloidæ derived their name from Aloeus, they were the sons of Iphimedia and Poseidon. They lived on grain and developed a superhuman strength. There is an interesting story of their controversy with Ares, which resulted in his imprisonment in a brazen vase for thirteen months, when he was released by Her mes. Some see in this story an expression of the antagonism between agriculture and war.

The Aloidæ made war upon the Olympian deities. They had piled Mount Ossa upon Mount Olympus, and Mount Pelion on Ossa, when they were slain by the arrows of Apollo.

AMYCUS [*Ă'mўkŏs*].

(TABLE B, 61.)

This giant was king of the Bebryces, and was celebrated for his skill in boxing. He was killed by Pollux (see DIOSCURI).

BUSIRIS [*Bousī'rĭs*].

(TABLE B, 62.)

Busiris was king of Egypt. The chief mention that is made of him is that he offered in sacrifice all foreigners who approached his shores. He met his death at the hand of Heracles. (See HERACLES.)

CYCNUS [*Kyk'nŏs*].

(TABLE B, 63.)

Cycnus was king of Calonæ in Troas. His sons were Tenes and Hemithea. Tenes was beloved by Philonome, the second wife of Cycnus, but as he did not return her affection, she made accusations to Cycnus of improper behavior on the part of Tenes, whereupon both Tenes and Hemithea were placed in a chest and thrown into the sea. Tenes escaped, and became king of Tenedos. Cycnus discovered the innocence of Tenes, and they became reconciled; they assisted the Trojans in the war, and were both slain by Achilles.

DEVELOPMENT OF SECOND TITANIC GROUP—OCEANUS AND TETHYS.

(TABLE A.)

OCEANUS [Ôkẹ'änŏs].

(TABLE C, I.)

Central Ideas.

The idea of water and moisture as sources of life and fertility is quite universal. In Hesiod's theogony *Oceanus* is a general term, signifying the great masses of water considered as the source of life-giving moisture and fertilizing streams.

It is in harmony with the early and grand idea that Eros harmonized all things in pairs; that the earth and the heavens were joined in marriage; and that prominent among their children were the ocean (Oceanus) and moisture (Tethys). And the same grasp of mind so characteristic of the Greeks, by which great relationships were personified, suggested the fine thought that Oceanus married Tethys; and since effects are called children, the Rivers were very naturally looked upon as their descendants. Oceanus as parent of streams and rivers is thus distinguished from Pontus, the salt sea, producing only troublesome or terrible monsters.

Homer, in the *Iliad*, used the term *Oceanus* as signifying a mighty river surrounding the earth, which was conceived of as a flat disk. In this circulating unknown ocean-stream at a very early period the sun and stars were supposed to rise and set. There, generally in the west, were located the Abode of the Dead and the Elysian Fields, or the Isles of the Blessed. After the time of Homer and Hesiod, when about the Mediterranean Sea were concentrated man's knowledge and interests, a new application was made of the term *Oceanus*, and it was applied to the waters that lay outside of the Pillars of Heracles, in contradistinction to the shore of the Mediterranean.

Early Legends.

Although Oceanus was one of the twelve deities called "Titans," he took no part in the Titanic War, but remained aloof. Even after Zeus assumed supreme command, Oceanus was never placed in a subordinate position, and therefore is not represented as attending the assemblies of the gods of Olympus.

TETHYS [*Tḗ'thys*].
(TABLE C, 2.)

Tethys seems to be but a reduplication of Oceanus; but little mention is made of her. It is related that she was the foster-mother of Hera.

RIVER-GODS AND RIVER-GODDESSES.
(TABLE C.)

In the old Pelasgic Nature-worship rivers were personified and worshipped. It is thought that in this earth-worship river-deities were associated with the lower world. We know that the entrance to Hades was generally marked out by a river. That traces of this idea lingered and were used by Homer is evinced in a story of Achilles. Peleus had promised that on their return home a lock of Achilles' hair should be dedicated to the river-god Spercheus. Achilles, knowing that he should not return home, yet placed a lock of his hair in the hands of the dead Patroclus, that his spirit might convey it to the river-gods in the lower world, as though that place were the home of those deities.

In Homer's time greater dignity was conferred upon the Rivers. They were associated with other deities, and were even invited to attend the Olympian assembly. These deities were supposed to live in the rivers, to control their changes, and to endow them with human actions.

The earliest representations were of figures partly human, partly animal; then succeeded those more distinctly human, and the smaller and less famous rivers were symbolized by youths bearing vases, river-plants, and other marks of fertility; while larger and more noted rivers were represented by dignified, aged men. In architecture the sculptured forms of river-gods were used with fine effect by being made to fill the angles of pediments.

(The relations of the river-deities with the other mythic beings are given in their respective places.)

Descendants of Oceanus and Tethys.

It is said that the children of this pair were very numerous, and some include among them the Naiades. (For list of river-deities see TABLE C.)

DEVELOPMENT OF THIRD TITANIC GROUP—CŒUS AND PHŒBE.

(TABLE A.)

CŒUS [*Koi'ŏs*].

(TABLE D, I.)

Of Cœus very little mention is made. He is called one of the most powerful of the Titans; also a deity of night. From the signification usually given to his name, "The Begetter," we may infer that he was a personification of the ancient ideas of some mysterious source whence issued new creations.

PHŒBE [*Phoi'bę*].
(TABLE D, 2.)

Even less is said of Phœbe than of Cœus, but the meaning assigned to her name "The Shining One," is suggestive of the possibility of union of seemingly opposite powers or beings.

DESCENDANTS OF CŒUS AND PHŒBE.
LETO [*Lę'tö*], OR LATONA.
(TABLE D, 3.)

Central Ideas.

It has been thought that the word "Leto" belongs to a class of words which signify the *obscure*, the *concealed*, and that this applies to Leto not as a physical power, but as a divinity quiescent and invisible, from whom issued the visible divinity with all its splendor and brilliancy.

Early Legends.

Throughout the persecutions of Hera, Leto was made to wander up and down the earth, the different peoples refusing to receive her—some accounting for this hesitation by saying that they were afraid to incur the vengeance of Hera; others, that they were afraid to receive the new divinity that Leto would bring forth. The latter view may have a hidden reference to the unwillingness with which men receive new light and truth.

After weary wanderings Leto reached an island called Delos. Zeus fastened the island to the bottom of the sea, and there were born the light-deities, Apollo and Artemis. (TABLE B, 18 and 19.)

ASTERIA [*Ästĕ'riä*].
(TABLE D, 4.)

Asteria's name is thought to mean "starry night." In order to escape from Zeus's attentions she fled in the form of a quail, and, leaving Olympus, threw herself into the sea, and was transformed into the island Asteria or Delos.

Descendants of Asteria (see PERSES, TABLE F, 9).

DEVELOPMENT OF FOURTH TITANIC GROUP—HYPERION AND THIA.

HYPERION [*Hypĕri'ŏn*].
(TABLE E, 1.)

The name of the Titan Hyperion seems to have a double meaning—first, that of *height;* second, that of *passing over head*—and it is thought that the sun was looked upon as a power or being combining sublimity and regular movement. May it not be that Hyperion, as a very distant, but still as an operative, power, faintly outlined what afterward in Helios was made more definite—as a deity who radiated glorious influences, and at the same time had vast controlling power in the heavens?

THIA [*Thei'a*].
(TABLE E, 2.)

If we have the correct apprehension of the early idea of Thia when we take for its synonym *order*, she forms a harmonious complement to the regulated and regulating Hyperion. She was also regarded as the source of light.

Descendants of Hyperion and Thia (see TABLE E).

HELIOS [He′lĭŏs], (THE SUN-GOD).
(TABLE F, 3.)

Central Ideas.

We have seen that light, in its illuminating, energizing power, typified Apollo; but while it indicated that the god was operative in the physical world, as sending blessings of fertility and health or chastisements of pestilence and death, all such operations were but *symbols* of his lordship over intellectual activities and spiritual powers. But there was recognized a sphere, subject to constant observations, which was filled with the splendor of day, the loveliness of night, or the changing hues or growing brightness of the morning—a sphere where reigned in unfailing succession Helios, Selene, or Eos.

HELIOS.

The earliest Greek idea of Helios as sun-god was quite impersonal. Either a bright being or his bright symbol rose from the distant waters of Oceanus, moved in majesty and glory through the heavens, passed out of sight in the western sky, leaving night, but surely rising again, and thus ensuring the day. Later, the poets picture him as sailing in a golden boat (gift of Hephæstus) around half of the earth, thus reaching the place in the earth whence he was to rise and again make his circuit through the sky. As was the case with all deities, the offices of Helios increased and personal myths clustered about him. He had palaces in the East and in the West worthy of such a god, and herds sacred to him grazed in the Islands of the Blessed. Some interpreters of mythology trace very close affinities between the alternations of light and shade and the worship of Helios. (See HADES.)

Emblems.

The number seven was sacred to Helios.

A crown with seven rays, or sometimes with twelve rays.

Ripened fruit, cornucopia.

The cock, oxen, horses' heads.

Representation.

1. Figure of a youth with crown of rays or rays of hair.
2. Seated in a chariot, guiding his horses, with a whip.
3. " Colossus of Rhodes," a colossal statue one hundred and five feet in height.

Worship.

Location.—The island of Rhodes was the chief centre, but his worship was quite general.

Sacrifices. — Honey, lambs, goats, white rams, and white horses.

Grecian Comp. Myth.

Only in later times was Helios identified with Apollo.

Foreign Comp. Myth.

ROMAN, Sol; PERSIAN, Mithra; EGYPTIAN, Ra, also Osiris in certain phases.

Gladstone thinks that the consecration of Apis to Osiris may be the origin of the sacredness ascribed to oxen in the worship of Helios. He thinks that Helios was an Eastern deity, uniting Egyptian and Assyrian elements. Some identify Helios with Baal.

Descendants of Helios and Perseis (Perse), (see TABLE E).

CIRCE [*Kir'ke*].
(Table E, 4.)

This celebrated sorceress lived in the island of Ææa, and was attended by four nymphs. Her magical power was exhibited in turning into swine all who approached her island, and she exercised it by offering to her victims a draught of cordial which had power to work the transformation.

Assoc. Myths.

Ulysses sent some of his companions to explore the island, and they met the usual fate. Hermes prepared Ulysses to resist Circe's power by giving him an herb which could counteract the effect of the draught. Ulysses drank the cordial offered him, and Circe touched him with her wand, expecting to change him as she had the others; but he drew his sword and threatened to kill her unless she restored his friends to their proper form. This was done, and after that Circe treated them with great kindness for a whole year.

During his sojourn in this island Ulysses visited Hades to consult the seer Tiresias; he also saw and conversed with Achilles and Agamemnon.

Descendants of Circe and Ulysses.

Agrius, Telegonus.

ÆETES [*Aie'tes*].
(Table E, 5.)

Æetes was king of Colchis at the time that Jason came there for the Golden Fleece. The prominent events of his life were connected with the Argonautic Expedition.

Descendants of Æetes.

Absyrtus, Chalciope, Medea (see ARGONAUTIC EXPEDITION).

PASIPHAË [*Päsĕ′ phäę*].
(TABLE E, 6.)

(For the story of Pasiphaë see MINOS.)

DESCENDANTS OF HELIOS AND CLYMENE.
PHAËTHON [*Phä′ ĕthōn*].
(TABLE E, 8.)

Phaëthon signifies "the shining one." Different legends assign to this son of Helios different mothers, but many unite in thinking him the son of Clymene. Ambition prompted him to ask his father to permit him to drive the chariot of the sun for one day. It was said, however, that Epaphus had questioned the parentage of Phaëthon, thus inciting him to make the rash request. Helios granted the request, but Phaëthon was unable to hold or guide the fiery steeds, and they, leaving the regular course, came so near the earth that portions of it took fire. Some of the people were burned black, and even the rivers were heated to boiling. Zeus then struck Phaëthon with lightning, and thrust him from the chariot into the river Eridanus. Cycnus, the friend of Phaëthon, was changed into a swan.

HELIADES.
(TABLE E, 9.)

Lampetia, Phaëthusa, and Ægle (Phœbe) are generally called the sisters of Phaëthon, though some call them the daughters of the nymph Neæra. As the Heliades had favored their brother's rash act, they were changed into poplars and their tears into amber.

SELENE [Sĕlḙ'nḙ].
(TABLE E, 10.)

Central Ideas.

This moon-goddess sustained to Artemis a relation similar to that held by Helios to Apollo, though Artemis never rose to so great a superiority over Selene as did Apollo over the Sun-god. Later, just as Helios was confounded with Apollo (in Troy, for instance), so Selene and Artemis were considered identical.

Assoc. Myths.

The story of Selene's love for Endymion has been related (see ENDYMION).

Emblems.

The moon or crescent, a torch, a veil.

Representation.

1. Clothed in a long robe and a veil which covers the back of the head; sometimes on her brow a crescent, at others horns.
2. Long robe; veil rising over her head in an arch.
3. Riding on a mule.
4. Riding in a chariot drawn by two or by four horses.
5. Scenes illustrating the story of Endymion.

Grecian Comp. Myth.

In later times Selene was identified with Artemis.

Foreign Comp. Myth.

ROMAN, Luna.

Descendants of Selene (see DESCENDANTS OF ENDYMION).

EOS [E'ŏs].
(TABLE E, 11.)

Central Ideas.

Eos was the personification of the dawn, but was the

beautiful herald of Helios. She rose from Oceanus in a chariot drawn by four white steeds. At her approach the moon and the stars faded away, and only the glorious Helios preserved his brightness as he followed her through the heavens. When she was supposed to accompany Helios the whole day, she was not distinguished from Hemera, the day.

Assoc. Myths.

Eos loved fresh, young life, and carried away beautiful youths and obtained for them immortality. This was especially true of Cephalus, Orion, and Tithonus. The same delicacy that suggested the thought that those who died without any apparent cause had been gently removed by Apollo or Artemis, prompted the Greeks to explain the death of a youth in the morning of life by saying that Eos loved and carried him into immortal life.

Eos married Tithonus, but in asking for immortality for him she did not ask eternal youth; so he grew old and unlovely, and was finally changed into a grasshopper.

Representation.

1. Riding on the winged horse Pegasus.
2. Riding in a chariot drawn by four horses (*quadriga*), preceded by Lucifer; she has large wings is draped in white and purple robes, on her brow a star or diadem, and she bears a torch in her hand. Sometimes Hermes precedes her.
3. Floating in the air, pouring dew upon the earth.

In EGYPTIAN mythology, Eos was Ahi, the day, and she was the daughter of Pa-hra.

Descendants of Eos (see TABLE E).

EMATHION [*Ĕmä′thĭŏn*].
(TABLE E, 12.)

Emathion lived in Ethiopia, and was noted for his cruelty to strangers, in consequence of which he was slain by Heracles.

MEMNON [*Mĕm′nŏn*].
(TABLE E, 13.)

Memnon was of remarkable beauty. In the Trojan War he was slain by Achilles. Two exquisitely beautiful legends grew out of the sorrow of Eos for her beloved son. One is, that after his death the goddess never ceased weeping, and that her tears are the dew; the second, that Eos bore the body of her son to Ethiopia; that at Thebes, in Egypt, she erected the monument called the "statue of Memnon;" and that this statue had the remarkable power of giving forth music when the first sun-rays touched it.

> "God keeps a niche
> In heaven to hold our idols; and albeit
> He brake them to our faces, and denied
> That our close kisses should impair their white,
> I know we shall behold them raised, complete,
> The dust swept from their beauty, glorified—
> New Memnons singing in the great god-light."
> MRS. BROWNING.

DEVELOPMENT OF THE FIFTH TITANIC GROUP—CRIUS AND MNEMOSYNE.

CRIUS [*Kroi′ŏs*].
(TABLE F, 1.)

References to Crius very seldom occur. The synonym that is usually given for his name is "The Ruler," and it is possible that this Titan was an embodiment of a growing appreciation of the perfect adjustment of the universe resulting from controlled forces and powers.

MNEMOSYNE [*Mnemŏ'synę*].
(TABLE F, 2.)

There is a fine thought that the original office assigned to Mnemosyne was to preserve the recollection of great events, particularly of that great struggle, the Titanic War. Be that as it may, as a goddess that preserved ideas and principles already acquired she was recognized as furnishing materials for progress in the arts and sciences; she was therefore considered as the "Mother of the Muses," sharing with them the guardianship of the finer departments of human life (see NINE MUSES).

In representation, Mnemosyne's quiet, secret action is indicated by her arms being folded under drapery, while the whole figure, standing simply but fully draped, expresses deep meditation.

No children are attributed to Crius and Mnemosyne, but from Crius and Eurybia (TABLE I, 53) descended deities of the Stars, and the Winds and the mysterious Hecate.

Descendants of Crius and Eurybia (see TABLE F).

ASTRA (THE STARS).
(TABLE F, 4.)

The stars of heaven, considered collectively, are seldom brought into important relations with Greek mythology, though certain groups, as Pleiades, Hyades, etc., have some importance.

ASTRÆA [*Ăstrai'a*].
(TABLE F, 5.)

Whatever physical meaning attached to Astræa in the

early period, as in the case of most deities it merged into something higher, in this case even into the moral. She was regarded as a goddess of justice, was even said to be the daughter of Zeus and Themis, and is identified with the Horæ. It is said that she refused to unite with the Titans in their resistance to Zeus, and that during that great struggle she came and dwelt on earth.

This was the time of the "Golden Age." When the "Silver Age" followed, Astræa came from her mountain-home only in the dusky shades of evening. Then came the "Bronze Age," and the lovely goddess left the abodes of men for ever, the last of the immortals who had lingered on the earth. Zeus placed her in the heavens as one of the signs of the Zodiac, and we call her Virgo.

HESPERUS [*Hĕs'pĕrŏs*] AND HEOSPHORUS [*Hĕōs'phŏrŏs*].
(TABLE F, 6 & 7.)

The terms apply to the evening and the morning stars considered as identical and also as "light-bearers." Hesperus was very beautiful, and contended with Venus for the palm of beauty. The Romans called the morning star Lucifer.

ANEMOI [*Ă'nĕmoi*], (THE WINDS).
(TABLE F, 8.)

Many myths, principally local, grew out of the various winds, and the names indicated directions whence they came. Boreas was the north wind; Notus, the south wind; and Zephyrus, the west wind. The east wind, being considered injurious in its effects, was classed with those pernicious winds of which Typhœus was considered the parent.

PERSES.
(TABLE F, 9.)

The only prominence given to Perses grows out of the fact of his being the father of Hecate.

Descendants of Perses (see TABLE F).

HECATE [*Hĕ′kätę*].
(TABLE F, 10.)

Central Ideas.

This goddess was a strange compound of strange elements. Hesiod refers to her as a goddess who was permitted by Zeus to retain all the prerogatives that she had enjoyed before his supremacy, thus clearly intimating that she had long been in Grecian theogony, whether in her primitive form she came from Pelasgic Nature-worship, from Egyptian, or from Eastern systems of belief.

HECATE.

According to what may be called the physical theory of mythology, Hecate represented the moon in her invisible phases, and it was thought that when she was absent from the earth she was in the lower world.

At a very early period the power of this goddess was extended to varied departments. In Nature she had power over the nocturnal phenomena—particularly those of the moon—over the land, and over the sea. In relation to human life this goddess was supposed to have power over life, both in its birth and its close; as goddess of nocturnal phenomena she had control over the reason of men; she was invoked by kings and rulers when they sought prosperity, and was honored with offerings when such prosperity was obtained. As a nocturnal deity Hecate was closely associated with the dark, mysterious Hades. She was supposed to send from it weird spirits, and is even represented as accompanying wandering ghosts in their visits to the earth, her presence being announced by the whining of dogs.

Though the variety of her offices is so great, it is usually considered as triple; hence, as operating in the heavens, she is identified with Selene; in her influence on the earth, with Artemis; and as having power in the lower world, with Persëphone. Her character as moon-goddess would readily account for her power over the sea.

Representation.

1. As a woman having the head of a woman, or of a dog, or of a horse.
2. As a woman having two faces.
3. As a woman having three bodies, partly distinct and partly united, having three distinct faces united at the neck; such a figure was called "Triformis."
4. A bronze statuette of the Triformis, now in the Capitoline Museum at Rome, combines many symbols, but a few simple principles of interpretation will give unity to them: first, Night is often called the "parent of all things;" second, light is most closely associated with life; third, the lotus and the serpent both express life; fourth, now, remembering that when the moon was in-

visible Hecate was supposed to be in the lower world, we may conclude that the general signification of the strange figure is that of a goddess of light, of life, and death.

May not early life be symbolized by the figure that holds a torch, having on her brow a half-moon and a lotus-flower; mature life, by the figure that wears a Phrygian cap and diadem with rays, and has the full moon as her type, though the knife and divided serpent in her hands are more indicative of death; while the disk, possibly representing the dark phases of the moon, and the key and rope, may have to do with her character as mystic goddess and also as goddess of the lower world?

Worship.

Location.—Athens and Ægina, and a "grove" near Avernus, Italy.

Sacrifices.—Black female lambs, dogs, eggs, libations of milk and honey.

Festivals were held at night by torchlight; black lambs were then sacrificed.

"*Supper of Hecate.*"—On the last day of each month sacrifices of young dogs and of honey were offered in expiation. The remains of these offerings, with various kinds of food, were then placed in highways and cross-roads as a feast for the poor.

Statues were placed at the doors of the homes in honor of Hecate as patroness of families, and they were placed in cross-roads in view of her mystic character.

(For an interesting phase of the character of Hecate, shown in her relations to Persephone, see DEMETER.)

PALLAS [*Päl″läs*].
(TABLE F, II.)

Pallas was of no individual importance. The descendants of Pallas and Styx were Bia (strength), Cratos (power), Nike (victory), and Zelus (zeal). The story of Styx and her children in connection with Zeus has been given (see ZEUS).

NIKE, OR VICTORY.

Small statues of Nike have been of frequent occurrence, since they were used as symbols of power and triumph, and as such were placed in the hands of other deities.

DEVELOPMENT OF THE SIXTH TITANIC GROUP.

(TABLE A.)

IAPETUS [*Ĭă'pĕtŏs*].

(TABLE G, I.)

Great as is the subject of the creation of man, it is very faintly touched upon in Greek mythology. There was a later theory that Prometheus was the creator, but it was only a later theory.

When Zeus assumed control of the universe he found man already existing, and there is a generally-accepted theory that Iapetus was considered as the creator of man, though we find traces of a belief in human beings who sprang from the soil (autochthones).

Though, as a Titan, Iapetus was associated with Themis, he is said to have married Clymene (TABLE C), and she was the mother of the sons that are so prominent in mythology, while Themis was allied with Zeus (TABLE B).

At the close of the Titanic War, Iapetus and his son, Menœtius, were imprisoned in Tartarus, Atlas was condemned to uphold the solid vault of the heavens, while Prometheus, and measurably Epimetheus, entered into most important relations with man considered as the subject of Zeus.

Iapetus and his sons may be looked upon as representatives of the old Titanic dynasty, continued in the reign of Zeus, but as his antagonists; this antagonism culminating in Prometheus's championship of man.

THEMIS [*Thĕ'mis*].
(TABLE G, 2.)

As the personification of law and justice Themis held high rank in the theogony. She was even said to share the throne of Zeus, to give him counsel, to convoke the assemblies of the gods, and to preside over the moral laws of the universe. She foresaw the consequences of conformity or of nonconformity with moral law, and was therefore a prophetic divinity, and was said to have had control of the Delphic Oracle before Apollo assumed it.

Themis's symbol was a pair of scales, though on some coins she has a cornucopia.

Descendants of Iapetus and Clymene (see TABLE G).

MENŒTIUS [*Mĕnoi'tĭŏs*].
(TABLE G, 3.)

The only event of importance in the life of Menœtius has been related in the account of the Titanic War when it was stated that he was imprisoned with his father Iapetus in Tartarus.

ATLAS [*Ăt'läs*].
(TABLE G, 4.)

At the close of the Titanic War the triumphant Zeus inflicted punishment upon the Iapetid Atlas, "The Endurer," by obliging him to support the concave vault of heaven. Homer supposed him to bear a long column which keeps asunder the earth and the heavens. Later, and quite generally, 'Atlas is associated with mountains, as seeming to support the heavens; and this idea gave rise to several myths —one, that Perseus, being refused shelter by Atlas, through the power of the Gorgon's head changed him into Mount Atlas. At first this Mount Atlas was located at the extreme verge of the earth, then different localities were assigned to

ATLAS (from the Farnese Collection at Naples).

it, but it is probable that the true location of the mythical being was in the north-west of Africa. (The Atlantic Ocean derived its name from this myth.)

Another interpretation of Atlas is that he first taught astronomy and navigation.

The parentage of the groups usually named as the descendants of Atlas is so differently related that any classification can be only approximately correct.

DESCENDANTS OF ATLAS AND PLEIONE, OR ÆTHRA.

PLEIADES [*Plei'ädēs*].
(TABLE G, 7.)

The Pleiades were seven daughters of Atlas. Their names were Alcyone, Electra, Celæno, Maia, Merope, Taygete, and Sterope.

Sterope, having married a mortal, lost her brightness. Others say that the one whose light grew dim was Electra, and that she disappeared from the band on account of her grief at the fall of the house of Dardanus. Another legend calls them companions of Artemis, who, being pursued by the hunter Orion, prayed to the gods, and were transformed into doves and placed in the heavens. Still another legend is that they pined through grief at the fate of their father, and were placed as stars at the back of Taurus. By profound students of mythology the Pleiades are supposed to have close alliance with the old Nature-worship, and the daughters of Atlas, rain-clouds and doves, were placed in curious relations to each other.

HYADES [*Hy'ädēs*] AND HYAS [*Hy'äs*].
(TABLE G, 5 & 6.)

It is said that Hyas was another name for Atlas, the

father of the Hyades; hence their name. The legends as to the mother of these sisters vary, one calling her Pleione, another Æthra, while a third named her Bœotia. Hyas was a brother of the Hyades, and he was killed by a serpent or by a wild beast in Libya.

They are associated with the Pleiades in the following legend: The daughters of Atlas were twelve or fifteen, and the two groups were honored with a place in the heavens as a reward for the love they evinced for their brother Hyas.

A most suggestive explanation of the name "Hyades" is that which derives the term from a Greek word which signifies "to rain." When this constellation rises simultaneously with the sun raining weather follows.

The names of the Hyades are Ambrosia, Eudora, Pedile, Coronis, Polyxo, Phyto, and Thyene (or Dione).

HESPERIDES [Hĕspĕr'ĭdĕs].
(TABLE G, 8.)

There are conflicting accounts of the origin of the Hesperides, and in placing them as the daughters of Atlas we are departing from Hesiod's method, for he calls them the daughters of Nyx (TABLE K). The number is made to vary in different traditions, one naming only three — Ægle, Arethusa, and Hesperia; another giving four—*i. e.* Ægle, Arethusa, Erytheia, and Hestia.

These nymphs were supposed to dwell near Atlas; Hesiod placed them in gardens near the river Oceanus in the West, where Atlas stood supporting his burden. When Atlas was supposed to be in Libya their home was near him, and even when tradition located him in the northern regions of the Hyperboreans, the Hesperides and their beautiful gardens were moved thither.

The legend of the "Golden Apples of the Hesperides" is this : At the marriage of Zeus and Hera, Gæa brought as a bridal-gift branches of trees having on them golden apples. Hera, charmed with the gift, asked that they be planted in her gardens, near Mount Atlas. Her request was granted, and the gardens were placed in charge of the Hesperides, and were thereafter called the "Gardens of the Hesperides."

These nymphs were assisted by Ladon, a dragon-guard (see TWELVE LABORS OF HERACLES).

"*Hesperia.*—Hesperia, the "Land of the West," was supposed to be far remote from the habitations of the Greek tribes, so connected by the Archipelago. The sea which marked the western coast was not a Greek sea, but was called the Sicilian, as belonging to the land on the other side; as it was broad and devoid of islands in comparison with the Ægean, it resembled an ocean. The current (passing from west to east) was adverse to Greek vessels, and the skies appeared to the Greeks as dark and insecure; it was the night-side, where Phææces, the mariners of the dead, densely shrouded in clouds and mists, passed along their gloomy paths."

PROMETHEUS [*Prŏmē'theus*].
(TABLE G, 9.)

Central Ideas.

The character and the story of Prometheus present most profound problems. The subjects involved in these problems are the sublimest that the mind can dwell upon. The relations of man as free, yet subject to a supreme ruler; the displeasure of the ruler incurred by the subject; the championship of man assumed by an immortal god, the punishment of that champion because of wrong-doing, even though he did this in the service of man;

the voluntary services through which the sufferer is released; and the final adjustment of all the great issues in entire harmony with justice, righteousness, and mercy— these are some of the subjects involved in the story of Prometheus.

Early Legends.

At the close of the Titanic War, Zeus assumed supreme command of the universe, but, though Iapetus and his son Menœtius were imprisoned in Tartarus, and Atlas pressed by his stupendous burden, Prometheus, and measurably Epimetheus, were left free to act as disturbing elements in the government of Zeus.

Prometheus's forethought had foreseen that Zeus would triumph over the Titans; he had even advised them to use moderation in their operations, and finally allied himself with Zeus in the war; but after its close, when the new ruler was so displeased at the weakness and degeneracy of man that he determined to destroy the whole human race, then Prometheus stood as its champion.

In the old theogony Zeus was not called the creator of man—that title had been bestowed upon Iapetus—for when Zeus became ruler he found man already existing. Yet in spite of the fact that he was not assumed to be their creator, the question naturally arises, How could a ruler have such a feeling toward any beings coming under his control? Some one has said that in this myth the object is not so much to delineate a godlike character in Zeus as it is to depict him as a ruler who would firmly establish his new government. Remembering that he looked upon man, in his then existing state, as a weakening element in his government, for which he would gladly substitute a stronger one, the antagonism between Zeus and Prometheus is not inconsistent. The controversy began in this wise: The gods met at Mecone in order to adjust the privileges and duties of men. Prometheus offered in sacrifice a large steer, but in order that he might secure for man the portion most suitable for eating, he divided the animal into two portions, wrapped the flesh in the least valuable parts, while he enveloped the bones in the fair white fat. The sacrifice, thus divided, was placed before Zeus, that he might choose on the part of the gods. He chose the fat, and, though angry at the conduct of Prometheus, the choice of a god could not be reversed.

Now begins to develop that identification between Prometheus and humanity that forms so grand an element in this story. In punishment for Prometheus's deceit and unjust appropriation of the sacrifice, man was to suffer; though Hesiod says that man, having countenanced Prometheus, was equally guilty of offence against the gods. Zeus determined to withhold fire from man, partly because of the offence against the gods in the matter of sacrifices, partly because fire was so purely a celestial element that it should not be used in the service of inferior beings, and partly because Zeus foresaw what arrogance it would awaken on the part of man. Prometheus succeeded in obtaining some of the celestial element, and, bringing it to earth in a hollow reed, gave to man the priceless gift of fire. This sacred gift was a talisman by which man was to unlock the treasuries of gold and gems that the dark earth concealed; by its power he was to compel the great forces of the world into his service; by its power he was to fill the earth with creations so exquisite or so grand that even divine beings must pay them the tribute of admiration. In giving man this talisman, by which he might almost wrest secrets from the gods themselves, Prometheus had openly rebelled against the will of Zeus, and, though the gift of the fire was secured to man, expiation must be made for Prometheus's sin—expiation of Prometheus on Mount Caucasus, expiation by man through Pandora.

PUNISHMENT OF PROMETHEUS.

An important fact must now be considered. The prophetic power of Prometheus enabled him to foresee the possibility of an event that should cause the overthrow of Zeus's government, and he alone knew how that danger could be averted; and as man through his gift of fire became lord over Nature, so he through his great secret had power over gods. And he went to his punishment and bore it as a great nature always endures. He was fastened to a rock of Mount Caucasus. Daily a vulture consumed his liver, which nightly grew again—a god, yet all alone, only with the cold companionship of the winds and the stars. Io in her wanderings visited him, and he foretold his own deliverance by one of her descendants after thirteen generations had passed.

The generations slowly passed; Zeus could not release the rebellious god who would not deliver up his secret, even if the sins of the god had been expiated. Prometheus would not reveal the secret, for in so doing he would yield allegiance to a god whom he deemed unjust, and would also give into the absolute power of that god the race for which he aimed to do such godlike service. But Prometheus knew that deliverance would come.

PANDORA.

At the command of Zeus, Hephæstus took precious materials and made a being so perfect in form and features that the gods soon saw that they themselves had served as models, and they added grace after grace, until

Pandora (the All-gifted) became the title of one who had received all the graces that even gods could give.

Prometheus had warned his brother Epimetheus against receiving any gift from the gods, but the warning was not heeded when Pandora was the gift; and so she came to bring misery to man, and she became the bride of Epimetheus (afterthought), whose whole life was a repentance over mistakes that he should have avoided.

In the house of Epimetheus was a chest in which had been enclosed all the ills and sorrows that could afflict mankind, and he had been forbidden to open the chest. Through curiosity or through mischief Pandora raised the lid, and out from the home of Epimetheus, out into the homes of all mankind, passed only cares, sorrows, woes. Pandora closed the lid, keeping back Hope; so, though Hope still lingered on earth, she was helpless and unhelpful. The thirteen generations foreseen by Prometheus passed away. The talisman of fire had wrought its work, that, like its own nature, seemed celestial in power, use, and beauty; gods and fair women had loved each other, and earth had been blessed by a race of heroes so human in sympathy for needing humanity that they became godlike in giving themselves to its service.

In all the splendid line of heroes, transcendent in godlike, self-giving sympathy and service, shone Heracles. Yet, before the apotheosis, were the shiver of pain, the torture of strained nerve, the humiliation of obeying one who was too contemptible to be worthy even of the lowliest place in the service of Heracles. While yet in his human form Heracles reached Caucasus, and Prometheus found in him a deliverer. By consent of Zeus the vulture was slain by an arrow of Heracles, so that Zeus's act of justice became one of mercy. Prometheus, recognizing (as had Heracles) that service is sublime only when wrought in harmony with the will of the gods and the decrees of Fate, admitted his own error, and consented to reveal to Zeus the secret by which he could maintain his throne. The secret was, that Zeus must not marry Thetis, for should he do so a son would be born who would usurp his father's throne.

The culminating act in this great drama was one of self-giving substitution. It had been decreed that Prometheus should remain in Caucasus until some one would voluntarily take his place. The centaur Chiron, who had uttered so many wise words, and who had taught so many heroes, was suffering from an incurable wound (see CHIRON). Though immortal, he had asked that he might find rest in Hades, but he voluntarily took the place of Prometheus. So Prometheus was freed from his weary pain—freed through the human instrumentality and divine substitution.

This myth, so great in its outlines, has always been wrapt in much obscurity; we have tried to give the earlier phases.

Æschylus assumed that the theft of fire was the initial act of the drama; and as the group of stars that we call a " constellation " is resolved into suns and systems, so the myth of Prometheus is but an expression of the depth and height of human thought, questioning, fear, hope, and belief, and is therefore a drama of human life and destiny.

Early Legend.

It was taught in later times that Prometheus, assisted by Athena, had formed man from clay and water, and that the winds breathed life into the newly-formed being.

Representation.
1. The older and rarer illustrations are of the "Chained Prometheus" and "the Prometheus delivered by Heracles."
2. Scenes connected with the formation of man.
3. On sarcophagi, in connection with Eros and Psyche. According to the Orphic Philosophy, Eros signified the state of the soul before imprisonment in the body (see ORPHIC PHILOSOPHY); Prometheus signified the imprisonment of the soul in the body that he had formed; and Psyche, the soul after death, happy and immortal.

Worship.
At the time of the Panathenaic festival, in the evening, was a torch-race in honor of Prometheus. A torch was lighted at the altar of that deity, passed from one competitor to another, and he who succeeded in longest preserving it lighted was successful.

DESCENDANTS OF PROMETHEUS.
DEUCALION [*Deukä'liön*].
(TABLE G, 10.)

Deucalion married Pyrrha, daughter of Epimetheus and Pandora. Zeus determined to destroy the degenerate race of man, but Deucalion and Pyrrha, on account of their piety, were preserved. Deucalion built a ship, in which he and Pyrrha floated in safety, while a nine-days' flood devastated Hellas. The ship rested at last on a mountain—some say on Mount Parnassus; others, on Mount Othrys. They consulted Themis as to the restoration of the human race. She said that they must throw the bones of their mother earth behind them. Interpreting their meaning as referring to stones, they threw stones behind them, and from those that Deucalion cast sprang men, while from those that Pyrrha cast sprang women; so the earth was again peopled.

Descendants of Deucalion.
Hellen, Amphictyon (TABLE G, 7). Hellen was king of Phthia, in Thessaly.

Descendants of Hellen.
Æolus (Æolians), Dorus (Dorians), Xuthus. Sons of Xuthus—Achæus (Achæans) and Ion (Ionians).

Amphictyon was sometimes called king of Attica, and said to have been expelled by Erichthonius. He was said to have founded the Amphictyony of Thermopylæ.

EPIMETHEUS [*Ĕpimę' theus*].
(TABLE G, 11.)

The stories of Epimetheus and of Pyrrha (TABLE G, 12) have been told in the preceding stories of Prometheus and Deucalion.

GROUPS IN THE LINE OF URANUS.
REBELLION OF THE CHILDREN OF URANUS.
(TABLE H, 1.)

GIGANTES [*Gĭgän'tĕs*], (SERPENT-LEGGED GIANTS).

Alcyoneus, Enceladus, Cromedon, Porphyrion, and Rhœtus are mythical beings, in regard to whom opinions have greatly varied. Homer thought them savage, gigantic men, destroyed on account of insolence. Hesiod, as we have seen, considered Gæa their mother, although they seem to be the children of Uranus.

Later writers thought them to be monsters with tails of dragons.

Gigantomachia.—Grote thinks the "war of the Giants only a reduplication of the war of the Titans." In the later legends the Giants that sprang from the blood of Uranus (TABLE A, 32) rebelled against the authority of Zeus under the leadership of Porphyrion. From the plains of Phlegra, in Thessaly, they sought to storm Olympus by piling Pelion on Ossa. Victory declared in favor of Zeus, and the Giants were banished to Tartarus. It is said that this war was succeeded by a Silver Age, and that it lasted until Zeus determined to destroy the whole race by a flood. (See DEUCALION.)

MELIÆ [*Mĕ'liai*], OR MELIAN NYMPHS.

(TABLE H, 2.)

These nymphs are of no importance; indeed, they are scarcely known in mythology. By some they are called "nymphs of oak trees," by others, "nymphs of ash trees." There is a supposition that they had special care of the oak trees, from which were made shafts for spears that were to be used in war.

ERINYES [*Ĕrin'yĕs*], OR THE FURIES.

(TABLE H, 3.)

The Erinyes (Latin, *Furiæ*) were placed by Homer in the obscurity of Erebus, suddenly appearing when some crime demanded punishment. While Hesiod called them the children of Uranus, he also considered Gæa as their mother (TABLE A, 34). Æschylus called them the children of Night. Erinyes, the oldest name, indicated their keen power in detecting crime. The most commonly-received idea was that of avenging deities, visiting with special severity all violations of the laws of hospitality and filial obedience. Their names were Alecto (relentless), Megæra (the grim one), Tisiphone (avenger of murder).

The early representations depicted them as beings of terrific appearance, with snakes instead of hair; they were sometimes winged. They were clad in black, and carried a torch, a sword, a knife, a whip, or a serpent.

The name was changed to Eumenides (the well-favored goddesses). In explanation of this, one theory is that the new name was merely one of the euphemisms common with the Greeks. Another is, that when Orestes was acquitted after his trial in the Areopagus, the name of these hitherto dreadful beings was changed. (See ORESTES.)

FURIES (from a painted vase).

The Erinyes were generally supposed to dwell near the entrance of the lower world, but they often appeared on earth, inflicting deserved punishment. Their worship was universal and of the most solemn nature. Their priests formed a tribunal before whom no one dared appear without having taken an oath on the altar of the Eumenides to speak only the truth. *Sacrifices*—black sheep, turtle-doves. *Libations*—honey and wine. *Offerings*—branches of cedar, alder, saffron, and juniper.

Later Grecian artists represented the Erinyes as young

280   GREEK MYTHOLOGY.

and beautiful, sometimes with and sometimes without serpents around the head.

APHRODITE [*Ăphrŏdĭ'tē*], OR VENUS.
(TABLE H, 4.)

Central Ideas.

Greek life was moved and moulded by that power which moves and moulds all human life—love.

We have hitherto used the term Love as the synonym for Eros, but since Hesiod makes distinct mention of

APHRODITE, OR VENUS.

Aphrodite as the goddess of love, we naturally ask what was the relation of the two deities. We have seen that at the time that Hesiod wrote his wonderful story of the gods there was a general recognition of a power that swayed human hearts, and they called it Love; while in charming union with this power, as though it were its complement, was ever found Beauty—each a world-power; united, they were irresistible.

Enshrined as the divinity who through love and beauty touched all human hearts was Aphrodite, as though Eros had commissioned her to unite on earth human hearts, even as he did those that were divine, until her work, perfectly completed, should be deemed worthy of immortality. This could be true only of the highest ideal of Aphrodite; and though in the course of time that ideal, like all others, had many phases, we rejoice to find that an early Hellenic conception of this goddess, uncontaminated by Eastern influences, was high, pure, and noble.

Possibly, the earliest changes in the development of this mythic character corresponded to those noticed in the sketch of her associated deity, Eros, but their work was always in unison; therefore it is not strange that in later times there arose the fine legend that when the seaborn Venus Urania stepped on the earth she was welcomed by Eros.

APHRODITE OF DODONA.

Very little is known of this goddess. We have seen that in the Pelasgic Nature-worship, that centred at Dodona, Zeus was recognized as the creator of all things, and that Dione was the "mother-goddess," whose symbol was productive earth or fertilizing moisture. Now, there are indications that their daughter, Aphrodite, embodied attributes that pertained to human character and affections; so even in the oldest worship she was the "goddess of love." Her association in worship with Zeus and Dione constituted the third stage of that worship.

The symbol of Dodonæan Aphrodite was the dove, and, though the same symbol distinguished a partially-corresponding Phœnician deity, it is probable that its signification in the system of Dodona was entirely different from that used in the latter connection. In the former case it may have typified the gentle influences of love.

APHRODITE URANIA.

It is difficult, perhaps impossible, to follow the development of the respective worships of Aphrodite of Dodona and Aphrodite Urania. So early as the time of Hesiod it was believed, in at least portions of Greece, that this goddess was the daughter of Uranus, and that she was therefore Urania, the "heavenly one" (see page 57). Charming myths clustered about her coming. Whether Cythera or Cyprus was first honored by her footsteps, grass and flowers sprang up in greeting; the Graces attired her; and, as we have seen, Eros welcomed to earth one whose mission was so like his own.

Because she sprang out of the sea she was called "Anadyomene." Preller finds in this legend a wide meaning. Child of Uranus (celestial spirit) and of the sea (plenitude of matter), received by the earth, whose subjects were to become her own, and welcomed by the divine Eros, how could such a goddess lack worshippers?

Some mythologists say that all worships of this deity were of foreign—*i. e.* non-Hellenic—origin, but many of the most learned and impartial of interpreters assert that there was a distinctly Hellenic goddess whose offices, like those of Eros, were tender but noble, comforting but uplifting—such as were befitting one who was of the sea and earth, but who was also of the heavens. This early Hellenic deity presided over pure love, and was the protectress of conjugal fidelity and the sanctity of homes.

She was always represented with a serious, noble countenance and a dignified air, and was fully and modestly draped.

The idea of Aphrodite underwent great changes, and it seems probable that simultaneously in different localities in Greece different phases of her character were made prominent. As goddess of the nocturnal heavens she dispensed blessings of fruitfulness, especially through fertilizing dew; hence, as goddess of the damp night she was goddess of fertility, for damp night, next to light, was thought to be the most powerful origin of all things. (May it not be that in this apprehension of Aphrodite as the obscure origin of beings is involved that of her identity with the oldest Fate, who held the beginning of life?)

APHRODITE PANDEMOS.

Either through degradation of the early Hellenic idea or through foreign influences there existed in Greece the worship of Aphrodite Pandemos. It is possible that its predominating idea was but a modified form of the Pelasgic worship of Dione as productive earth, combined with that of her daughter as the patroness of human affection; or it may have been derived from that Oriental worship of which we shall speak under the head of ASTARTE. But the whole character of this worship was as opposed to that of Urania as the earthly is opposed to the heavenly. This goddess was installed as the goddess of earth-life considered in its productiveness, and as the deity that presides over the lower passions of mankind.

APHRODITE LIBITINA.

As goddess of the fertility of earth-life Aphrodite was supposed to have supervision over life even while it was in a torpid state; therefore she is sometimes identified with Persephone. The myth of Pygmalion is an interesting illustration of this phase of worship.

APHRODITE PONTIA.

In this phase the goddess presides over the tranquil sea. Professor Curtius thinks that the apprehension of Aphrodite as a sea-deity was Phœnician in origin. It is certain that those people had a corresponding deity who was the special protectress of their mariners, who never undertook a voyage without carrying her image with them. In the Grecian system she was installed as patron of navigation and harbors; in this capacity she was first worshipped at anchoring-places—then, later, farther inland.

Her symbol was the dove, but, unlike the Dodonæan idea, it here signified the bird " whose flight before the prow of vessels announced the vicinity of land." As a sea-deity her worship was associated with that of Poseidon.

APHRODITE IN HOMER.

Dione of Dodona and her daughter Aphrodite were transferred from that early system to the Olympian, but neither deity attained to a high position. Aphrodite became prominent through her relations to the Trojan War, but the whole history of her influence and actions in that connection delineated a goddess who was inferior in character, attributes, and power.

ASTARTE.

Under the names of Astarte, Ishtar, Mylitta, etc. ancient Asiatic races worshipped a deity nearly identical in character and attributes with Aphrodite. It may be that the remote origin of this goddess lay in the common tendency to associate with the creative energy, which was personified as a chief deity, a feminine principle potent throughout all Nature. In some systems this feminine principle seems to have been a mere abstraction; in others it became a sky-goddess, called "queen of the heavens," or "great lady," or by kindred titles.

As the chief god was more definitely conceived as a sun-god, or as a god of whose powers the sun was a fitting symbol, the chief goddess assumed astronomical characteristics, and was sometimes represented by the planet Venus. By reason of the observed connection between astronomical and solar influences and the phenomena of the seasons, very naturally the decay of vegetation in autumn and the desolation of winter became typical of the death of a god, while the return of life was the symbol of his return.

Festivals held in honor of such a deity were of a two-fold nature—first, harvest and winter lamentations by the bereaved goddess and her worshippers; second, vernal rejoicings over the return that was heralded by the returning life of the spring. In Astarte-worship such festivals were held in honor of her relations to Adonis, or Tammuz (See ADONIS.)

The fitness of Nature to symbolize, and its power to affect, human life suggested the existence of a subtle sympathy on her part, or on the part of her personification as Astarte, not only with the physical life and death, but with human feeling and passion, whether of pleasure or of pain; so, as human life became degraded, the central idea and accompanying rites of this worship became more grossly sensual, until it comprehended little save perversions and corruptions of that divine principle of love which, as heaven-sent, should have been a heavenward guiding-power in human life.

This form of worship was adopted by the Hellenic races of the west coast of Asia Minor, as well as by those of Greece proper, and it came to exercise a controlling influence in the islands of the Ægean Sea. In some localities Aphrodite was regarded as an embodiment of both the feminine and masculine principle. Since Astarte held the same relation to the Phœnician religious system, it would seem that this worship was but a modification of the Phœnician, though Cyprus became a chief centre.

Office and Archetypes (of Aphrodite).

Nature: 1. To preside over the development of all forms of physical life.
2. As goddess of the nocturnal heavens, to give light and to dispense fertilizing dew.
3. As goddess of the sea, to modify the powers of Poseidon and preserve a calm sea.

Human Life: 1. As goddess of beauty, to create ideals of physical beauty seemingly more than earthly, that they may worthily symbolize that immortal beauty that is to be the celestial benediction on human obedience to truth and purity.
2. As goddess of pure love, also of marriage ceremonies.
3. As protectress of families, to base the marriage relation upon such noble, self-giving love that earthly homes might typify the celestial home, heaven.
4. To preside over the pleasures and amusements of the young.
5. To preserve life during its torpid state, and to secure for it a resurrection.

Attendants.

To this incarnation of love and beauty were assigned

as attendants the Seasons (Horæ); the Graces (Charites); her son Eros or Cupid; Himeros (desire of love); Pothos (anxiety of love); and Peitho, or Suadela (persuasion of love).

Legends.

Aphrodite married Hephæstus, but her chief love was for Ares (Mars). Æneas, so famous in the Trojan War, was the son of Aphrodite and Anchises.

Assoc. Myths.

1. *Judgment of Paris.*—Prometheus had warned Zeus against marrying Thetis (see PROMETHEUS). She was given in marriage to Peleus, prince of Phthia, in Thessaly. All of the gods came to the marriage, save Eris, the goddess of discord. Angry at not being invited, she threw among the guests a golden apple inscribed "To the fairest," and Hera, Athena, and Aphrodite each laid claim to the apple. Paris, son of Priam, king of Troy, was at the time a shepherd on Mount Ida. The three goddesses asked him to award the golden apple, each offering a reward for a decision in her favor. Athena offered military fame; Hera, the empire of Asia; Aphrodite promised him the most beautiful woman in the world for a wife. Paris gave the apple to Aphrodite. (See TROJAN WAR.)

2. (See PSYCHE.)
3. (See ADONIS.)

Emblems (at Dodona).

> *Nature:* As goddess of the heavens—first, the moon, planet Venus, torch; second, a polos on her head.
> As goddess of fertility—first, a cone (Eastern in origin); second, hare, tortoise, swan, iynx.

As goddess of the sea, dolphin, dove (see APHRODITE OF DODONA).

Human Life: As goddess of love and beauty—first, lime tree, myrtle, rose; second, diadem, fillet, mirror.

As goddess who rules all hearts, armor, laurels, palm, apples.

As goddess of human births, a child or Cupid in her arms.

As goddess of youthful pleasures, ankle-bone (dancing), dice (games of chance).

As goddess of ornamental arts, a spindle, purple shellfish.

As goddess of torpid life, poppy, pomegranate (?).

As goddess of spring life, the month of April, flowers, swallow.

Theog.: As victorious over Ares, his shield and helmet.

As victorious over Athena and Juno, an apple (victory). (As the pomegranate was associated with Persephone as the goddess of torpid life, may not the apple (generally recognized as a symbol for victory) be the emblem of Aphrodite as more distinctly a goddess of the returning exuberant life of spring?)

Representations.

1. Most ancient, a conical pillar of wood or of stone.
2. Three wooden statues to Aphrodite as—first, celestial; second, popular (*pandemos*); third, one who persuades to pure love (*apostropia*).
3. Statues of wood, with hands and face of marble.
4. As goddess of pure love and marriage, with serious and noble countenance and mien; fully draped.

5. As goddess of human births, holding a child or Cupid.
6. As goddess of love, less noble and ideal than the fourth type.
7. As goddess of the sea—first, rising from the waves of the sea; second, seated on a dolphin, riding through waves.
8. As victorious over mankind (Victrix)—first, clothed in armor or one foot on a helmet; second, standing with one foot on a globe; third, with a spear or a sceptre, a laurel-wreath or a palm.
9. As victorious over Ares, one foot on his helmet and holding his shield.
10. As victorious over Athena and Hera, holding an apple—first, together with Eros (Cupid), accompanied by the Graces (Charites), the Seasons (Horæ), Himeros, and Pothos; second, surrounded by little winged figures called Erotes or Amorettes.
11. Undraped figures in graceful attitudes.
12. As goddess of torpid life (Libitina), as in the sleep of death on sarcophagi.
13. As embodiment of masculine and feminine princiciple, this goddess (an Eastern or Phœnician type) was represented as bearded.

Worship.

Location.—Cyprus, Cythera, and other islands; Athens, Corinth, and other Grecian cities; Cnidus and other cities in Asia Minor.

Festivals.—These, called "Aphrodisia," were general. The sacrifices were of rams and goats, and they were accompanied by offerings of incense and garlands of flowers; also by libations of wine, milk, and honey.

Grecian Comp. Myth.

Aphrodite combined some of the characteristics of Dione, Rhea, Hera, and Persephone.

Foreign Comp. Myth.

Assyrian, Ishtar; Babylonian, Mylitta; Egyptian, Athor; Phœnician, Astarte; Jewish, Ashtoreth; Roman—first, Venus; second, Libitina.

Literature.

Homer represents Aphrodite as a devoted ally of the Trojans during the Trojan War (see Judgment of Paris).

Art.

Every department of art is filled with the deity whose dominion was throughout the earth, the sea, and the heavens. The finest types are as follows:

Venus Melos, or Milo.—Lübke says of this marvellous statue that it is the only one which represents Aphrodite as *divine*. It is generally thought to represent the "Venus Victrix," and that it bore armor as a token of victory. K. O. Müller speaks of the Venus de Milo as having been twice restored in antiquity, the last time barbarously. If the last restoration placed in the hands an apple (the symbol of Melos, or Apple Island), may not that theory be correct which assumes that the people of Melos considered it an embodiment of the universal Venus, the lowly who was to be exalted, and, whatever had been its original home and central idea, adopted it as the protecting deity of their land? (Louvre.)

K. O. Müller refers to another figure like the Venus de Milo, which represents the goddess as triumphing over Ares.

Capuan Venus, taken from the amphitheatre of Capua, is of the same type as the Venus de Milo; the left foot is placed upon a helmet. (Naples Museum.)

Townley Venus.—This statue, of a noble type, was found in the ruins of the Baths of Claudius, and is one of the Townley Marbles in the British Museum.

Venus of Cnidus.—Overlooking the harbor of Cnidus was a statue to the "goddess of prosperous voyages," by Praxiteles. It is believed that the statue in the Vatican Museum named as above is a perfect copy of the Cnidian masterpiece.

The Venus de Medici must stand as the type of that period of art during which, according to K. O. Müller, Aphrodite was less a goddess than an exaltation of individual womanhood—when, through forms that held marvellous equipoise between the noble dignity of the matron and the severe contour of Diana, art reached its highest grade in depicting feminine beauty. Some critics have considered this Venus to be a free copy of the Venus of Cnidus by Praxiteles. (Uffizi, Florence.)

Modern Research.

Dodona.—A statue in simple drapery, holding an apple.

Cyprus.—First, a statue (probably of Venus), draped and sandalled; three tresses fall on either side of her neck, around which is a string of beads or pearls with a pendant. A long veil, surmounted by a diadem, falls from the back of her head. Second, a statue of a draped figure, bearing on her left arm a winged boy, is probably Aphrodite. This figure is much like Persephone, as it is fully draped and wears a crown bearing floral ornaments, while Aphrodite usually wears a diadem. (May not this represent Aphrodite as the goddess of life, wearing the emblems of Persephone as goddess of the returning life of spring?) Third, a bearded figure, draped, and holding in one hand a cup and in the other a dove, may represent a priest of Aphrodite, or it may be an embodiment of the goddess as combining both sexes.

(The statues from Cyprus are in the unique and magnificent Cesnola Collection in New York, and the above descriptions are those given by General di Cesnola.)

Nineveh.—Among the tablets that formed the library of Assur-bani-pal at Nineveh was one that bore the story of Ishtar (the Babylonian Venus) and Tammuz. (See ADONIS.) This tablet forms a part of the priceless treasures that Mr. George Smith, the great Assyrian discoverer, added to the British Museum.

Descendants of Aphrodite.

Aphrodite and Ares—1, Deimos; 2, Harmonia; 3, Eros, or Cupid; 4, Anteros. Aphrodite and Anchises—Æneas.

(For the story of Cadmus and Harmonia, see ARES; for that of Æneas, see TROJAN WAR.)

EROS, OR CUPID (AMOR).

We have already distinguished between the cosmogonic Eros of Hesiod and the more personal Eros of the philosophers and early poets, and we must regard as a still different being Eros, the son of Aphrodite. This last conception of Eros was at first represented by a youth whose face was radiant with a beauty of which it is said, "It comes from God and it leads to God."

Later, a lighter ideal of Aphrodite's son, better known as Cupid, was represented as a mischievous boy with a quiverful of golden arrows, with which he made merciless havoc among human hearts.

ANTEROS.

The myths of this brother of Cupid are vague and conflicting. One is, that he strove to undo the work

EROS.

of his brother, while a second makes him the avenger of unrequited love. The first theory is favored by a statement of Pausanias: "At Elis there is a Cupid and the divinity which is called Anteros. Cupid holds in his hand a branch of a palm tree, and Anteros endeavors to take it from him."

PSYCHE.

Psyche was the daughter of a king, and was the youngest of three sisters. She was so beautiful that people neglected the worship of Aphrodite for that of Psyche, and in revenge the goddess sent her son Eros to fill the heart of Psyche with love for some inferior being. Eros went in quest of the lovely maiden, but when he saw her his own heart was filled with love for her. This love increased, and he even asked his mother's permission to marry Psyche, and finally received it, but with this proviso—that he must never be seen by his bride.

After her marriage the sisters of Psyche came to see her, and, jealous of her happiness, they wished to destroy it; so they persuaded their sister that her husband was a monster, and that he had imposed the strange condition that she must not see him for the purpose of concealing his deformity. The unhappy bride foolishly yielded to their influences. So one night she went with a lighted lamp to solve the mystery of her husband's appearance. She beheld the marvellous beauty of Eros, but while she was gazing in entranced wonder a drop of oil from her lamp fell on the shoulder of the sleeping god; he awoke and fled from her presence. Then the penitent Psyche sought long and sorrowfully for her Eros. After many disappointments they were reunited and received the blessing of Aphrodite.

PSYCHE.

According to the Orphic Philosophy, the soul exists before it is in the body; the body is like a prison-house in which the soul is to be disciplined and purified; it is drawn toward earthliness by an earthly love, and toward heavenliness by a heavenly love; the latter triumphs, and the soul, wedded to the heavenly, has immortal blessedness.

PYGMALION.

This king of Cyprus carved a statue so beautiful that he fell in love with it, and prayed that Aphrodite would impart life to it. The goddess granted his request, and the statue became a lovely maiden, whom he married. Some see in this myth a reference to Aphrodite as breathing the life of spring into the cold earth.

ADONIS.

Under the head of ASTARTE we have given what might be called the *motive* of the cycle of myths that in every great system of mythology has centred around a sun-god as the active principle in Nature, and a goddess that seemed to have a dual nature, in that she was queen of heaven and yet was personified as productive earth. Then the Chaldæan Dumuzi, the Egyptian Osiris, the Babylonian Tammuz, and the later Adonis may all be considered as " an incarnation of the sun as in a state of passion and suffering, in conjunction with the apparent changes in its celestial position, and with respect to the terrestrial metamorphoses produced under its influence upon vegetation."

When the diminishing of the fervor and power of the winter sun was conceived as a disappearance or a dismemberment of a god, there must needs be lamentations, such as come only from hearts that love; so Ishtar enters the dreadful gloom of Hades to dispute with Allat (the Babylonian Persephone) possession of the beloved Tammuz; while in Syria, as the summer glory faded, the worshippers of Astarte believed that her beloved Adonis, torn by the cruel tusks of a wild-boar, was sleeping in death; so the nation joined in her mourning, but when her love was restored to her, or Adonis was found, a nation united in her rejoicing.

In the Grecian form of the myth Adonis was a son of Cinyras and Metharme (daughter of Pygmalion). He was so exceedingly beautiful that he was beloved both by

Aphrodite and Persephone. He was killed by a wild-boar, and each goddess besought Zeus to permit her to retain her beloved. Zeus consented that the youth should spend a portion of the year with each goddess.

One can readily interpret this myth. Adonis is the universally-recognized active principle of Nature; the decay of autumn and the torpor of winter signify its suspension and apparent death (caused by the sharp frosts); during the time of torpor Adonis was with Persephone, but in the spring he returned to the rejoicing Aphrodite.

LINUS.

[From K. O. Müller's *History of Grecian Literature.*]

Linus belongs to a class of demigods of which many instances occur in the religions of Asia Minor and of Greece. Boys of extraordinary beauty are supposed to be drowned, or devoured by raging dogs, or destroyed by wild beasts, and their death is lamented in the harvest or in other periods of the hot season. The real object of this lamentation was the tender beauty of the spring destroyed by the summer heat, and similar phenomena, all first invested with a personal nature, then represented as being of a divine nature.

According to Argive tradition, Linus was a youth who sprang from divine origin, but who grew up with shepherds among the lambs. He was torn in pieces by wild dogs, whence arose a "Festival of Lambs," at which dogs were slain. Doubtless this festival was celebrated during the period of greatest heat, at the time of the constellation Sirius, the emblem of which, among the Greeks, was a raging dog. At the time of grape-picking or of corn-cutting plaintive songs were sung, in which was expressed, not the misfortune of a single individual, but a universal and perpetually-recurring cause of grief.

By a natural confusion of this tradition, Linus came to be considered as a minstrel, some calling him the son of Apollo and a Muse; others, son of Amphimarus and Urania. It was said that Linus presumed to enter into a musical contest with Apollo, and that the god destroyed him in punishment for his temerity.

Pausanias speaks of a statue of Linus near the Grove of the Muses in Helicon, and says, " They perform funeral sacrifices every year to this poet before they sacrifice to the Muses."

GROUPS IN THE LINE OF GÆA AND PONTUS.
(TABLE I.)

PONTUS.

In the early ages water was considered as a source of life, but before Eros had given new energy to all things Gæa had brought forth the great mass of salt, unfertilizing waters that afterward became the home of sea-monsters; this mass of waters was called Pontus.

Descendants of Gæa and Pontus (see TABLE I).

NEREUS.
(TABLE I, 2.)

Nereus is a sea-god in a limited sense; he had special control over the Ægean Sea and a limited one over the Mediterranean Sea. Nereus had the power of changing his appearance, was noted for truthfulness and wisdom, and had the prophetic power. It was said that he foretold the evils that Paris would bring upon his family and people. In his representations sea-weed takes the place of hair.

NEREIDES.
(Table I.)

Doris, the mother of the Nereides, was the daughter of Oceanus and Tethys (TABLE C, 34). This title applied to the sea-nymphs that were supposed to be in the Ægean Sea and in the Mediterranean Sea. They are generally represented as beautiful undraped maidens, though they sometimes have the lower part of the body like a fish. The worship of these nymphs was associated with that of Poseidon.

Reference to individual nymphs will be found in several places: Amphitrite (see POSEIDON), Galatea (see POLYPHEMUS).

THETIS [*The'tis*].
(Table I, 52.)

Thetis was of considerable importance in mythology. We have learned that the secret which Prometheus finally revealed to Zeus was in reference to Thetis. Themis had said that when Thetis was married she would have a son who would be greater than his father; and it is said that this prophecy prevented not only Zeus, but also Poseidon, from making her his bride.

Thetis was given in marriage to Peleus (son of Æacus), king of Phthia, in Thessaly. It was at this marriage that Eris threw the golden apple among the guests (see APHRODITE).

Assoc. Myths.

Dionysus visited Thetis, when, persecuted by Lycurgus, king of the Ædones, he leaped into the sea. Thetis treated him with great kindness, and received from him a golden urn. When Hephæstus was thrown from Olympus, Thetis united with Eurynome in showing to him great kindness. In the Trojan War, Thetis had a prominent place, growing out of the prominence of her son Achilles.

Descendant of Thetis and Peleus.

ACHILLES.

This world-renowned hero was "greater than his father," and lent glory even to his divine mother's name. He had for instructors Phœnix and Chiron. While Achilles was still young his mother had foretold for him either a short life, full of hardship, but crowned with glory, or a longer life of inglorious ease. Achilles chose the former, and in the Trojan War won immortal fame (see TROJAN WAR).

EURYBIA [*Eurў'bia*].

(TABLE I, 53.)

Eurybia is of importance only as being the mother of Astræus, Pallas, and Perses (TABLE F).

CETO (TABLE I, 54; see PHORCYS).

THAUMAS [*Thau'mäs*].

(TABLE I, 55.)

The name of this son of Pontus is significant, for its meaning is "wonder" or "astonishment." The descendants of Thaumas exhibited great differences. On the one hand were the deformed, fierce Harpies; on the other hand, the heavenly Iris.

IRIS [*I'ris*], (RAINBOW).
(TABLE I, 56.)

The glimpses that we have caught of this lovely goddess have revealed her only in her heavenly offices, yet she is in the line of Pontus, the barren sea—barren of all beautiful life. Is not the myth of Iris an exquisite expression of the mind's recognition of the possibility that earth-born creations may put on unearthly loveliness?

Iris may be more than the rainbow, more than the messenger from Olympus, for her highest message spans the earth and the heavens. Our life must have three cycles. There is one which is of the earth, earthy; its symbol is the heavy vapor that lifts upward for a while, but returns again, maybe to stagnate in the marsh. There is a cycle that is celestial; its symbol is light—the light that is not of the earth, but is the life of the earth, its truth, its hope, its joy, the perpetual benediction of the presence of God. Between these lies a border-land where the divine may become incarnate, into which the human may rise and dwell through blessed apotheosis. Its symbol is the rainbow—born of the earth, but so reflecting the glory of the celestial that the soul, recognizing the smile of a Father, looks upward to his face.

The development of the ideal of Iris is a lovely one —how her messages grew in grandeur until we see her coming with Hermes to lead the spirit of Heracles into Olympian immortality. (For the outlines of her life see HERA, HADES, THE STYX, and HERACLES.)

THE HARPIES [*Härpui'ai*].

(TABLE, I, 57.)

According to the advocates of the physical theory of interpreting mythology, the Harpies were personified whirlwinds; certainly, at an early date these were associated with those demons that directed their movements. Homer thought of them as suddenly carrying away human beings. Hesiod thought them to be winged maidens whose flight was swifter than that of birds; he mentions only Ocypete and Aëllo. Later poets depict them as having bodies of birds, claws of lions, with faces of maidens, but pale and emaciated. These poets named three—Aëllo (storm), Celæno (obscurity), Ocypete (rapidity). It was said that these beings would suddenly carry away food from those whom they wished to punish (see PELEUS).

A HARPY, BRITISH MUSEUM (from a tomb at Xanthus).

PHORCYS [*Phör'kys*].

(TABLE I, 58.)

Phorcys has no individual importance, but the long line of his strange, dark descendants cannot be omitted from mythology.

Descendants of Phorcys and Hecate (see TABLE I).

SCYLLA [Skȳl'la].
(TABLE I, 59.)

Between Italy and Sicily are two rocks, one of some height, in which is a cave where Scylla was once supposed to dwell. Many origins are assigned to this monster, and different causes are given for her deformity. One is that Scylla was beloved by Poseidon, and that Amphitrite changed her into a monster. Another is that Glaucus loved Scylla, and asked Circe to aid his suit. Circe loved Glaucus, and, jealous of his affection for the maiden, threw herbs into the well wherein Scylla went to bathe; in bathing she was changed into a monster, the lower part of whose body was a serpent surrounded by dogs, while the upper portion remained a fair woman. Others pictured her as having six long necks, with a terrific head armed with three rows of teeth. This monster preyed upon human beings, whom she seized from passing vessels.

Opposite the rock where Scylla dwelt was a lower rock. This contained a large wild fig tree, under which dwelt Charybdis, who three times each day swallowed and disgorged the dark water. The ancients located these rocks in the Straits of Messina. Ulysses passed between these dreaded beings; Scylla removed six of his men, while Charybdis engulfed Ulysses, but, having hold of the branches of the fig tree, he was set free again.

Descendants of Phorcys and Sterope (see TABLE I).

SIRENES [Seirę'nĕs], OR SIRENS.
(TABLE I, 60.)

Homer located the island of the Sirens near the rock of Scylla. They were sea-nymphs, who had the power of luring to ruin by their charming voices. At one time only two were recognized—Aglaopheme and Thelxiepia;

then there were three—Aglaope, Pisinoe, and Thelxiepia. Later writers describe them as having wings. The contest of the Sirens with the Muses has been given. (See NINE MUSES.) The Sirens endeavored to attract Ulysses and his companions to their ruin, but he stuffed the ears of his men with wax and lashed himself to the mast of the vessel, and thus escaped. The Sirens attempted to draw the Argonauts from their course, but their singing was drowned by the sweeter music of Orpheus.

Descendants of Phorcys and Ceto (see TABLE I).

Ladon, the dragon-guard of the Hesperides (see HERACLES).

GRÆÆ [*Grai'ai*], ("THE OLD ONES").
(TABLE I, 62.)

It is thought that these were sea-deities, and they seem to have been the product of a freak of the imagination. They had but one eye and one tooth in common, each one borrowing it when needed. The believers in the physical theory of mythologic interpretation think that these creatures were personifications of the gray fog that hangs about caverns near the sea, and is dangerous to mariners. The Grææ were believed to dwell in a cave near the entrance of Tartarus. These beings befriended Perseus when he went to slay Medusa.

GORGONES [*Görgŏ'nes*], OR THE GORGONS.
(TABLE I, 63.)

The Gorgons, Medusa, Euryale, and Stheno, have importance chiefly through the first. Medusa, the only one of the three that was mortal, was a beautiful maiden, but having with Poseidon profaned the temple of Athena, that goddess caused the hair of Medusa to become snakes, while her face became endowed with the strange and fearful power of turning into stone everything that it looked upon. We have related the story of the death of Medusa at the hands of Perseus (see PERSEUS).

Descendants of Medusa and Poseidon.

When Perseus cut off the head of Medusa, from her blood sprang Pegasus and Chrysaor.

PEGASUS [*Pĕ'gäsŏs*], OR THE WINGED HORSE.
(TABLE I, 65.)

After the birth of this winged horse from the blood of Medusa, he went to Olympus, and was employed by Zeus in carrying his thunderbolts. By some he was considered as belonging to Eos (Aurora).

When Bellerophon was preparing to attack the Chimæra, he found that he must have the assistance of Pegasus, but thought it would be impossible to catch the winged creature. By advice of a seer, Bellerophon passed a night in the temple of Athena. The goddess appeared to him, and advised him to offer sacrifice to Poseidon; she also gave him a golden bridle, which he found when he awoke. Bellerophon offered the sacrifice, and with the golden bridle caught Pegasus while the horse was drinking at the well of Pirene. Later writers connect Pegasus with the Muses.

There is a curious legend to the effect that when the nine daughters of Pierus entered into a contest with the Muses (see MUSES), everything grew dark; but when the Muses sang, earth, sky, and heaven all stood still to listen; even Mount Helicon rose upward in delight. Then Poseidon bade Pegasus strike the mountain with his hoof, and from the mountain issued the well of Hippocrene, the inspiring well of the Muses. Another version of the story of Hippocrene is that Pegasus caused it to spring up that he might allay his thirst.

CHRYSAOR [*Chrysä'or*].
(TABLE I, 64.)

This giant, who, with Pegasus, sprang from the blood of Medusa, was so named from wielding a golden sword. He married Callirrhoe, daughter of Oceanus.

Descendants of Chrysaor and Callirrhoe (see TABLE I).

GERYON [*Gĕrў' ŏnĕs*].
(TABLE I, 66.)

This monster had the bodies of three men united, cohering in the upper part, but dividing in the lower. He lived in the island of Erythea, where grazed his famous oxen of a purple hue; these were guarded by Orthrus (see ECHIDNA) and by the herdsman Eurytion. The tenth labor of Heracles was to bring these oxen to Eurystheus. He reached Erythea in the golden cup of Helios, passed the night on Mount Abus, and on the next day carried away the oxen after killing the guards. Menœtius, who was keeping the oxen of Hades in this same island, told Geryon of his loss. Geryon pursued Heracles, but was killed by him. Heracles then placed the oxen in the sun's golden cup and brought them to the main land. Some see in this myth only physical phenomena.

ECHIDNA [*Ĕchĭd'na*].
(TABLE I, 67.)

This monster had the upper part of the body like that of a beautiful maiden, while the lower part was that of a serpent. Hesiod spoke of her as living in a cave with Typhaon, though other writers locate her in Scythia.

Descendants of Heracles and Echidna (see HERACLES).
Descendants of Typhaon and Echidna (see TABLE J).

GROUPS IN THE LINE OF GÆA AND TARTARUS.

(TABLE A, 4 and 5.)

TYPHOEUS [*Tÿphō'eus*].

(TABLE J, 1.)

According to Hesiod, Typhoeus was a giant, not unlike the Hecatoncheires in nature, having many heads and voices. After the close of the Titanic War, Typhoeus entered into personal contest with Zeus, but he was subdued and thrust down to Tartarus under Mount Etna.

TYPHAON [*Tÿphä' ōn*], OR TYPHON.

(TABLE J, 2.)

Typhaon seems to have been a personified wind of the nature of a hurricane. His precise relation to Typhoeus is not known, but by some he was said to be his son.

PERNICIOUS WINDS.

(TABLE J, 3.)

These winds, as opposed to beneficent winds, are attributed to Typhoeus.

Descendants of Typhaon and Echidna (see TABLE J).

Cerberus, Hydra (TABLE J, 5; see HERACLES); Orthrus (TABLE J, 6; see GERYON); Chimæra.

CERBERUS [*Kĕr'bĕrŏs*].

(TABLE J, 4.)

This was the triple-headed monster that was placed as guard in Hades (see HADES; also HERACLES).

CHIMÆRA [*Chimai'ra*].
(TABLE J, 7.)

This was a fire-breathing monster. Hesiod pictures her as having one body with three heads, one being that of a lion, one of a goat, and the third of a dragon. This creature devastated the country of Lycia, but was slain by Bellerophon. Chimæra was sometimes represented as having the fore part of her body like a lion, the middle like a goat, and the third part like a dragon.

Descendants of Chimæra.

Nemean lion, the Sphinx.

NEMEAN LION (TABLE J, 8; see HERACLES).

• THE SPHINX.
(TABLE J, 9.)

The myth of the Sphinx was probably of Egyptian origin, and the central idea may have been different from the Grecian, as was the mode of representation.

According to Wilkinson, the Sphinx had the body of a lion in a lying attitude, while the upper part was that of a human being, but not of a woman, unless in rare instances that of a queen. The same author gives the following forms: First, an *androsphinx* had the head of a man and the body of a lion having human hands, signifying either the union of physical and intellectual power, or they may have represented deities. Second, a *criosphinx* had the head of a ram and the body of a lion; this may have symbolized Chnoumis, the ram-headed deity. Third, a *hiercæosphinx* had the head of a hawk and the body of a lion; probably represented the god Ra. Winged sphinxes were rare.

Wilkinson's views on this subject seem to confirm the theory that the Sphinx was employed as a symbol of kingly power and commemoration, for he says that it was called Ha or Akar, meaning "lord." He also states that the Sphinx symbolized the god Harmachis, and that it represented a king in that character; further, that its earliest appearance was in the fourth dynasty.

Near the second Pyramid in Egypt is a remarkable figure, everywhere known as "The Sphinx." The body is that of a lion, while the upper portion is thought by many to be that of a woman, by others to represent a king. The body, one hundred and twenty-five feet in length, is mostly formed from solid rock; the paws are of masonry, and they extend fifty feet from the body; between the paws was a little temple formed of sculptured tablets, and in front of it was a square altar.

Plutarch says that sphinxes before temples signified the enigmatical nature of theology; and in confirmation of this idea is the fact that rows of sphinxes lined the approaches to the temples. Besides being the symbol of mystery, it would seem that in some localities a sphinx had a mortuary signification, and in the ancient legend of Ishtar's descent into Hades (see ADONIS) it is said that the sun-god induced Hea, the god of wisdom, to create a sphinx of a doglike shape, which should visit Allat and demand the liberation of Ishtar. (Is there not in this legend a key to the frequent presence of the dog in the mortuary collections of General di Cesnola?)

THE GRECIAN SPHINX.

In Hesiod's theogony this monster is said to have descended from Chimæra (TABLE J). As an emblem it was of a more complex nature than was its prototype, and shows Phœnician as well as Egyptian influences. It is represented in different positions and in varied forms—sometimes as having the body of a winged lion, with the breast and head of a woman; at others, as a winged lion with the tail of a serpent, while the face was that of a woman. In the Grecian mythology this emblem may have retained much of its ancient meaning of mystery and power, but in addition it was considered as the emblem of fertility, and as associated with Athena may have signified wisdom.

ŒDIPUS.
THE RIDDLE OF THE SPHINX.

Œdipus was the son of Laius and Jocaste of Thebes, in Bœotia. An oracle having said that King Laius was destined to perish at the hand of his son, when a son was born they pierced his feet and exposed him on Mount Cithæron. Some shepherds in the employ of Polybus, king of Corinth, found the child, and from his swollen feet called him Œdipus. He was adopted by King Polybus, but after he became a youth, having been told that he was not the son of the king, he consulted the Delphic Oracle as to his parentage. The oracle did not answer his inquiries, but foretold that he would murder his father and commit incest with his mother.

Œdipus, supposing that he was the son of Polybus, in order to avoid the terrible crimes foretold, determined not to return to Corinth; but on his road between Delphi and Daulis he met King Laius, his real father, and becoming involved in an altercation with the charioteer of the king, he slew both the charioteer and his father.

At this time strange events were occurring in Thebes. Hera, jealous of Thebes as the city of Dionysus, had sent a terrible monster, the Sphinx, to lay waste the surrounding country. This creature sat upon a rock, and with a human voice propounded this riddle: "A being with four feet has two feet, then three feet, yet only one voice; when it has most feet it is weakest." Any one failing to guess this riddle was destroyed by the Sphinx.

In their great distress the Thebans proclaimed that whoever should solve this riddle and free them from the monster should be made king of Thebes and should marry Jocaste.

Œdipus came forward and gave the solution by saying, "It is man, who in infancy crawls upon all fours, in manhood stands upon two feet, and in old age supports himself with a staff." This answer so enraged the Sphinx that she threw herself down from the rocks, and thus killed herself.

Then followed the fulfilment of the oracle's dreadful prophecy. Unaware that Jocaste was his mother, Œdipus married her, and their children were Antigone, Eteocles, Ismene, and Polynices. Though this alliance of mother and son was the result of ignorance on the part of both, yet it was a violation of the moral order which is an expression of the will of the gods; hence Thebes was afflicted with a terrible plague, and an oracle announced that it would not abate until the murderer of King Laius was expelled from the land. Œdipus then pronounced a solemn curse and sentence of exile upon the unknown murderer, but was overwhelmed with horror and anguish when Tiresias told him that he himself was the murderer of his father and that his wife was his mother. This sad legend further says that Jocaste hung herself, that Œdipus put out his eyes, and that, through the rebellion of his sons, the remaining years of the wretched king were filled only with trouble and grief.

GROUPS IN THE LINE OF NYX AND EREBUS.

(TABLE A, 6 and 7.)

NYX, OR NIGHT.

(TABLE K, 1.)

Central Ideas.

We have found that during the earliest periods of Greek life there was a general but confused idea of some mysterious, inexhaustible source whence issued the new beings that constantly appeared. It was quite natural that Nyx should be identified with that source, and we find that the oldest writers thought of Night as the parent of all things. So vague were their ideas of both Nyx and Erebus that their relations to each other could never have appeared very definite.

We have already outlined the possible development of the respective ideas until we found that Night was supposed to dwell with her children in a palace in the lower world. Homer dwelt more on the awful obscurity that enveloped Night, and said that even Zeus stood in awe of her. But the abstract idea was lost, and Night became more closely identified with Nature and with human life.

According to the principle that "from obscurity springs brightness," Night gave birth to Hemera, the day, but as darkness may cover evil things, she was also the mother of care, ills, and death.

Early Legends.

Night, with her two sons, Death (Thanatos) and Sleep (Hypnos), dwelt in a palace in Hades. Hemera, the day, shared this palace, and she and Night alternately rode forth to minister to the world. Night rode in a chariot drawn by black steeds, and she was accompanied by the stars. She made the circuit of the sky, and then returned to her palace.

Representation.
First Type.—With or without wings, clothed in black drapery and having a starry veil; riding in a chariot, and accompanied by the constellations.
Second Type.—With starry veil floating in the air, coming toward the earth, as if to extinguish a flaming torch which she carries in her hand.
Third Type.—A floating figure clad in a long black robe, carrying in her arms Death and Sleep. Death is draped in black and holds an inverted torch, while Sleep is robed in white, and has for his symbol the poppy.
Fourth Type.—Sitting beneath a tree, distributing poppies to Morpheus and his brothers. Morpheus, the god of dreams, receives the poppies, while his brothers bend to gather the falling leaves.

Worship.
Sacrifices.—Black sheep. A cock was offered to her, because that bird announced the coming of the day even in the presence of Night. Nyx was identified with the moon-goddess, and her statue was placed in the great temple of Diana at Ephesus.

Descendants of Nyx (see TABLE K).

EREBUS [*Er'ĕbŏs*].
(TABLE K, 2.)

We need merely give a brief résumé of the changing ideas of Erebus. When night was thought to be a vast dark void surrounding the earth, Erebus was thought of as a still more vast and dark realm surrounding that of Night. At that time the lower world was called Tartarus. Then Erebus was supposed to include all the lower world, and within it was Tartarus, used as a prison for the gods. Still another change in the application of the term made Erebus apply to a dark region through which shades passed when after death they went down to the lower world. To the region into which they passed through Erebus the term "Hades" was applied.

DESCENDANTS OF EREBUS AND NYX.

ÆTHER [Äi'thĕr].
(TABLE K, 3.)

In speaking of Æther as a type of the highest deities we have indicated the meaning of the term. It seemed to be considered as the source of fire, light, spirit, and life, yet was spoken of as "fields of ether," as the "abode of Zeus," but in the same way in which the ocean and its waves were spoken of as the home of Poseidon.

HEMERA [Hĕ'mĕra], THE DAY.
(TABLE K, 4.)

Hemera seems to have been merely an abstraction. We have an interesting survival of this abstraction in the word *ephemeral*, "lasting but a day."

DESCENDANTS OF NYX.

MOROS [Mŏ'rŏs], DESTINY OR FATE.
(TABLE K, 5.)

The word "destiny" or "fate" may be of stupendous signification. It may be the synonym for the relation that must exist between the supreme will of the universe

CLOTHO. LACHESIS. ATROPOS.

MŒRÆ, OR THE FATES.

and the order of events through all ages. Whether or not Hesiod used the word "Moros" or any other word in that wide sense cannot be known, but there are clear indications that there was in every age an apprehension of an all-controlling necessity or power to whose decrees the gods were subject.

We know that Hesiod calls Zeus "supreme ruler of gods and men," even calls the Mœræ (the Three Fates) the daughters of Zeus and Themis, but he may have had an apprehension of a power whose decision even Zeus must obey, and he may have used the term "Moros" as a name for such power. The same indefiniteness attaches to the word "Ker," that seems to be another word for "Fate."

MŒRÆ [*Moi'rai*], THE FATES.

(TABLE K, 6.)

The Mœræ were also called Parcæ; either of the terms signifies "a share," in the sense of allotting to every man his share.

Early Legends.

At Delphi only two Fates were recognized, but three became the general number. As to their parentage, Hesiod in one place calls them daughters of Zeus and Themis, and in another classes them with the children of Nyx. It is said that the last-mentioned classification occurs in an interpolated passage; but while we admit that the first classing harmonizes with Hesiod's exalted idea of Zeus, the general character of the rest of the descendants of Nyx clearly indicates that he looked upon Nyx as closely related to human destiny; so they seem properly placed in that group. The idea prominent in the earliest conception of the Mœræ was *controlling power*, but later they were regarded as goddesses of birth, destiny, and death, and the line of life was symbolized by a thread which was spun or divided. Their names had reference to their respective offices: Clotho, "the spinning Fate," who spins the thread of life; Lachesis, "the Allotter," who determines its duration; Atropos, "the Inevitable," who divides the thread of life.

Offices.

1. To see that the fate assigned by eternal law to every human being may take its course.
2. To assign to the Erinyes their duties, and with them to direct all destinies according to the law of necessity; hence called "sisters of the Erinyes."
3. To preside over the duration of human life, by determining its beginning, continuance, and close.
4. To reveal the future.
5. Goddesses of death, to accompany the infernal Erinyes.
6. In the spring, in company with the Horæ, to lead Persephone from Hades to the earth.

Representations.

1. *Earliest.*—With serious faces, fully draped, each holding a staff as a symbol of dominion.
2. Poets describe them as aged, hideous women.
3. Clotho, seated, spinning; one distaff before her; another behind her; at her feet a comic and a tragic mask. Lachesis, standing, leaning against a pillar; a distaff in her left hand, while her right plays with that thread of destiny on which depends the limit of all things.
4. Clotho has a spindle; Lachesis holds a roll of parchment on which is inscribed human destiny; Atropos holds a balance.

5. Clotho, a spindle or a roll (book of fate); Lachesis, a staff, pointing to a globe; Atropos, pair of scales, a sun-dial, or a cutting instrument.

Worship.
Their worship was general.
Sacrifices.—Ewes, flowers, and honey.

THE KERES [*Ke'rēs*].
(TABLE K, 6.)

This term is rarely used, and is quite indefinite as to meaning in mythology, but the Keres are said to accompany the Fates.

NEMESIS [*Nĕm'ĕsĭs*].
(TABLE K, 7.)

Central Ideas.
Nemesis may be regarded as a personification of conscience, therefore as the goddess who rewards or punishes right- or wrong-doing. In practical life, Nemesis was curiously associated with Tyche, or Fortune. There was a common belief that the gods were envious of those who had too great happiness. Tyche, or Fortune, was very lavish in her gifts to some, but Nemesis was supposed to act as a check upon these favorites; she also inflicted chastisement upon the arrogant.

Attendants.
Dice (justice), Pœna (punishment), Erinyes (vengeance).

Emblems.
A rod or a sceptre, sovereignty.
A bridle or a yoke or a rudder, restraint.
A lash or a sword, punishment.
A balance or a cubit's length, measurement.

A wheel, swiftness and certainty of retribution.

An apple-branch, reward of well-doing (?).

Representations.

1. A queenly figure with wings; on her head a diadem; in one hand an apple-branch, while the left arm is bent at the elbow and the fore finger extended, thus marking a cubit, "the gesture of Nemesis" (?); at the feet, a wheel.
2. A noble figure holding a rod or sceptre, at her feet a wheel.
3. Riding in a chariot drawn by griffins, holding a sword.
4. Pressing her finger to her lip as a token of self-restraint (?).
5. It is said that Nemesis sometimes took the emblem of Tyche, or Fortune.

Worship.

As Nemesis preserved the relics and memory of the dead from desecration, a solemn festival called "Nemesia" was celebrated in memory of the dead.

Modern Research.

Olympia.—A statue of Nemesis, bearing a vessel, supposed to be an ell, the symbol of measure.

THANATOS [*Thä′nätŏs*], OR DEATH.
(TABLE K, 8.)

The earlier representations of this god show that all associations with his work were of terror and gloom. Afterward, in literature and in art, there was a softened expression of the soul's submission to destiny or the dawn of the apprehension of the soul's immortality.

Representations.
1. In the Florentine Gallery, Death is represented as a skeleton, sitting on the ground and resting one hand on an urn.
2. The poets speak of him as in sacrificial robe, holding a sword with which he cuts off a lock of a dying person and devotes it to the lower world.
3. Large figure, with fierce countenance and having great wings.
4. As a youth leaning against a tree, with his arm resting on his head, indicating eternal repose.
5. As a youth winged, holding an extinguished torch reversed, standing beside an urn on which lies a wreath of flowers.
6. In the arms of Night (see Nyx).

It is known that there were sacrifices offered to Death, but no temples have been discovered.

The Roman deity answering to Thanatos was Mors.

HYPNOS [*Hyp'nŏs*], OR SLEEP.
(TABLE K, 9.)

Hypnos (Latin, *Somnus*) was the twin-brother of Thanatos (Death), and dwelt within the palace of their mother Nyx in the shadows of Hades. His office was to give rest and freedom from pain.

Representations.
1. With his brother Thanatos, in the arms of Nyx.
2. As a sleeping child on a couch, holding poppies, which also serve for a pillow; Morpheus and dreams attend him.
3. His head on a lion or lion's skin; in one hand poppies or a horn of poppy-juice.
4. Winged, with a lizard at his feet.

5. As a youth, holding a horn, or a poppy from which dew is dropping on sleeping mortals.
6. As an aged, bearded man.
7. On his head the wings of a hawk or a night-bird; near him a lizard (because it sleeps half the year).

In the British Museum is a bronze head of Hypnos, having wings like those of a hawk growing from the temples.

MORPHEUS [*Mör'pheus*], GOD OF DREAMS.
(TABLE K, 9.)

Morpheus formed dreams as the gods needed them when they wished to send them to man. He was assisted by Icelos (dreams that appear real), Phobetor (alarming dreams), and Phantasos (strange, false dreams).

It was said that dreams lived in a palace near the western Oceanus. They were of two kinds—one deceptive, the other prophetic; the former class passed out through ivory gates, while the true, prophetic dreams passed out through gates of transparent horn.

ONEIROS was a personification of dreams, and was represented as a man of middle age, with two large wings; also on his head are two small wings.

HESPERIDES.
(TABLE K, 10; also TABLE G, 8.)

While Hesiod groups the Hesperides with the children of Nyx, according to the general belief they were the daughters of Atlas, and we have considered them in that connection.

MOMUS [*Mŏ'mŏs*], (CRITICISM AND REPARTEE).
(TABLE K, 11.)

Momus was the critic and wit of Olympus, but he so

exercised his privileges as to make himself exceedingly unpopular. His comment upon the man formed by Prometheus (or by Vulcan) was that the new being would have been much more complete if there had been a window in his breast, through which one could see his thoughts and intentions. A house which Athena constructed did not please Momus, because it was not movable, and therefore could not be taken from a bad neighborhood.

There are two versions of the story in regard to Aphrodite. One is that Momus tried in vain to detect some flaw in her beauty, but, failing to do this, he sneeringly said that the noise of her feet when walking was altogether too loud for the "goddess of beauty;" the other is that, failing to find a single imperfection in her, he vexed himself to death over it. Probably the first version was the one generally accepted, for it is said that in consequence of his unlovely and unjust spirit Momus was banished from Olympus.

This god was represented as holding a small figure in his hand and raising a mask from his face.

ERIS [*É'ris*], OR STRIFE.
(TABLE K, 13.)

Eris (Latin, *Discordia*) was employed by the gods to incite mortals to disputing and strife. Her spirit was so similar to that of Ares that she was sometimes called his sister or his wife, and is frequently represented as accompanying him in his fierce combats. It was she who at the marriage of Thetis and Peleus threw among the guests the golden apple that caused the strife between Hera, Athena, and Aphrodite (see APHRODITE, JUDGMENT OF PARIS).

The emblems of Eris are a whip, dagger, or flaming torch.

Descendants of Eris (see TABLE K).

DESCENDANTS OF EREBUS.

CHARON [*Chä′rōn*].
(TABLE K, 14.)

Charon was the ferryman that carried the shades across the river Styx into Hades (see HADES).

Many of the ideas and customs connected with death and burial among the Greeks resembled those of the Egyptians. With the Egyptians vital importance was attached to the character of the deceased. After a body was embalmed and ready for interment it was placed in a hearse, which was placed upon a sledge, and then taken in solemn procession to a sacred lake over which it was to be borne for burial, if the rite of burial should be granted. The body remained on this shore (opposite to the place of burial) until the character of the deceased had been judged. Forty-two judges were appointed to conduct the trial. If the departed one was found to have led a virtuous life, the hearse was deposited in a boat under the direction of a boatman called Charon, and was then conveyed across the sacred lake (Acherusia) to the place of burial. Before the deceased was taken across the lake a piece of gold or silver was placed in the mouth as a token of his virtuous character. The Greeks believed that Charon would not receive the shades of their deceased friends unless the bodies had received all proper tokens of respect, in addition to sacrifices and mourning. A coin (obolus or danace) was placed in the mouth of the dead, perhaps more as an expression of the loving appreciation of friends than as a fee for the boatman Charon. The superstition that unless the coin were placed in the mouth the shade must wander on the shore of Styx for a hundred years may have had the moral meaning that any person might so live as to deserve some tribute of respect, and thus obtain a burial.

Hermes as Psychopompus (conductor of shades) had the privilege of constant passage into and from the boat of Charon. Living mortals could not enter Charon's boat unless they bore a golden bough from the Cumæan Sibyl (oracles of Apollo at Cumæa). The heroes Heracles and Theseus by their valor, Orpheus by his music, and Æneas by his piety, were made exceptions to this law.

Representation.
As an aged, wrinkled man, with long gray beard and with ragged garments.

CURETES, OR CORYBANTES, Etc.

These mysterious beings have caused much discussion in mythology as to their origin, nature, and offices.

1. Those who resolve all myths into mere personifications of physical phenomena will readily believe the following theory: The Curetes were the children of Poseidon and Thalassa (troubled sea), and their archetypes were the heavy vapors born of the sea, that settled around the mountains (*volcanic?*). The office assigned to them by this myth was nourishers of fruits and givers of wine to the Argonauts, who passed on their way to Colchis.

2. Somewhat in harmony with this myth is another to the effect that the Curetes sprang from the sides of the mountain (*volcanic?*)—that they were the first beings who assumed human form.

3. Still another theory is that these beings, and also the Cyclopes, were descendants of Hephæstus—that they assisted the Cyclopes in inventing practical arts for the use of man and in making thunderbolts and weapons for the gods. Is it not possible that the internal action of volcanic mountains, around whose sides sea-born vapors rested, suggested the existence of beings having compound powers of working in metals or of caring for the vine? This would be analogous to the relations supposed to exist between Hephæstus and Dionysus (see HEPHÆSTUS).

4. Strabo says that the Telchines that accompanied Rhea to Crete were called Curetes, and that they must have been Phœnicians, who introduced practical arts.

By some the Curetes are said to have been the most ancient people of Crete—that the infant Zeus was entrusted to their care (see LEGENDS OF CRONUS AND RHEA). We know that the priests of Rhea were called Corybantes, and that the Corybantes, Curetes, Idæan Dactyli, Cabiri, and Telchines were often confounded. May not the theory suggested by Burney (*History of Music*) be a correct one?—

The Phœnicians who came into Greece with Cadmus brought not only new doctrines and knowledge, but practical arts. Among them were men skilled in metal-working, who were called Curetes. These Phœnicians settled in different places and were called by different names. Those in Phrygia were called Corybantes; in Crete, Idæan Dactyli; in Rhodes, Telchines; in Samothrace, Cabiri. When they settled they first wrought in copper or bronze, then in iron. They made armor and danced in it at sacrifices with tumult, clamor, bells, pipes, drums, striking one another's armor at regular intervals, making a kind of music. We know that there is a theory that the Idæan Dactyli invented rhythm and music; and there is a close connection between Tubal Cain and music. Now, by following the lines of thought that may be suggested by the facts above given, is there not a possibility of harmonizing the apparently conflicting theories in regard to these groups of beings that have so strange a place in mythology?

TYCHE [*Tўˊchɛ*], OR FORTUNE.
(Table C, 61.)

Tyche (Roman, *Fortuna*) was the goddess who presided over the fortunes of mankind (see Nemesis).

Emblems.

A rudder, her guidance of all human affairs.

A globe, her control over the fortunes of all men.

Cornucopia, lavishness of her gifts.

A wheel or a ball, unsteadiness of Fortune's gifts.

Worship.

Athens was the chief centre, but her worship was quite general throughout Greece.

Tyche, or Fortune.

Art.

Small statue, draped in a tunic and peplus; on her head a modius (corn-measure); in her right hand a rudder resting on a globe; in her left, a cornucopia filled with corn and fruits of various kinds. (British Museum.)

Modern Research.

Olympia.—A statue of Tyche in simple drapery; the right hand places a rudder upon a wheel resting against her shoulder, but the left hand holds, instead of the customary cornucopia, a vessel resting against the shoulder.

MYTHOLOGIC CHARACTERS OUTSIDE OF HESIOD'S GROUPS.

MYTHOLOGIC CHARACTERS OUTSIDE OF HESIOD'S GROUPS.

DIONYSAN CYCLE.
PAN.

PAN was the son of Hermes and an Arcadian nymph. The traces of Pelasgic Nature-worship that lingered about Hermes grew and remained prominent in his son; so Pan was accepted as a deity who presided over rural life, but who had a special care over the interests that lay in the animal kingdom. The shepherds and herdsmen saw in him a beneficent deity to whose power and kindness they could appeal for increase and protection of their flocks and herds; fishermen besought his blessing upon the waters; and huntsmen propitiated him previous to their expeditions, and inflicted imaginary punishment upon the god by bestowing lashes upon his statue if he withheld from them expected success.

Not alone with the employments of rural life was this deity identified, but even more closely with its relaxations and amusements; hence the exuberant, undisciplined animal life of his worshippers found expression in music cheerful or exciting, and in amusements simple, wild, or riotous.

Such was the popular apprehension of Pan, but perhaps those thoughtful minds that search for the deeper and subtler meaning of all things saw in this strange

PAN.

being a coining of the recognition by the common mind not only of the interdependence of animals and man, but of that interdependence and close sympathy between that department of man's nature called and symbolized as the animal, and those higher attributes that entitle him to companionship with gods; and as the immediate influences of Dionysus lay in the sphere of interdependence between the moral and the social, so those of the god Pan lay between the social and the sensual.

Pan was supposed to have prophetic powers. This high endowment seems almost incongruous with the characteristics generally assigned to him, but such endowment may have resulted from a closer identification of the god with the general processes of the earth that were often called oracular; or, on the other hand, it may have resulted from the expansion of the whole idea of Pan by adding new attributes and offices, some saying that he was oracular because he founded the religion of the country. We know that his worship was for a long time limited to Arcadia, but at the battle of Marathon it was believed that this god assisted the Greeks; hence the Athenians adopted his worship. Some have supposed that the association of Pan with the worship of Cybele arose from his love of wild music and excitement. Be this as it may, as his own worship spread it seemed to receive elements of an Eastern origin, for it more and more assimilated to their character. Some have interpreted the name of this deity as signifying universal power, but his worship was never general and exalted in the widest, highest sense.

Abode and Attendants.

Pan's principal abode was wild, lonely forests, and there he frightened any travellers who might break the solitude. He was supposed to be attended by little wood-spirits called Panisci, though no distinct class of beings was suggested by the name. Notwithstanding the love that this god bore to the forests, he often led the dance in which the Oreads joined; at other times the Satyrs danced to his music.

Assoc. Myths.

1. Pan was the inventor of the syrinx, in this manner: He loved a nymph named Syrinx; she did not return his love, and one day, fleeing from him, she was changed into a reed by Gæa. Pan divided the reed into seven unequal pieces, and joined them so as to form the instrument named after the nymph.

2. It is said that Pan had a terrific voice, and that he used it in frightening the Titans in their war with the gods.

3. Various causes are assigned for the origin of the word "panic." One is, that the sense of loneliness and fear belonging to dark forests was ascribed to Pan; hence any alarm arising from an unknown cause might be called a *panic*.

4. Pan ventured to challenge Apollo to a trial of musical skill; Midas, king of Phrygia, decided in favor of Pan. Apollo in punishment caused the ears of Midas to grow like those of an ass, but permitted his hair to grow long to cover them. Midas told this to his wife as a great secret, but she, being unable to remain entirely silent, threw herself upon the ground and whispered it to the reeds. As the air passed through the reeds they repeated the words, "King Midas has the ears of an ass." The poor king, hearing this, besought Bacchus to aid him. In compensation that god granted him the power of turning into gold whatever he might touch. So distressing did this golden plague become that he prayed for relief, and he obtained it by washing in the river Pactolus; hence that river has golden sands.

Representation.
1. Human form, with horns growing from the forehead, holding a shepherd's crook and the syrinx.
2. In human form, playing on the flute.
3. In connection with religious ceremonies.

Later.—4. With legs, feet, horns, and ears like a goat, playing on the syrinx; near him a shepherd's crook.
5. Same form as above; dancing and playing on the flute or syrinx.

Worship.
Location.—Chief centres in Arcadia, at Athens, etc.

The caves in which flocks might find protection were sacred to Pan; one in Mount Hymettus (Attica) was dedicated to Pan and the nymphs and the pastoral Apollo. Plato was taken to this cave to sacrifice to those deities. There was a grotto in the Acropolis sacred to Pan.

Sacrifices.—Cows, rams, goats, lambs, sometimes dogs and new wine, milk, and honey.

Foreign Comp. Myth.
ROMAN, Faunus, Inuus, or Lupercus.

SATYRS, OR FAUNS.

Dionysus was attended by a class of beings that represented in forms other than those already considered the luxuriant life of Nature as everywhere abounding and under the control of Dionysus.

1. The forms of the Satyrs, or Fauns, presented great variety, for the ideals had wide range. The highest type was of a beautiful youth with delicate form, in which every nerve was an avenue of the pure pleasures that came from earth, sun, and sky; this type was sensi-

tive, not sensual. The indications of the departure from the human type are pointed ears; and this type, like the exquisite conception of Hawthorne's *Marble Faun*, has the ears partly concealed by waves of hair.

2. In other types the animal nature began to exhibit more decided characteristics: horns sprouted from the temples; then, one after another, the parts of a goat, and in some cases the tail of a horse, were added, until in an almost entirely animal form were embodied the lowest phases of human nature.

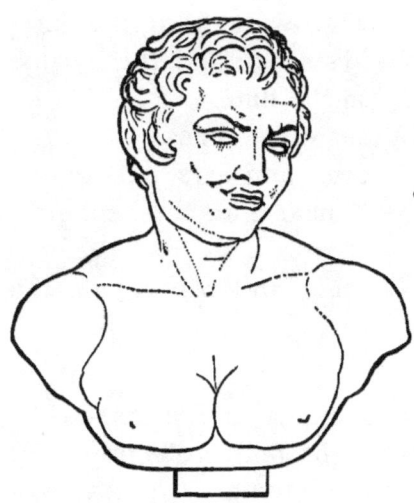

HEAD OF SATYR.

SILENUS AND SILENI.

The oldest Satyrs were called Sileni—some have said from having flat noses.

Great prominence was given to one of these Sileni under the name of Silenus. He was foster-father of Dionysus, and was his constant companion after that god commenced his journeys of conquest.

The ideals and representations of Silenus vary, as in

SILENUS.

the cases of the other Satyrs. The finest type is that of Silenus holding the infant Dionysus (Villa Borghese).

CENTAURS.

The home of the Centaurs was in Thessaly, near Mount Pelion. The original inhabitants of this region were savage people, one of whose customs was hunting

CENTAUR (metope from the Parthenon).

the bull on horseback; and it is possible that other peoples may have supposed the man and horse but parts of the same animal, as our native Indians thought of the Spaniards and their horses. Some writers apply the term "Centaur" only to the primitive Thessalians, and to the compound of the human being with a horse they apply the term "Hippocentaur."

Representation.

The body of a man down to the waist attached to the body of a horse.

In early times, instead of the fore legs of a horse, they had the legs of a man.

Assoc. Myths.

In Thessaly was another people called the Lapithæ, with whom the Centaurs had frequent warfare. The celebrated legend of the Battle between the Centaurs and Lapithæ has been given.

Chiron, called "the wise centaur," had the form, but nothing of the nature, of a centaur. He dwelt in a cave in Mount Pelion, and there he instructed some of the most noted heroes, as Achilles and Jason. He was a friend of Heracles, but in attempting to make peace between him and the Centaurs he was accidentally shot by one of the poisoned arrows of Heracles. (For his heroic release of Prometheus see PROMETHEUS.)

LEGENDS OF HEROES.

LEGENDS OF HEROES.

THESEUS.

PANDION II., king of Attica, in whose line descended the illustrious Theseus, must not be confounded with Pandion I. (son of Erichthonius). Pandion II. succeeded Cecrops II. (see DESCENDANTS OF HEPHÆSTUS).

Descendants of Pandion.

Ægeus, Lycus, Nisus, Pallas. Theseus was the son of Ægeus and Æthra, daughter of Pittheus of Trœzen.

When Ægeus left Æthra at Trœzen, he placed his sword and sandals under a great rock, and told her that when their child should be able to lift the rock he might come to him at Athens, bringing the sword and sandals. When fifteen years of age Theseus accomplished this feat and departed for Athens.

On his way to Athens he was the hero of several exploits. He slew the giant Periphetes, who killed all travellers with his iron club; he killed the robber Sinis, and founded the Isthmian Games in honor of his victory; he threw the robber Sciron from a rock into the sea; he slew the Crommyon boar, also the powerful Cercyon. At Eleusis he slew Procrustes (Damastes), the cruel robber who killed his victims by placing them on a bed that was either too long or too short, and making the body conform to the length of the bed by removing a portion if longer than the bed, and by stretching the body if too short.

Theseus now reached Athens, and was obliged to be purified from the blood that he had shed, although he had done it in noble service. Now commenced a service of heroic enterprises. The sons of his uncle Pallas conspired against the life of Theseus in hope of securing the throne of Ægeus. Theseus easily overcame these Pallantides. At Marathon he captured a furious bull that was devastating the land, led it to Athens, and sacrificed it to Athena.

We have given the story of the Minotaur (see MINOS), also of the tribute that Minos demanded of the Athenians; now Theseus offered himself as one of these victims, and arrived at Crete.

Ariadne, the daughter of Minos, conceived a deep affection for Theseus, and when he sought to enter the Labyrinth which Dædalus built for the Minotaur, she gave him a clew by which he could find his way back again. Theseus slew the monster, thus freeing Athens from the tribute of seven youths and seven maidens. Theseus, accompanied by Ariadne, now left Crete, but he deserted her on the island of Naxos, whence she was taken as the bride of Dionysus. (See DIONYSUS.)

Theseus now returned to Athens. He had promised his father Ægeus to raise a white flag in signal of success when he should sight Attica; the delight of his return caused him to forget this promise. Ægeus, who was waiting for his return, saw the black colors with which he left Athens, and, supposing his son to be dead, put an end to his own life.

Assoc. Myths.

Theseus and Pirithous; Battle of the Centaurs and the

Lapithæ (page 91); Rescue from Hades; Theseus joined Heracles in the expedition against the Amazons, and carried off Hippolyte, whose girdle Heracles was to obtain; a great body of Amazons invaded Attica, but were repulsed by Theseus. This hero was with the Argonautic Expedition.

Closing Events.—Theseus succeeded his father Ægeus in the government of Athens. He united the towns of Attica, with Athens at the head; he gave new importance to the Athenæa established by Erichthonius. (See PALLAS ATHENA.) He also established the Pyanepsia, in honor of Apollo; the Oschophoria, in honor of Dionysus; in Delos, a festival for whose games the prize was a wreath of palm. The beautiful temple called the "Theseum," at Athens, was erected in honor of Theseus.

BELLEROPHON.

Bellerophon was son of Glaucus, king of Corinth. Having accidentally slain Bellerus, a Corinthian noble, he was obliged to be purified, and he went to Argos for that purpose, and was received kindly by the king, Prœtus. Sthenebœa, the queen, made false charges against Bellerophon of improper conduct toward her, and Prœtus sent the youth to Iobates, king of Lycia and father of Sthenebœa, with a letter written in strange characters, exhorting the Lycian king to put Bellerophon to death.

Iobates thought that he could best accomplish this by sending the youth on a dangerous expedition, so he ordered him to slay the Chimæra (see CHIMÆRA); and, having obtained the assistance of the wonderful horse Pegasus (see PEGASUS), Bellerophon arose in the air above the reach of the monster, yet not too far for deadly use of his spear; so the Chimæra was slain. Iobates then sent him on an expedition against the Solymi, a neighboring tribe, and after that against the Amazons, in both of which he was victorious. The last effort of the king to bring about the death of Bellerophon was the placing in ambush his bravest warriors, but they were all slain

BELLEROPHON.

by the hero; and he was now rewarded for his great valor: the king's daughter was given to him in marriage and he received large tracts of fertile lands.

In accordance with the general belief that the gods are jealous of excess of happiness on the part of mortals, they prepared a catastrophe for this hero who had been so crowned with success: he became insane and wandered away from the sight of men.

THE HUNT OF THE CALYDONIAN BOAR.

Œneus and Althæa, king and queen of Calydon, were parents of Deianira, wife of Heracles. At the birth of their son Meleager the three Fates appeared to Althæa, and Atropos told her that her infant's life would continue only so long as a certain brand then burning in the fire would remain unconsumed. The mother snatched it from the flames and carefully concealed it.

Meleager reached manhood and developed great heroism. He took part in the Argonautic Expedition, but his great enterprise was the Calydonian Hunt. Calydon was devastated by a terrific wild-boar. Meleager determined to slay this creature, and invited the assistance of many heroes. Atalanta from Arcadia, Ancæus, Admetus, the Dioscuri (Castor and Pollux), Idas and Lynceus, and many others joined in the hunt. Meleager entertained the hunters for nine days; then they set out on their expedition. Meleager killed the boar with a spear, so the head and skin fell to him as a trophy of his skill. Atalanta had first wounded the monster, so Meleager gave her the skin; but the brothers of Althæa, claiming a better right to it, robbed Atalanta of it as she was returning to Arcadia.

Meleager, wishing to defend Atalanta's right to the trophy, entered into a contest with his rivals, and they were all slain. Althæa, enraged at the death of her brothers, seized the brand upon which depended the life of her son, and which had up to this time been so carefully preserved, and threw it into the fire, where it was consumed. True to the warning of Atropos, Meleager's life closed. Althæa in deep remorse slew herself.

ATALANTA.

Atalanta was a daughter of Iasus. At her birth her father, greatly disappointed that he had not a son, caused Atalanta to be exposed on the Parthenian hill, where she was suckled by a she-bear (symbol of Artemis).

After a time Iasus acknowledged her as his daughter, and desired her to marry, but she made this condition: any one who sought her in marriage must compete with her in the foot-race; if he were victorious she would bestow her hand upon him, but if she were victorious the suitor should be slain by her hand. Milanion conquered in this manner: Aphrodite gave him three golden apples; these he dropped in the path of Atalanta, who stooped to gather them, thus enabling her suitor to first reach the goal; she therefore became his bride. (Atalanta is sometimes confounded with Artemis.)

THE ARGONAUTIC EXPEDITION.

The hero of this renowned expedition was Jason (or Iason), son of Æson, rightful king of Iolcus. Æolus, son of Hellen (see HELLEN), died, leaving the kingdom of Iolcus to his son Æson. Pelias, his step-brother, drove Æson from the throne and ascended it. An oracle had bid Pelias "beware of a man with a single sandal." A grave cause of alarm soon appeared in the form of Jason.

Jason determined to reclaim the throne to which he was heir. On his way to Iolcus he found the river Enipeus much swollen. Hera appeared in the form of an aged woman and bore him across, but he lost one of his sandals in the stream. Pelias recognized Jason as soon as he arrived at Iolcus, but he was unwilling to resign the throne, and in order to prevent Jason from demanding his right Pelias sent him to fetch the Golden Fleece from Colchis. Jason consented to undertake the expedition. Athena and Hera assisted him to build the great ship Argo, and when it was finished Jason gave a general invitation to the heroes of Greece to join him in his enterprise. Prominent among those who came were Admetus, Boreas, Castor and Pollux, Heracles, Calais, Meleager, Neleus, Orpheus, Peleus, Pirithous, Theseus, and Zetes.

THE GOLDEN FLEECE.

Amathas, uncle of Jason, married Nephele, and their two children were Helle and Phryxus. Nephele died, and Amathas married Ino, and their sons were Learchus and Melicertes. Ino, conceiving a hatred for her stepchildren, tried to destroy them, but the shade of their mother came to their aid by bringing a large ram with a golden fleece, on which they were to make their escape by the sea. They started on their journey, but Helle fell into the sea and was drowned; so the sea was called Hellespont. Phryxus passed over in safety to the opposite shore. He then went to Colchis, and sacrificed to Zeus the ram that had carried him in safety, and he hung its golden fleece in the temple of Ares.

SAILING OF THE ARGONAUTS.

When everything was in readiness Jason sacrificed to Zeus, and as a sign of his favor Zeus answered by thunder.

The Argo went first to Lemnos, where it remained for a long time. Here Jason married Hypsipyle, and she bore a son whom she called Euneus. The Argonauts left Lemnos and passed on to Cyzicus. Here occurred the loss of Hylas, the search for him by Heracles (see HERACLES), and the loss of the ship of the latter. They then went to Scutari, where occurred the contest with, and victory over, Amycus by Pollux (see DIOSCURI).

They now passed toward the entrance of the Black Sea, and found the unfortunate Phineus, who was so tormented by the Harpies (see PHINEUS). They freed him from those dreadful creatures, and in return he gave them wise directions by which they passed in safety through the Symplegades, two great cliffs that had the power of moving together and crushing anything that attempted to pass between them. Phineus advised them to let a pigeon fly between the cliffs, then follow in the wake of the bird; they did this, and passed in safety to Colchis. The king of Colchis, Æetes, was a son of Helios. He refused to yield the Golden Fleece to the Argonauts unless they would undertake certain hazardous enterprises.

The Golden Fleece was suspended from an oak tree in the temple of Ares. It could be obtained only by the following heroic deeds: Æetes owned some bulls that emitted flames from their nostrils, and had brazen feet; he who aspired to the honor of taking the fleece from the oak tree must plough the Field of Ares with these terrible creatures, and must then sow the field with dragons' teeth, from which armed men must spring.

Medea, the daughter of King Æetes, was a sorceress, and, having conceived for Jason a violent love, she assisted in the capture of the fleece by furnishing him with a magic mixture which rendered him proof against fire or sword. Jason procured the Golden Fleece, and, taking Medea and her brother Absyrtus with them, the Argonauts started on their homeward journey.

King Æetes soon missed his daughter, and started in pursuit. He was about to overtake them when Medea used this terrible stratagem to divert his attention: she took her brother Absyrtus, divided him in pieces and threw them into the sea. Medea and Jason thus escaped.

After other adventures the Argonauts reached Iolcus, and consecrated their ship to Poseidon in the grove sacred to him. Jason now presented the long-sought Golden Fleece to Pelias and demanded his throne. Pelias refused to yield it; so Jason slew him and became king of Iolcus and also of Corinth.

Jason now formed a strong attachment for Creusa, daughter of Creon, king of Corinth. Medea, infuriated with jealousy, sent to her rival a poisoned robe and wreath, and thus caused the death of Creusa. She then murdered her own two children, and in consequence fled to Athens, where she lived with King Ægeus. She here made an attempt on the life of Theseus, and was obliged to flee. It is said that she returned to Colchis.

Jason's death was caused in this manner: in great depression of spirits Jason sought relief in the sacred grove of Poseidon, in which had been consecrated the Argo. As he passed near the ship a portion of it fell upon him and caused his death.

THE TROJAN WAR.

In the story of "The Rescue of Hesione" we learned that when Heracles inflicted punishment upon Laomedon, of all the house of that king only Hesione and Priam were spared; that Priam was placed upon the throne of Troy, while Hesione was given in marriage to Telamon; that Priam resented the detention of his sister by the Greeks; and that their refusal to return her to Troy was one of the causes of the Trojan War (see HERACLES). But the leading cause of that great event was the abduction of Helen, wife of Menelaus, king of Sparta, by Paris, son of Priam.

Before the birth of Paris, Cassandra, daughter of

Priam and Hecuba, prophesied that woe and ruin would come to their house and kingdom through the birth of a son. The infant Paris was therefore exposed on Mount Ida, but was preserved and cared for by shepherds.

In the story of "The Judgment of Paris" (see APHRODITE) it was related that Aphrodite had promised to Paris the most beautiful woman in the world for a wife. That woman was Helen of Sparta, and not as a shepherd, but as a Trojan prince, was he to woo her.

The Trojans were to offer oxen in sacrifice, and two sons of Priam, Hector and Helenus, were sent to Mount Ida to procure them. The brothers selected, among others, one that was a favorite of Paris. A strife followed, which would have ended in bloodshed but for the appearance of Cassandra, who told them that the young shepherd was their brother Paris. Paris was restored to his family, the prophecy was forgotten, and he enjoyed all the privileges of a prince of Troy.

About this time Priam determined to bring back from Greece Hesione, the sister that had once saved his life. A fleet was prepared and placed under the control of Paris. Aphrodite made known to him that she was to fulfil her promise, and, accompanied by Æneas, he set sail for Greece with instructions to bring back Hesione.

HELEN.

Helen, the sister of the Dioscuri, was wife of Menelaus of Sparta. In the story of "The Dioscuri" reference was made to her abduction by Theseus, to her release by her noble brothers, and to her return to Sparta. Her marvellous beauty brought to her feet suitors from all parts of Greece, but she chose for her husband Menelaus. It is asserted by some, and denied by others, that before a decision was made in reference to the bestowal of the hand of Helen the suitors entered into a league to support the one on whom the choice might fall.

Paris arrived at Sparta, became the guest of Menelaus, won the affection of Helen, and, taking advantage of her husband's absence, persuaded her to flee with him to Troy. On their voyage they encountered a terrific storm sent by Hera, the glorious protectress of sacred marriage. Hera, not content with manifesting her anger against the guilty ones, sent Iris to tell Menelaus of the sorrow and disgrace that had fallen upon him.

In this great crisis Menelaus consulted Nestor, and was told that nothing but a combination of all the armies of Greece would be sufficient to punish the great crime committed by Paris, and endorsed by his father and countrymen in that they would not oblige him to return Helen to Greece. The Greeks prepared for war with Troy. A large fleet was gathered, and over the whole was placed Agamemnon, king of Mycenæ and brother of Menelaus; with him were associated, in addition to Menelaus, Achilles, Ajax (son of Telamon), Ajax (the Lesser), Diomedes, Idomeneus, Machaon, Nestor, Podalirius, Patroclus, Philoctetes, Sthenelus, Thersander, Ulysses. (See GREEK GENEALOGIES.)

More than one thousand ships formed the Grecian fleet. It sailed across the Ægean Sea, and landed, by mistake, in Mysia. The Greeks prepared to conquer the country, but Telephus, the king, opposed them with great bravery. Telephus was wounded by the spear of Achilles, and finding that it would not heal, he consulted an oracle, and was told that it could be cured only by him who caused it. At the same time the Greeks had learned from an oracle that Telephus should conduct their fleet to Troy. The way in which Telephus was cured of his wound and became the guide of the Greeks can be given only in connection with

THE STORY OF IPHIGENIA.

From Mysia the Greek fleet returned to Aulis. Agamemnon's love of the chase caused great trouble; he saw a fine stag, and, though it was sacred to Artemis, he killed it. This so offended the goddess that she detained the fleet in Aulis for many weeks, and she finally made known the only condition of reconciliation; which was, that Agamemnon should sacrifice to her his daughter Iphigenia.

Agamemnon sent a message to his wife Clytemnestra to bring Iphigenia to Aulis, that she might wed Achilles. She obeyed, and when Agamemnon received his daughter, for the sake of the great cause which he had espoused he prepared to offer her in sacrifice to Artemis. That goddess, satisfied with the spirit in which her commands had been obeyed, provided an animal for the sacrifice and bore Iphigenia away as her priestess. (See ARTEMIS.)

When Clytemnestra brought her daughter to Aulis, she also brought her infant son Orestes. One day Telephus managed to enter the tent where this child was lying, and threatened to take its life unless his wound could be healed. Ulysses accomplished this by applying to it some rust from the spear of Achilles. Telephus now offered to conduct the fleet, and for the second time it sailed toward Troy.

FIRST STAGE OF THE WAR.

The Greeks reached Troy. They were opposed in their landing by the Trojans, led by the heroic Hector, the oldest son of Priam. The Trojans were repulsed.

The Greeks made an attempt to take the town by storm, but failed, and they resolved to commence a siege. The ships were brought to the shore; around them was built a fortified camp, and, thus protected, the Greeks made frequent raids upon Trojan towns.

On one of those expeditions Pedasus was taken, and when the spoils were divided Chryseis was given to Agamemnon as a captive. This lovely maiden was the daughter of Chryses, a priest of Apollo in the island of Chrysa. To Achilles was given as captive Briseis, who was as fair as was Chryseis.

The priest Chryses implored Agamemnon to return his daughter, but his entreaties failed. He then prayed to Apollo for aid. Not alone in defence of his own priest, but in his character as a god who severely punished disrespect to all gods, Apollo sent a plague that devastated the Greek camp. Agamemnon consulted the priest Calchas as to the cause of the plague. The priest, having been assured of the protection of Achilles, announced that the cause was the detention as a captive of the daughter of the priest of Apollo. Chryseis was restored to her father, but Agamemnon accused Calchas of being in league with Achilles. Achilles resented this, and threatened to avenge the insult, but he was restrained by Athena. Agamemnon was now offended at the threat of Achilles, and required as a satisfaction the captive Briseis. Whether in deference to Agamemnon's superior position or in submission to the stern decrees of necessity, Achilles yielded to a demand that he knew to be unjust, but he withdrew from the service; and this "wrath of Achilles" affected the whole character of the early years of the war. Thetis, the mother of Achilles, now besought Zeus to compel Agamemnon to atone for his injustice to her son; her prayer was granted, and it was decreed that the Greeks should have only defeats so long as Achilles remained apart from the service.

The withdrawal of Achilles emboldened the Trojans to make frequent attacks upon their invaders, and the latter were finally driven within their camp. Achilles was entreated to return and lend his mighty aid to his distressed countrymen. Agamemnon offered to restore Briseis—to give him in marriage his own daughter with a dowry of seven towns; but Achilles remained apart in his wrath.

Under the leadership of Hector the Trojans stormed the very camp of their foes, set their ships on fire, and, could men be independent of the gods, would have decided the issue of the war, had not Patroclus, the friend of Achilles, clad in that hero's armor, led the Myrmidons against the Trojans with such fury that they fell back in dismay. Patroclus single-handed pursued the retreating enemy until Hector turned and engaged him in single combat, slew him, took from him the armor of Achilles, but magnanimously allowed his body to remain that it might have honorable interment.

Now a new passion took possession of the breast of Achilles. Uncontrollable grief at the loss of his friend—grief that could be allayed only by the death of Hector—and desire for vengeance moved to action the heart which the need of his country had no power to reach. Arrayed in the armor made by Vulcan, with god-like bearing Achilles sought to meet Hector in single combat. They met; Hector was slain, and his body dragged at Achilles' chariot-wheels three times around the walls of Troy, and then thrown into the dust within the camp of the Greeks.

Even the gods were indignant at the ferocious anger

of Achilles, and they cared for the body of Hector by preserving it from corruption. Zeus softened the heart of Achilles, so that when Priam came to beg the body of Hector, he who with a god-like bearing had taken the life of his foe now in a god-like spirit did reverence to a father's love. He shared his own tent with King Priam, and gave to him the body of his son.

The Trojans now found allies in the Amazons. Penthesilea, the beautiful leader of the Amazons, met Achilles in single combat, but was vanquished by that hero. Achilles gently supported the dying heroine in his arms, and nobly returned her body to the Amazons, praising her beauty and valor. Thersites alone was base enough to discern evil in the noble conduct of Achilles, and he even thrust his spear into the lifeless remains of Penthesilea. Achilles dealt the wretch a blow that felled him to the ground lifeless. This punishment, severe as it was, was approved by all the Greeks save Diomedes, who, being kinsman of Thersites, demanded the sum of money usually given as reparation. Offended that he had not been at once and in every way upheld in the course he felt to be just, Achilles again withdrew from the Greeks, but was persuaded by Ulysses to return to the camp.

Tithonus and Memnon, the husband and son of Eos (Aurora), now appeared as allies of the Trojans. Memnon and Achilles met in single combat, and at the same time Thetis and Eos appeared before Zeus, each asking aid for her son. Zeus replied that the issue of the matter must be decided by Fate; and on placing in a golden balance the fate of the two contending heroes, that of Memnon sank, thus denoting his death. Achilles fought with renewed courage, but soon met his fate through an arrow from the hands of Paris. Words could not tell the grief of the Greeks; even the Muses joined in the dirge of Achilles. The armor of the hero was given to Ulysses.

Shortly after this great event the Greeks captured Helenus, son of Priam, and compelled him to use for them the gift of prophecy with which he was endowed. When asked by what means Troy could be taken, he replied that three things were necessary—the bow and arrows of Heracles; the assistance of Neoptolemus, son of Achilles; and the possession of the Palladium, then in Troy. Two of these conditions were complied with. The bow and arrows were obtained from Philoctetes, to whom Heracles gave them at his death; Neoptolemus joined the Grecian ranks; and there remained only to obtain possession of the Palladium.

Ulysses went in disguise to Troy, managed to enter, and was detected by no one but Helen, who, to her praise be it said, gave clear indications of her sorrow at her conduct and of her affection for the husband whom she had deserted. Ulysses returned to the Greek camp and obtained the assistance of Diomedes, and then brought from Troy the Palladium, on the possession of which depended the fate of Troy. This Palladium had been given by Zeus to Dardanus, the great founder of the Trojan line; its loss could presage only ruin.

Ulysses now planned the downfall of the doomed city. A horse was constructed of sufficient size to hold a large number of Greeks. This image was filled with armed men, and the Grecian forces were gathered into the ships, and the Trojans saw the whole fleet sailing from their shores. They rushed to the camp of their enemy, but found only the great structure, called the "wooden horse," that contained those whose entrance to their city should secure its fall. Thinking that this structure must have a religious meaning, they determined to preserve it; so it was taken to the city-gates.

If we are right in thinking that the fall of Troy was decreed by the gods as a penalty for the violation of moral law in upholding Paris in his sin, then we can understand

THE STORY OF LAOCOÖN.

This was a priest of Apollo, who with his two sons

LAOCOÖN (from the group at the Vatican).

had come to offer a sacrifice to his god. He raised a voice of warning against receiving in their city anything of Greek workmanship; and he was turning the whole tide of feeling toward the removal or destruction of the horse; and they would have thus saved their city. But the gods had decreed its downfall, whereas the tenor of the advice of Laocoön was opposed to that decree; so, in order to move the Trojans to act to their own destruction, the influence of the priest must be counteracted. Two serpents came from the island of Tenedos and crushed in their folds Laocoön and his sons. The Trojans readily believed that some deity had thus punished Laocoön for sacrilegious treatment to the horse, and they were thus prepared to work their own ruin.

When the Greek fleet sailed, they left behind them Sinon, so bound that he presented the appearance of a victim that had been prepared for the sacrifice. Sinon assumed this character, and upon being asked what the great horse was, he told them that it was a very sacred object, and that if taken into the city it would preserve it as effectually as the Palladium itself. The Trojans decided to receive the wooden horse into their city, and because the gates would not admit the immense image they broke through a portion of the walls.

The Trojans, believing that the siege of their city had been abandoned, and that they now had a sacred object in the place of the Palladium, abandoned themselves to festivities, until, exhausted, they were sunk in deep sleep. The Greek fleet, which had merely withdrawn to Tenedos, now quietly approached the shore, and co-operating with those in the doomed city, the Greeks were in possession of Troy. The city was soon in flames.

Among the few who escaped was Æneas, who bore

on his own shoulders his aged father, Anchises. After tarrying at Mount Ida, Æneas, it is said, went to Italy and founded the Roman nation. Menelaus received the penitent Helen, and the fleet returned to Greece.

AGAMEMNON.

On the return of Agamemnon to his home he found that his wife, Clytemnestra, had married Ægisthus, a son of Thyestes. Cassandra, the daughter of Priam, had been awarded to Agamemnon as a part of the spoils of war, and she now used her prophetic powers in his behalf. She told him that Clytemnestra and Ægisthus plotted his death. Believing that his wife's professed joy was genuine, he would not receive the warnings of Cassandra. At last, on emerging from the bath one day, he was enveloped in a net by his perfidious wife and then slain by Ægisthus. Orestes, their young son, escaped and fled to Phocis.

ORESTES.

When Orestes reached manhood an oracle of Apollo commanded him to avenge the murder of his father Agamemnon. He went to Mycenæ, revealed himself to his sister Electra, and in order to find whether or not there was any change for the better in the heart of his mother, he announced himself as one who came to inform her of the death of her son Orestes. The joy that the unnatural mother displayed at news that should have been so sad convinced Orestes that she was as unworthy as ever. He then slew her, and his friend Pylades murdered Ægisthus.

Great as had been the crime of Clytemnestra, and though Orestes had killed his mother under the sanction of Apollo as the god of just punishment, yet the universal law that forbade the murder of a parent became paramount to other considerations, and Orestes was given over to the terrible Erinyes. These avengers pursued him relentlessly. On reaching Delphi he was told by Apollo that he should bring from Taurus the statue of the goddess Artemis.

The people of Taurus were in the habit of offering as sacrifices all strangers who approached their shores, but it will be remembered that when Agamemnon had evinced his willingness to sacrifice Iphigenia to Artemis, that goddess had borne the maiden away to be her priestess. She brought her to Taurus; so the priestess of the temple in which Orestes would have been sacrificed was his own sister. He told her his commission to bring away the statue of Artemis. By her assistance they accomplished it, and the statue was brought to Greece (see ARTEMIS).

The Furies were not yet satisfied with the expiation of Orestes; so, through the advice of Apollo, he went to Athens and asked for a trial in the Areopagus, where sat a court appointed to judge in cases of murder. The Furies appeared as his accusers. Apollo pleaded that Clytemnestra's death was deserved. The votes were cast. There being an equal number for and against acquitting him, Athena added the white voting-stone in favor of Orestes, and he was acquitted. The Furies were satisfied, and it was said it was on this occasion that their name was changed from Erinyes to Eumenides.

Orestes now ascended the throne of Mycenæ, married Hermione, the daughter of Menelaus and Helen, and at their death he added to his own possessions the throne of Sparta.

ODYSSEUS (ULYSSES).

We need only briefly outline the order of events in the life of Odysseus, as the individual occurrences have been referred to in connected myths.

Long after the other heroes had reached Greece, Odysseus, who had left Troy in a fleet richly laden with spoils, was on the sea meeting adverse fate. His adventures in the cave of Polyphemus have been related under the head of POLYPHEMUS; his tarrying in the island of Circe was related under her story (see CIRCE); his escape from the perils of the Sirens has been already told (see SIRENS).

When Odysseus visited Hades from the island of Circe, the shade of Tiresias warned him against landing on the island of Trinacria. Notwithstanding this warning, he and his companions landed on that island, and his companions plundered the sacred flocks of Helios (see HELIOS). In punishment, they were overtaken by a fearful storm, and only Odysseus escaped. He was then driven on an island in possession of the beautiful nymph Calypso. This goddess detained him for eight years, offering him immortality if he would remain with her; but he besought the gods to favor his return to his home, and they persuaded Calypso to release him.

Odysseus constructed a raft and put out to sea, but Poseidon, unappeased for the death of his son Polyphemus, sent a storm that overwhelmed him, and he would have perished but for the aid of Leucothea. He swam to the shore of the island of the Phæacians; he was discovered by Nausicaa, the charming daughter of the king, Alcinous. He received from these hospitable people every kindness and the richest presents, and was presented with a well-manned ship that he might return to Greece in a manner befitting such a hero.

He reached his home, and found that Penelope had despised the offers of the suitors for her hand. With the aid of Telemachus, his son, he slew those that had so annoyed the queen, and long reigned over Ithaca.

MYTHOLOGY OF HOMER

ARRANGED FROM "JUVENTUS MUNDI" (GLADSTONE).

HESIOD, the Bœotian, worshipped and faithfully portrayed the splendid retinue of deities that peopled the realm of religious belief at his time. Homer was more than a worshipper: he was a creator.

Homer found ready for his use grand materials: 1st, ancient Pelasgic gods were stationed as awful guardians of the under-world, were propitiated as bestowers of blessings on fields and flocks, and were worshipped in the pure flame of mountain-altars; 2d, the Hellenic imagination had wrought marvellous creations, and had already peopled earth and sky with beings that ranged in rank from the grotesque to the sublime; 3d, constant streams of Phœnician influence mingled with these native elements portions of the half-mystic worships of Egypt or the corrupting sensualism of Oriental countries.

These masses of materials were first unified in the mighty mind of Homer through his perfect comprehension of the phase presented by their combined whole; then, in the potency of his transcendent genius, he created a new phase and established therein a new unity. To accomplish this he threw into a neutral or shadowy background those Nature-powers that the expanding Greek mind had begun to recognize as too material in their offices longer to command the old reverence. He then marshalled in the foreground the already existing deities that the Hellenes had endowed with superior attributes; and adding to these attributes others so imposing that the transfigured gods shone in a new splendor, and placing them in complex relations to each other and to mankind, he became "the maker not only of poems, but of a language, of a nation, and of a religion."

In an abstract necessarily brief we cannot give even in outline an adequate idea of Gladstone's admirable treatment of this subject as he notes the central ideas contributed by the varied component mythic systems, or traces the connections that even the highest Olympian gods seemed to maintain toward Fate, Right, and Retribution; and we can give only in classes his statement of the characteristics and prerogatives of the Homeric creations; but, selecting such sentences or parts of sentences as suit our purpose, we give the following as the principles that he considers fundamental in the Homeric mythology:

1st. In order to comprehend the *method* of the poet, we must bear in mind (*a*) that many deities, afterward completely naturalized, were in his day only making the first steps of their way into Greece; (*b*) that deity is with him a most elastic idea, susceptible of infinite diversities in point of both virtue and power; (*c*) that he has a vivid conception of intercommunication between the two natures, divine and human.

2d. Anthropomorphism, or "the tendency to cast the divine in human forms"—its skilful employment by Homer, acting as a principle which found its way to the mind of man through his sympathies and propensities.

3d. Adjustment by distribution of offices—the anthropomorphic idea greatly favoring the application of this principle, since it gave to the poet all the varied functions and orders of human society, both domestic and political, as a framework after which to arrange his Olympian personages.

Finally. We find that the Homeric formation consists of a polity framed on the human model, with a king, an aristocracy, and even a people or multitude, and that its seat is on Olympus. The king is Zeus. The aristocracy consists of a number not precisely defined; but since Hephæstus prepared seats or thrones for twenty deities, we must suppose this to have been the number who were entitled to attend the councils of the gods, though only eight or ten took part in the debates of Olympus. This is the body of which the feastings are so gorgeously described, and in it are probably included all the deities who had obtained more than a narrowly local recognition in the Greece of Homer.

NUMBER OF OLYMPIAN DEITIES.

CHILDREN OF CRONUS.

1. Zeus; 2. Poseidon; 3. Hera; 4. Aides, or Hades.

WIVES OF ZEUS.

Chief wife, Hera.
Secondary wives: 1. Dione; 2. Demeter; 3. Leto.

CHILDREN OF ZEUS.

Pallas Athena, Apollo, Artemis, Ares, Aphrodite, Hephæstus, Hermes, Persephone.

PERSONAGES PERFORMING GENERAL OFFICES.

Themis, the summoner; Iris, the envoy; Hebe, cup-bearer; Paieon, the healer; Helios, taking part in Olympian proceedings.

RANK OF OLYMPIAN DEITIES.

SUPERIOR DEITIES.

GROUP A.

(PRE-EMINENT IN MORALITY, POWER, AND ACTIVITY.)

PALLAS ATHENA, APOLLO.

ZEUS, as traditional representation of Providence and of the theistic idea.

GROUP B.

(LOWER IN MORAL TONE OR IN ATTRIBUTES.)

ZEUS, in his Olympian personality.

HERA, POSEIDON.

INFERIOR DEITIES.

Limitations of these inferior deities are—

1. They know of human events only through sight or sound;
2. They do not know what is in the mind;
3. They shriek or cry aloud from emotion;
4. When they move, it is (*a*) by gradual progression, (*b*) with means of conveyance;
5. They are liable to be hurt and wounded;
6. Human warriors can contend against them;
7. Their worship is peculiar to some races or places;
8. They are even liable to disparagement in communications held by the highest gods with men;
9. They have little or no command over outward Nature and the elements;
10. They do not habitually repair to Olympus;

11. Their partialities and propensities are without system, policy, or governing mind;

12. They neither have divine foreknowledge, nor, in many cases, have they prudence or forethought equal to the human;

13. They are not able immediately to influence the human mind.

"All except the highest gods may be said generally to be subject to the above liabilities and limitations."

NATURE-POWERS.

SUPERIOR DEITIES.

OCEANUS, source of deities.

TETHYS, mother of deities.

GÆA, presiding in the under world.

CRONUS. According to Welcker he was a reflection of Zeus, for in Homer Zeus alone was called Cronides.

RHEA. Welcker thinks Rhea was an ancient earth-goddess, associated with Oceanus and Tethys.

NEREUS, deity of the sea.

AMPHITRITE, moaning sea (? Phœnician).

INFERIOR DEITIES.

RIVERS.

Æsopus, Alpheus, Axius, Enipeus, Spercheus, and Scamandrus.

NYMPHS.

A (THOSE WHO HAD TAKEN PART IN THE OLYMPIAN ASSEMBLY).

DAUGHTERS OF ZEUS, mountain nymphs, grove nymphs, fountain nymphs, meadow nymphs, and the nymph Abarbarée.

B (Nymphs of the Sun).

Lampetia, Phaëthusa.

C (Nymphs of the Sea.)

Nereides, the sisters of Thetis.

WINDS.

Zephyrus, Boreas.

FOREIGN (? PHŒNICIAN) DEITIES.

Helios and Perse.
  | |
Æetes.   Circe.

Atlas, bearer of pillar and sea-explorer.
Calypso, daughter of Atlas.
Maia, mother of Hermes (Mercury).
Thoosa.
Proteus (? Egyptian).
Phorcys, ruler of the sea.
Sirens (two in number).
Æolus (semi-deified mortal).
Leucothea (deified mortal).

REBELLIOUS POWERS.

Cronus and the Titans (probably).
The Giants.
Tityus.
Otus and Ephialtes.

MINISTERS OF DESTINY AND DOOM.

KER, plural KERES.
>Ker approaches most frequently to a distinct impersonation. It is the destiny of an individual, not of a law governing the world.

CATACLOTHES, or spinnners, like Keres.

ÆSA (moral law), destiny of a particular person, or the moral law for the government of conduct.

MŒRA. May be the divine will embodied. Nothing in Homer is actually done contrary to Mœra, but such things seem to be regarded as not beyond the bounds of possibility.

POETICAL IMPERSONATIONS.

THE MUSES, daughters of Zeus.

THE FATES (Keres, Cataclothes, etc.).

THE PRAYERS (Litæ), with Ate.

OSSA (Rumor), ERIS (Discord).

DEIMOS (Terror), PHOBUS (Panic), CUDŒMUS (Tumult).

THANATOS (Death).

HYPNOS (Sleep), ONEIROS (Dream).

ALCE (Might), IOCE (Rout).

HARPYIÆ (Storm-winds).

PODARGE, mother of the Storm-winds, also of the two immortal horses, Xanthus and Balius.

GENEALOGICAL TABLES,

BASED UPON

GROTE'S HISTORY OF GREECE.

GENEALOGY OF IAPETIDS.

[TABLE I.] GENEALOGY OF IAPETIDS (TABLE G).

IAPETUS and CLYMENE.

- Menœtius.
- Prometheus.
  - Deucalion and Pyrrha.
    - Hellen and (Orseis).
      - Dorus.
      - Xanthippe.
      - Æolus.
        - *Daughters:* Alcyone, Calyce, Canace, Peisidice, Perimede.
        - *Sons:* Athamas, Deion, Cretheus, Magnes, Perieres, Salmoneus, Sisyphus.
      - Xuthus and (Creusa).
        - Achæus. ACHÆANS.
        - Ion. IONIANS.
      - Amphictyon.
- Epimetheus.
- Atlas.
  - Protogenia and (Zeus).
    - Aethlius. (See TABLE II.)

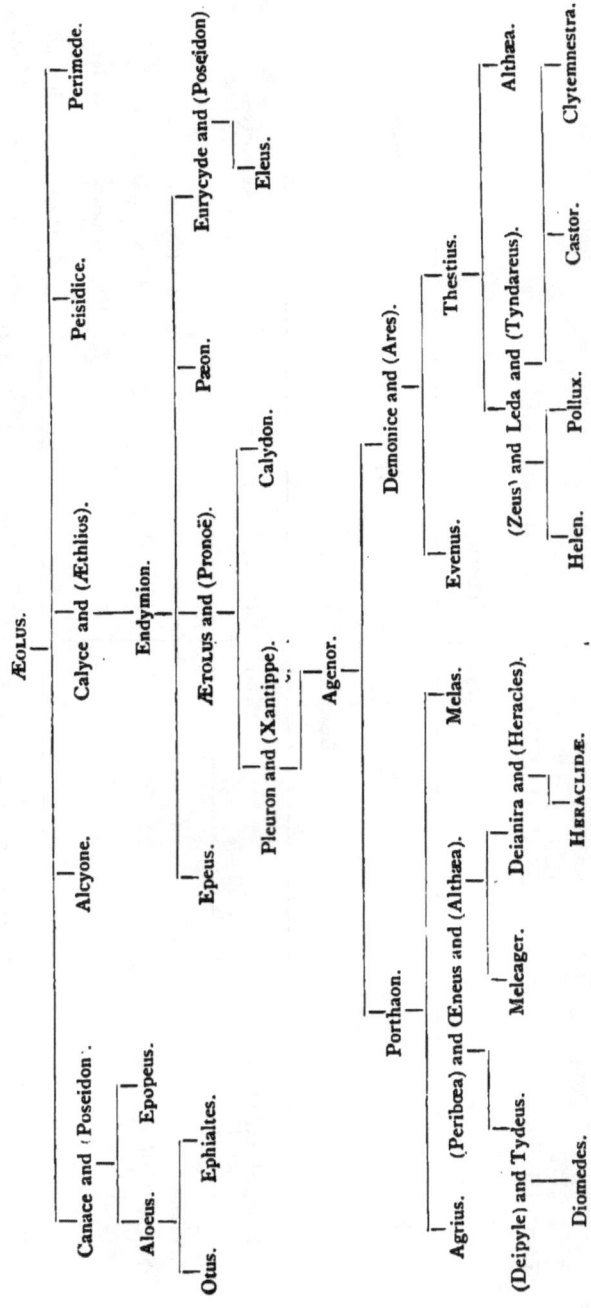

GENEALOGY OF ÆOLIDS.

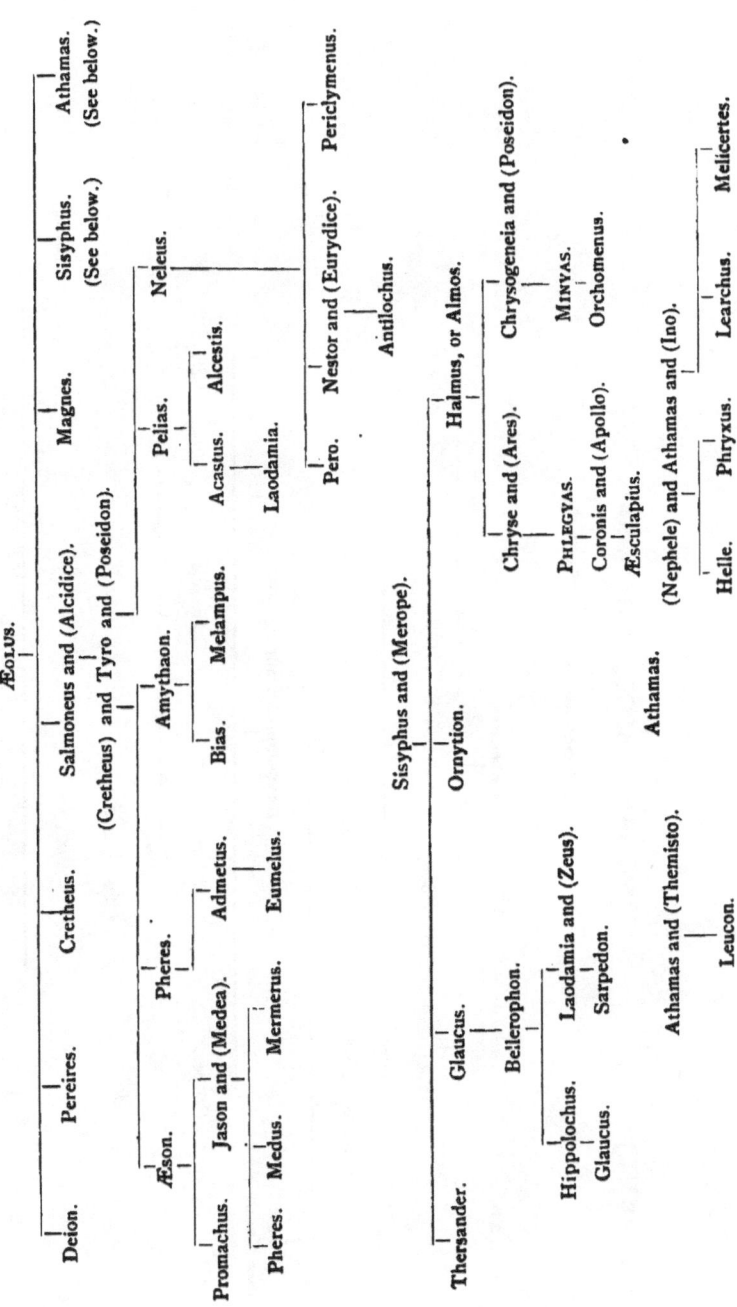

ÆOLIDS—SONS (TABLE I).

32

GREEK MYTHOLOGY.

TABLE III.] GENEALOGIES OF ARGOS.

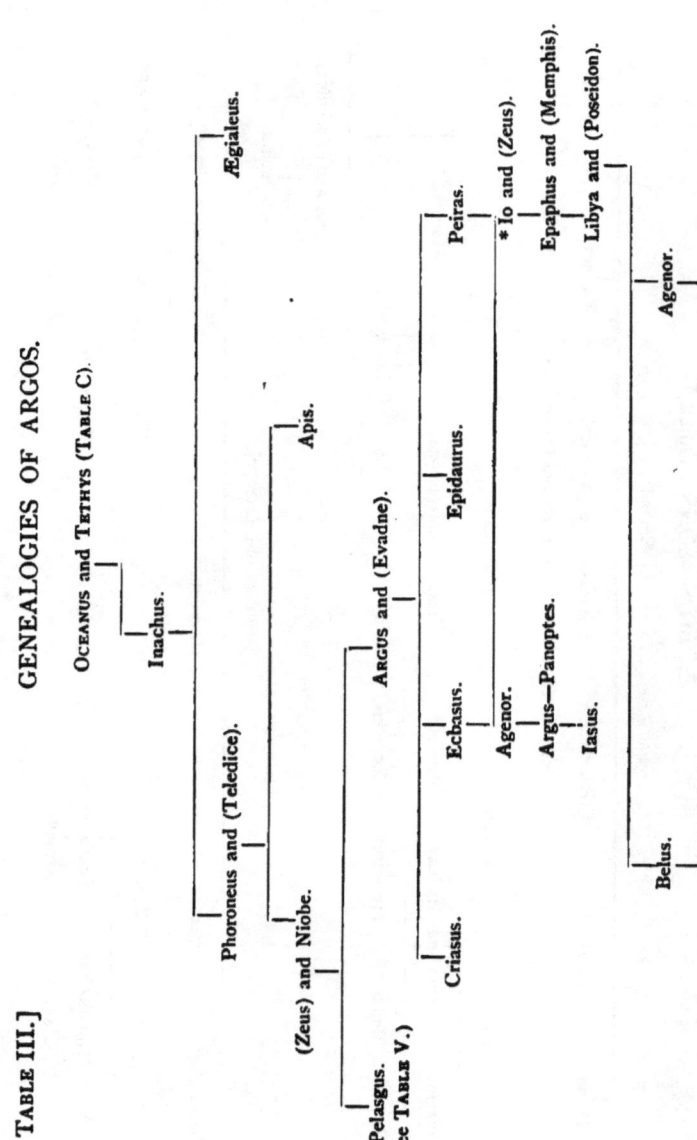

GENEALOGIES OF ARGOS.

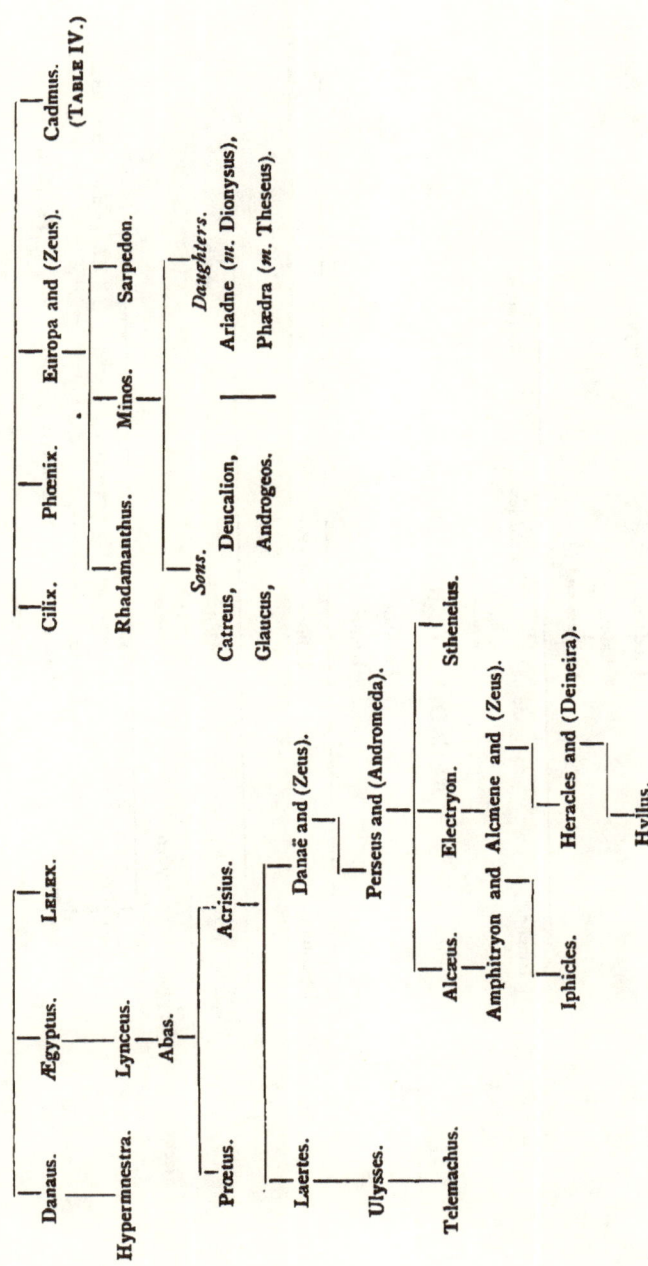

* From Io to Ægyptus I have followed the genealogies usually given.—S. A. S.

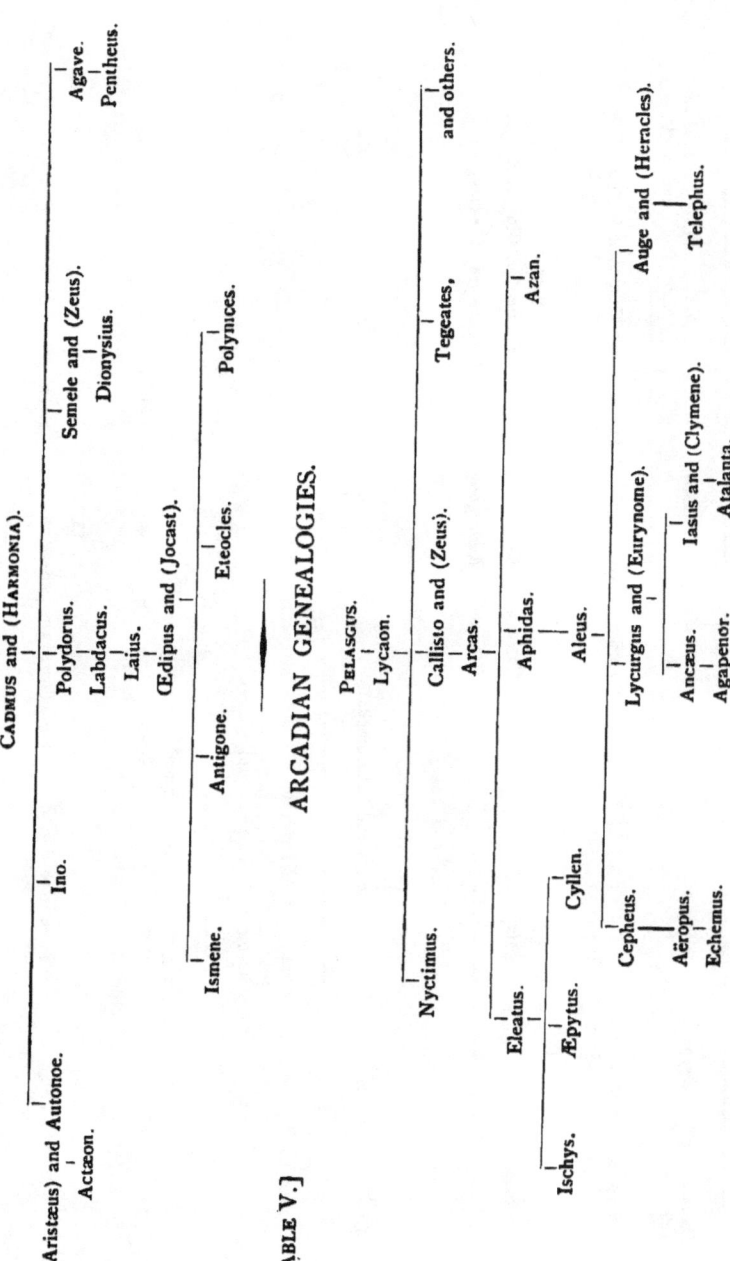

TABLE VI.]   GENEALOGY OF THE PELOPIDÆ.

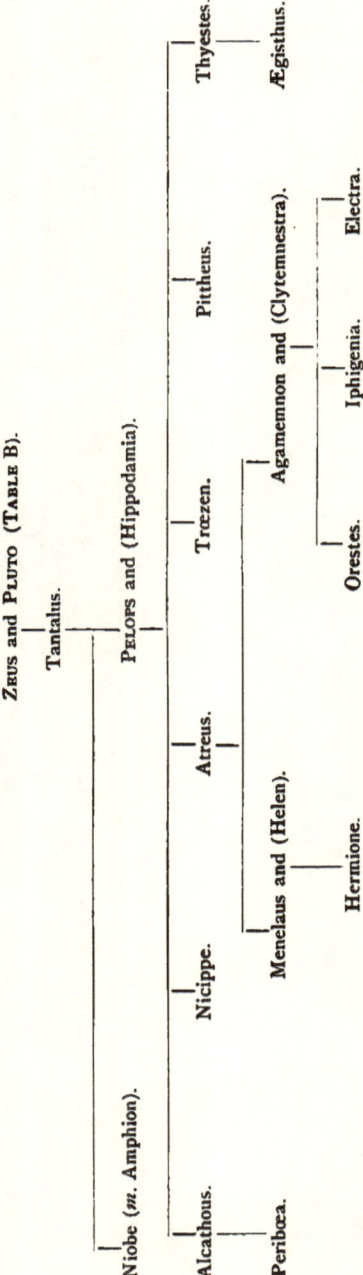

GENEALOGIES OF ATTICA.

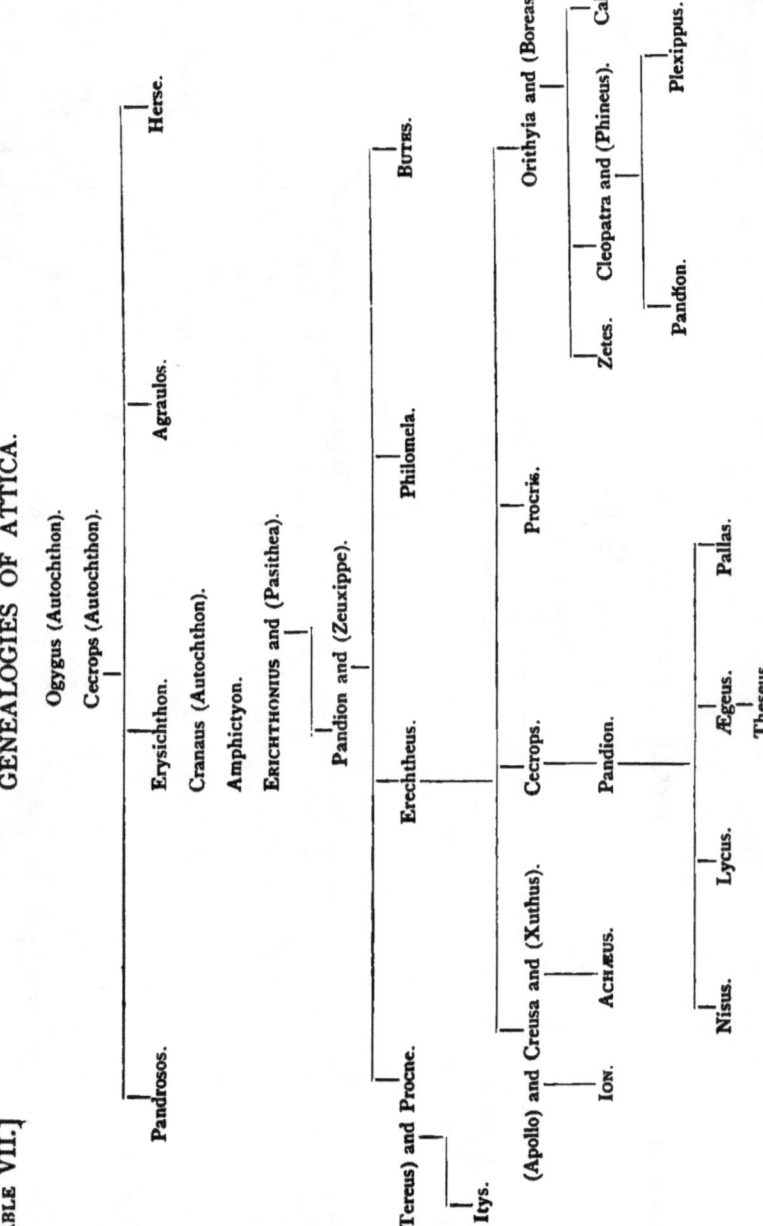

TABLE VII.

GENEALOGIES OF LACONIA, MESSENIA, ETC. 379

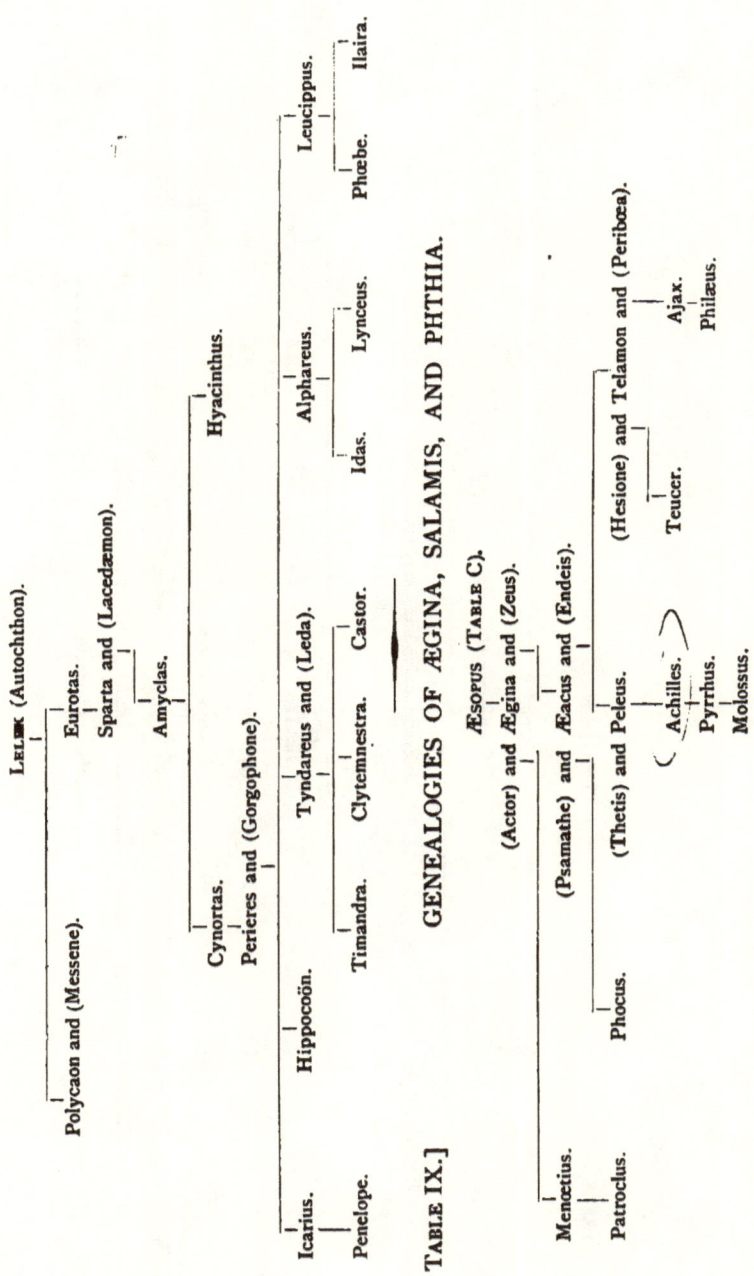

TABLE IX.] GENEALOGIES OF ÆGINA, SALAMIS, AND PHTHIA.

[TABLE X.]

TROJAN GENEALOGIES.

```
Zeus and Electra (Table B).
         |
Dardanus and (Batea).
         |
Erichthonius and (Astyoche).
         |
        Tros.
         |
    ┌────┴────┐
Ganymedes.   Ilus I.   Ilus II.   Assaracus.
              |                      |
           Laomedon.               Capys.
              |                      |
        Priam and (Hecuba).    Anchises and (Aphrodite).
              |                      |
   ┌──────────┼──────────┐         Æneas.
 Paris.  (Andromache)  Cassandra.
         and Hector.
              |
          Astyanax.
```

INDEX.

For convenience of reference the spelling throughout the book has been made to conform with that used in Smith's *Classical Dictionary*.

The leading features of deities are found by consulting in connection the places indicated by the tabular references, and by the page reference which follows the abbreviation *Descp*.

Abarbareë, 365.
Abas, 246, 375.
Absyrtus, 256, 346.
Abyla, 218, 249.
Acalle, 225.
Acaste, Tab. C, 29.
Acastus, 240, 373.
Achæus, 277, 371, 378.
Achelous, Tab. C, 3.—79.
Acheron, 101.
Acherusia, 101, 322.
Achilles, descp. 299.—223, 235, 247, 249, 255, 259, 350, 351, 379.
Acis, 238.
Acrisius, descp. 246.—226, 375.
Actæa, Tab. I, 4.
Actæon, 164, 243, 376.
Actor, 379.
Admete, Tab. C, 28.
Admetus, 150, 218, 343, 345, 373.
Adonis, descp. 295.—201.
Adrastia, 66.
Adrastus, 91.
Æacus, Tab. B, 30; descp. 194.—102, 379.
Æetes, Tab. E, 5; descp. 255.—346, 366.

Ægeon, 55.
Ægeus, descp. 339 and 347.—378.
Ægialeus, 374.
Ægina, 194, 379.
Ægistheus, descp. 357.—377.
Ægle, Tab. E, 9; descp. 256.
Ægle (dr. of Atlas), 269.
Ægyptus, Tab. B, 58; descp. 246.—375.
Aëllo, Tab. I, 57; descp. 301.
Æneas, 292, 323, 348, 356, 380.
Æolus, 277, 344, 366, 371, 372, 373.
Æpytus, 376.
Aëropus, 376.
Æsa, 367.
Æsculapius, descp. 158.—114, 150, 373.
Æson, 239, 240, 344, 373.
Æther, Tab. K, 3; descp. 313.
Æthlius, Tab. B, 28a.—371, 372.
Æthra, 197, 339.
Æthra, 269.
Ætolus, 372.
Agamedes, 241.
Agamemnon, descp. 349.—156, 161, 255, 357, 377.
Agapenor, 376.

381

Agave, Tab. I, 3.
Agave (dr. of Cadmus), 243, 376.
Agenor, Tab. B, 57; descp. 242.—372, 374.
Agenor, 374.
Aglaia, descp. 185.—235.
Aglaope, 303.
Aglaopheme, 302.
Aglaric, 184.
Aglaurus. See AGRAULOS.
Agraulos, 132, 378.
Agrius, 255, 372.
Ahi, 258.
Aïdes. See HADES.
Ajax (son of Telamon), 349, 379.
Ajax (son of Oileus), 349.
Akar, 308.
Alcæus, 208, 228, 375.
Acathous, 377.
Alce, 367.
Alcestis, 218, 240, 373.
Alcidice, 373.
Alcinous, 241, 359.
Alcippe, 141, 142.
Alcmene, 208, 375.
Alcyone (dr. of Atlas), 268.
Alcyone (dr. of Æolus), 371, 372.
Alcyoneus, Tab. H, 1; descp. 277.
Alecto, Tab. H, 3; descp. 279.
Aleus, 376.
Alexiares, 223.
Algea, Tab. K, 13.
Allat, 295, 308.
Alöeus, Tab. B, 59; descp. 246, 372.
Aloidæ, 246.
Alphareus, 379.
Alpheus, Tab. C, 4.—160, 365.
Althæa, 342, 372.
Amalthea, 66.
Amazons, 86, 353; Queen of, 214, 217, 342.
Ambrosia, 269.

Ammon, 89.
Amphictyon, descp. 277, 371, 378.
Amphilogeai, Tab. K, 13.
Amphimarus, 297.
Amphion, Tab. B, 28; descp. 192 and 193.—377.
Amphiro, Table C, 30.
Amphitrite, Tab. I, 5.—302, 365.
Amphitryon, 208, 375.
Amun, 74.
Amyclas, 198, 379.
Amycus, Tab. B, 61; descp. 247.
Amymone, 238.
Amythaon, 373.
Ancæus, 343, 376.
Anchises, 292, 357, 380.
Androgeos, 225, 375.
Androktasai, Tab. K, 13.
Andromache, 380.
Andromeda, 227, 375.
Annit, 65.
Anouki, 126.
Antæus, Tab. B, 45; descp. 237.—216.
Antea. See STHENEBŒA.
Anteros, descp. 292.—142.
Anthesteria, 205.
Anticetus, 223, 376.
Antigone, 310, 376.
Antilochus, 373.
Antiope, 192.
Anubis, 172.
Aoide, 177.
Apate, Tab. K, 12.
Apaturia, 236.
Aphidas, 376.
Aphrodisia, 289.
Aphrodite of Dodona, descp. 78 and 280.—100.
Aphrodite (dr. of Uranus), Tab. A, 35; descp. 57 and 282.—115, 185, 189, 235, 321, 348, 363, 380.

INDEX.

Apis, 374.
Apollo. See PHŒBUS APOLLO.
Arachne, 132.
Arcas, Tab. B, 32; descp. 196.—376.
Arche, 177.
Archegallus, 64.
Ardescus, Tab. C, 5.
Ares, Tab. B, 15; descp. 139.—90, 214, 242, 321, 372, 373.
Arethusa (dr. of Atlas), 269.
Arethusa, 160.
Arges, Tab. A, 17; descp. 55.
Argonautic Expedition, 240 and 344.
Argus, Tab. B, 29; descp. 193.—374.
Argus Panoptes, 95, 170, 193, 374.
Ariadne, 203, 225, 340, 375.
Arion, 117.
Aristæus, descp. 158.—243, 376.
Artemis, Tab. B, 19; descp. 159.—86, 143, 148, 164, 251, 263, 350, 363; as Ephesian Diana, 162.
Asaracus, 191, 380.
Ascalabus, 110.
Ascalaphus, 110, 142.
Ashtoreth, 290.
Asia, Tab. C, 31.
Asine, 198.
Astarte. See APHRODITE.
Asteria, Tab. D, 4; descp. 252.—58.
Asterion, 224.
Astra, Tab. F, 4; descp. 260.
Astræa, Tab. F, 5; descp. 260.
Astræus, Tab. F, 3.
Astyanax, 380.
Astyoche, 191, 380.
Atalanta, descp. 343.—376.
Ate, Tab. K, 13.—367.
Athamas, 202, 345, 371, 373.
Athena. See PALLAS ATHENA.
Athenæa, 132, 136, 341.
Athor, 290.

Atlantides, 188.
Atlas, Tab. G, 4; descp. 267.—67, 94, 214, 228, 366, 371.
Atreus, 377.
Atropos, Tab. K, 6; descp. 316.—343.
Atys, descp. 66.
Auge, 223, 376.
Augeas, 213.
Auno, 184.
Auræ, 188.
Aurora. See EOS.
Autochthe, 228.
Autolycus, 173.
Autonoë, Tab. I, 6.—376.
Autonoë, 243.
Avernales, 188.
Axius, 365.
Azan, 376.

BAAL, 74, 156, 254.
Bacchæ, 188.
Bacchus. See DIONYSUS.
Bacidæ, 188.
Bætylus, 63, 65.
Balius, 367.
Batea, 191, 380.
Bellerophon, descp. 341.—304, 373.
Bellerus, 341.
Belus (Oriental), 74, 89.
Belus, Tab. B, 58; descp. 245.—374.
Benthesicyme, Tab. B, 46.—240.
Bia, Tab. F, 12; descp. 265.—68, 80.
Bias, 373.
Boreas, descp. 261.—240, 345, 366, 378.
Brauronia, 161.
Briareus, Tab. A, 16; descp. 55.—94.
Briseis, 357.
Brontes, Tab. A, 17; descp. 55.
Bronze Age, 261.
Bubastis, 166.

Busiris, Tab. B, 62; descp. 247.
Butes, 135, 136, 237, 378.

CABIRI, 324.
Cacus, 216.
Cadmus, Tab. B, 57; descp. 242.—324, 375, 376.
Caicus, Tab. C, 14.
Calais, 345, 378.
Calchas, 351.
Callidice, 106.
Calliope, 183.
Callirrhoë, Tab. C, 45.—191.
Callisto, 160, 196, 376.
Calpe, 218, 249.
Calyce, 371, 372.
Calydon, 372.
Calydonian Boar, 343, 164.
Calypso, Tab. C, 43; descp. 359, 366.
Canace, 371, 372.
Capys, 380.
Carpo, 174.
Cassandra, descp. 347.—357, 380.
Cassiopea, 227.
Castor, descp. 228.—189, 343, 345, 372, 379.
Cataclothes, 367.
Catreus, 225, 375.
Cecrops, 131, 132, 135, 378.
Cecrops II., descp. 237.—339, 378.
Celæno, descp. 301.
Celæno, 268.
Celeus, 106, 107.
Centaurs, descp. 335.
Centaurs and Lapithæ, descp. 91.—86, 135, 158.
Centimani, 54.
Cephalus, 173, 258.
Cepheus, 227, 376.
Cerberus, Tab. J, 4; descp. 215 and 306.—101.

Cerceis, Tab. C, 44.
Cercyon, 339.
Ceres. See DEMETER.
Ceto, Tab. I, 54.
Ceto, Tab. I, 62.
Chalciope, 256.
Chalkeia, 236.
Chaos, Tab. A, 1; descp. 47.—48.
Charis, 184, 234.
Charites, Tab. B, 24; descp. 184.—94, 149, 204.
Charitesia, 186.
Charon, Tab. K, 14; descp. 322.—102.
Charybdis, descp. 302.
Chelone, 93.
Chimæra, Tab. J, 7; descp. 307.—308, 341.
Chione, 240.
Chiron, descp. 336.—275, 299.
Chloris (dr. of Niobe), 239.
Chnoumis, 89.
Chromius, 239.
Chrysaor, Tab. I, 64; descp. 305.
Chryse, 373.
Chryseis, Tab. C, 32.
Chryseis, 156, 351.
Chryses, 351.
Chrysogenia, 373.
Chthonia, 237.
Cilix, Tab. B, 57; descp. 244.—226, 242, 375.
Cinyras, 295.
Circe, Tab. E, 4; descp. 255.—302, 366.
Cleisidice, 106.
Cleopatra (dr. of Boreas), 244, 378.
Clio, 183.
Clita, 184.
Clotho, Tab. K, 6; descp. 316.
Clymene, Tab. C, 46; descp. 266, 371, 376.

INDEX. 385

Clytemnestra, 350, 357, 372, 377, 379.
Clytie, Tab. C, 47.
Clytie, 152.
Coelus. See URANUS.
Cœus, Tab. A, 23; descp. 250.
Coeytus, 102.
Comasia, 185.
Core, 112.
Corœbus, 87.
Coronis, 269, 373.
Corybantes, descp. 323.—64, 324.
Cottus, Tab. A, 16; descp. 55.
Crambis, 244.
Cranaus, 378.
Cratos, Tab. F, 12; descp. 265.—68, 80.
Creon, 219.
Cretheus, 239, 371, 373.
Creusa (of Attica), 237, 371, 378.
Creusa (of Corinth), 347.
Criasus, 193, 374.
Crius, Tab. A, 27; descp. 259.—58.
Cromedon, Tab. H, 1, descp. 277.
Cronia, 60.
Cronids, 61, 69.
Cronus, Tab. A, 19; descp. 58.—55, 57, 60, 64; legends of, 66, 67, 68, 69, 70, 101, 365, 366.
Cudœmus, 367.
Cumæan Sibyl, 323.
Cupid, 292.
Curetes, descp. 323.—66, 224, 234, 324.
Cybele. See RHEA.
Cyclopes, Tab. A, 17; descp. 55 and 324.—54, 57, 80, 100, 234, 324.
Cycnus, Tab. B, 63; descp. 247.
Cycnus (son of Sthenelus), 256.
Cyllen, 376.
Cymatolege, Tab. I, 26.
Cymo, Tab. I, 27.

Cymodoce, Tab. I, 28.
Cymopoleia, 55.
Cymothoë, Tab. I, 29.
Cynortas, 379.
Cyparissus, 152.
Cypselus, 96.

DACTYLI, 324.
Dædala, 95.
Damastes. See PROCRUSTES.
Danaë, 226, 375.
Danai, 246.
Danaides, 245.
Danaus, Tab. B, 58; descp. 245.—375.
Daphne, 152.
Dardanus, Tab. B, 27; descp. 190.—354, 380.
Death. See THANATOS.
Death Genius, 173, 189.
Deianira, 219, 372, 375.
Deimos, 141, 367.
Deion, 371, 373.
Deipyle, 372.
Delphine, 149.
Demeter, Tab. B, 10; descp. 69 and 104.—74, 126, 127, 363.
Demo, 106.
Demonice, 372.
Demophoön, 107.
Dendrophores, 64.
Deucalion of Crete, 225, 375.
Deucalion, Tab. G, 10; descp. 276.—371.
Diana. See ARTEMIS.
Diana of Ephesus, descp. 162.—64, 65, 165, 166, 312.
Diasia, 72.
Dice, 175, 317.
Diomedes (of Argos), 141, 349, 353, 372.
Diomedes, 213.

Dione of Dodona, descp. 77.—53, 65. 79, 91, 97, 100, 281, 363.
Dione, Tab. C, 33.
Dione (dr. of Atlas), 269.
Dionysia, 206.
Dionysus of Thebes, Tab. B 36; descp. 198 and 331.—74, 172, 223, 234, 235, 298, 332, 340, 375, 376.
Dionysus Zagreus, 206.
Dioscuri. See CASTOR AND POLLUX.
Dirce, 192.
Discordia. See ERIS.
Divine Principle, Tab, A, 2; descp. 47.
Doris, Tab. C, 34.
Doris, Tab. I, 7.
Dorsanes, 221.
Dorus, 277, 371.
Doto, Tab. I, 8.
Dragon, Colchian, 190.
Dragon-Guard of Hesperides, Tab. I, 61; descp. 303.—270.
Dreams. See ONEIROS.
Dryades, 187.
Dsom, 221.
Dumuzi. See ADONIS.
Dunamene, Tab. I, 9.
Dyaus, or Dyu, 60, 89.
Dysnome, Tab. K, 13.

EARTH. See GÆA.
Ecbasus, 193, 374.
Echemus, 376.
Echidna, Tab. I, 67; descp. 305.
Echo, 189.
Eleatus, 376.
Electra, Tab. C, 35.
Electra (dr. of Atlas), 268, 380.
Electra (dr. of Agamemnon), 357, 377.
Electryon, 208, 375.

Eleusinian Mysteries, descp. 107, 113, and 240.
Eleus, Tab. B, 65.—372.
Elysian Fields, 101, 103, 115.
Emathion, Tab. E, 12; descp. 259.
Enceladus, Tab. H, 1; descp. 277.
Endeis, 379.
Endymion, Tab. B, 33; descp. 196, 372.
Enipeus, 239, 365.
Enyo, Tab. I, 62.—140, 141.
Eos, Tab. E, 11; descp. 257.—253, 353.
Epaphus, Tab. B, 38; descp. 224, 374.
Epeus, 372.
Ephialtes, Tab. B, 60; descp. 246, 141, 366, 372.
Epidaurus, 193, 374.
Epimelian Nymphs, 188.
Epimetheus, Tab. G, 11; descp. 274 and 277, 371.
Epopeus, Tab. B, 59.—192, 372.
Epoptæ, 115.
Erato, Tab. I, 11.
Erato (a Muse), 181.
Erebus, Tab. A, 7; descp. 49 and 101.—48.
Erebus (as a deity), Tab. K, 2; descp. 312.
Erechtheus I. See ERICHTHONIUS.
Erechtheus, or Erechtheus II., descp. 132 and 237.—240, 378.
Erichthonius, Tab. B, 44; descp. 132 and 236.—133, 135, 136, 378.
Erichthonius (son of Dardanus), 191, 380.
Eridanus, Tab. C, 7.
Erinyes, Tab. A, 34; descp. 57 and 278.—102, 317, 358.
Eris, Tab. K, 13; descp. 321.—141, 287, 367.

INDEX.   387

Eros as a Nature-power, Tab. A, 8 and 12; descp. 49.—48, 50, 52, 248.
Eros, of 2d Epoch, descp. 50.—57, 58, 280.
Eros (son of Aphrodite), descp. 292. —142, 276.
Eros, as Cupid, descp. 292.
Ersa, Tab. B, 26.
Erymanthian Boar, 212.
Erysichthon, 109, 378.
Erytheia, 269.
Eteocles, 310, 376.
Ether. See ÆTHER.
Eucrato, Tab. I, 13.
Eudora, Tab. C, 36.
Eudora, Tab. I, 12.
Eudora (dr. of Atlas), 269.
Eulimene, Tab. I, 14.
Eumelus, 373.
Eumenides, 279, 358.
Eumolpus, Tab. B, 51; descp. 240.— 109.
Euneus, 345.
Eunice, Tab. I, 15.
Eunomia, 175.
Euphrosyne, 185.
Eupompe, Tab. I, 16.
Europa, Tab. B, 57; descp. 224 and 242.—375.
Eurotas, 197, 379.
Euryale, Tab. I, 63.—227, 303.
Eurybia, Tab. I, 53; descp. 299.
Eurycyde, 372.
Eurydice, 198, 373.
Eurydice, a nymph, 190.
Eurynome, Tab. C, 37.—233, 299, 376.
Eurystheus, 209.
Eurytion (centaur), 91.
Eurytion, 214.
Eurytus, 219.

Euterpe, 178.
Evadne, Tab. B, 64.—193, 374.
Evagore, Tab. I, 17.
Evarne, Tab. I, 18.
Evenus, Tab. C, 8.
Evenus (son of Ares), 372.

FATE, as all-controlling Destiny. See MOROS.
Fates, Three. See MŒRÆ.
Faunus, descp. 333.
Faunus, 333.
Fortuna. See TYCHE.
Furiæ, or Furies. See ERINYES.

GÆA, as Nature-power, Tab. A, 4; descp. 48.—50, 61, 91.
Gæa, as Earth-goddess, Tab. A, 12; descp. 52 and 57.—48, 65, 94, 106, 126, 149, 365.
Galatæa, Tab. I, 19; descp. 238.
Galaxaure, Tab. C, 38.
Galene, Tab. I, 20.
Galli, 64.
Ganymeda, 145.
Ganymedes, descp. 191 and 192.— 80, 144, 380.
Gelasia, 185.
Geras, Tab. K, 12.
Geryon, Tab. I, 66; descp. 305.— 214.
Giants. See GIGANTES.
Gigantes, Tab. A, 32; descp. 57 and 227.—366.
Gigantomachai, or War of the Giants, descp. 278.—68, 131.
Glauce, Tab. I, 21.
Glauconome, Tab. I, 22.
Glaucus (son of Minos), 225, 375.
Glaucus (son of Sisyphus), 373.
Glaucus (son of Hippolochus), 373.
Golden Age, 68, 26 .

Golden Summer, 150.
Gorgons. See GORGONES.
Gorgones, Tab. I, 63; descp. 227 and 303.
Gorgophone, 228, 379.
Graces. See CHARITES.
Grææ, Tab. I, 62; descp. 303.
Granicus, Tab. C, 9.
Gyges, Tab. A, 16; descp. 55.

HADES, Tab. B, 9; descp. 69 and 99.—55, 80, 106, 111, 197, 215, 218, 363.
Hades (Lower World), descp. 59, 100, 101, and 102.—107, 169, 172, 249, 313.
Haliacmon, Tab. C, 11.
Halimedes, Tab. I, 23.
Halirrhothius, Tab. B, 56; descp. 242.—141.
Halmus, 373.
Hamadryades, 187.
Harmachis, 308.
Harmonia, descp. 142 and 243.—376.
Harpies. See HARPYIÆ.
Harpyiæ, Tab. I, 57; descp. 301.—245, 367.
Hea, 308.
Hebe, Tab. B, 17; descp. 143.—220, 363.
Hecate, Tab. F, 10; descp. 262.—106, 107, 112, 166.
Hecatoncheires, Tab. A, 16; descp. 55.—54, 67.
Hector, descp. 350, 348, 380.
Hecuba, 348, 380.
Hegemone, 184.
Helen, Tab. B, 41; descp. 229 and 348.—197, 372, 377.
Helenus, 354, 348.
Heleus, 228.

Heliades, Tab. E, 9; descp. 256.
Helios, Tab. E, 3; descp. 253.—106, 120, 155, 252, 258, 359, 363 366, 371.
Helle, descp. 345, 373.
Hellen, descp. 277.
Helli, or Helloi, 75, 78.
Hemera, Tab. K, 4; descp. 313.—49, 258, 311.
Hemithea, 247.
Heosphorus, Tab. F, 7; descp. 261
Hephæstus, Tab. B, 43; descp. 232 —56, 135, 136, 253, 299, 363.
Heptoporus, Tab. C, 12.
Hera, Tab. B, 8; descp. 69 and 91.—53, 80, 81, 120, 141, 143 185, 202, 207, 209, 220, 224, 235 251, 309, 344, 349, 363, 364.
Heracles, Tab. B, 37; descp. 208.—81, 86, 131, 151, 197, 239, 246 259, 274, 300, 323, 336, 345, 372 375, 376.
Heræa, 96.
Hercules. See HERACLES.
Hermæ, 170, 172.
Hermæa, 172.
Hermaphrodite, 172.
Hermaphroditus, 173.
Hermes, Tab. B, 20; descp. 166.—80, 94, 95, 102, 107, 125, 135 202, 205, 206, 220, 255, 300, 323 363.
Hermione, 358, 377.
Hermus, Tab. C, 10.
Hersa, 132, 378.
Hesione, 216, 347, 379.
Hesperia, 269.
Hesperia, Land of, 270.
Hesperides, Tab. G, 8; also Tab. K, 10; descp. 269 and 320.—94, 188, 214.
Hesperus, Tab. F, 6; descp. 261.

INDEX.

Hestia, Tab. B, 12; descp. 69 and 122.—87.
Hestia (dr. of Atlas), 269.
Hierophant, 113.
Hilaira, 379.
Himeros, 287.
Hippo, Tab. C, 39.
Hippocentaur, 335.
Hippocoön, 379.
Hippodamia (dr. of Œnomaus), 90, 377.
Hippodamia (dr. of Adrastus), 91.
Hippolochus, 373.
Hippolyte. See QUEEN OF THE AMAZONS.
Hipponoë, Tab. I, 24.
Hippothoë, Tab. I, 25.
Horæ, Tab. B, 22; descp. 173.—94, 149, 261.
Horkos, 68, 86.
Horus, the younger, 156.
Hurricane, Tab. J, 1.
Hyacinthus, 151, 379.
Hyades, Tab. G, 6; descp. 269.—188, 202.
Hyas, Tab. G, 5; descp. 269.
Hydra, Lernean, Tab. J, 5; descp. 306.—211, 219.
Hylas, 217, 345.
Hyllus, 223, 375.
Hymnia, 160.
Hyperion, Tab. A, 25; descp. 252.—58, 67.
Hypermnestra, 245, 246, 375.
Hypnos, Tab. K, 9; descp. 319.—101, 231, 311, 367.
Hypsipyle, 345.
Hyrieus, Tab. B, 54; descp. 241.
Hysminai, Tab. K, 13.

IACCHOGOROI, 114.
Iacchus, 114, 117, 207.

Ialmenus, 142.
Iamus, 158.
Ianira, Tab. C, 42.
Ianthe, Tab. C, 40.
Iapetids, 81, 371.
Iapetus, Tab. A, 29; descp. 265.—67, 101, 371.
Iasion, 117.
Iason, 193.
Iasus, 374.
Iasus, 376.
Icarius, 379.
Icarus, 225.
Icelos, 320.
Ida, 66.
Idæa, 244.
Idæan Mother, 65.
Idas, 230, 343, 379.
Idomeneus, 349.
Idyia, Tab. C, 41.
Ilaira. See HILAIRA.
Ilithyia, Tab. B, 16; descp. 142.—42.
Ilithyiæ, 94.
Ilus (son of Dardanus), 191, 380.
Ilus II. (son of Tros), 191, 380.
Inachus, Tab. C, 13 a —193, 374.
Indra, 89.
Ino, 202, 243, 345.—359, 366, 373, 376.
Inuus, 333.
Io, 81, 95.—170, 193, 224, 273, 374.
Iobates, 341.
Ioce, 367.
Iolaus, 212, 219.
Iole, 219.
Ion, 158, 277, 371, 378.
Ione, Tab. I, 10.
Iphicles, 209, 375.
Iphigenia, descp. 350.—161, 358, 377.
Iphimedia, 246.

Iphitus, 239, 218.
Irene, 175.
Iris, Tab. I, 56; descp. 94 and 300.
—80, 102, 107, 220, 363.
Ischys, 376.
Isdrus, Tab. C, 13.
Ishtar, 284, 290, 292, 308.
Isis, 65, 115, 224.
Isles of the Blessed. See ELYSIAN FIELDS.
Ismarus, 240.
Ismene, 310, 376.
Isthmian Games, 121.
Itys, 237, 378.

JAPETUS. See IAPETUS.
Jason, descp. 344.—346, 373.
Jocaste, 309, 376.
Jove. See ZEUS.
Jumala, 54.
Juno. See HERA.
Jupiter. See ZEUS.

KER, Tab. K, 5. See MOROS, also p. 367.
Keres, Tab. K, 6; descp. 317. See p. 367.
Kneph, 89.

LABDACUS, 192, 244, 376.
Lacedæmon, Tab. B, 35; descp. 197.—379.
Lachesis, Tab. K, 6; descp. 316.
Ladon, Tab. C, 15.
Ladon. See DRAGON-GUARD OF HESPERIDES.
Laertes, 375.
Laius, 309, 376.
Lampetia, Tab. E, 9; descp. 256.—366.
Laocoön, descp. 355.
Laodamia, 373.

Laodice, 223.
Laomedia, Tab. I, 30.
Laomedon, descp. 217.—120, 150, 347, 380.
Lapithæ, 91.
Latona. See LETO.
Learchus, 244, 345, 373.
Lecoris, 185.
Leda, 229, 372, 379.
Leichas, 223.
Leimoniades, 187.
Lelex, Tab. B, 58; descp. 246.— 375. 379.
Lethe, Tab. K, 13.
Leto, Tab. D, 3; descp. 251.—143, 148, 363.
Leuce, 103.
Leucippus, 379.
Leucon, 373.
Leucothea. See INO.
Leucothoë, 152.
Liagore, Tab. I, 31.
Libya, 224, 374.
Libys, 173.
Limniades, 188.
Limos, Tab. K, 13.
Linæa, 206.
Linus, descp. 296.—151.
Litæ, 367.
Logos, Tab. K, 13.
Lucifer, 261.
Lucina. See ILITHYIA.
Luna. See SELENE.
Lupercus, 333.
Lycaon, 196, 376.
Lycurgus, 376.
Lycus (son of Pandion), 339, 378.
Lycus (son of Hyrieus), 241, 192.
Lycus, Tab. B, 53; descp. 241.
Lynceus, 230, 343, 375, 379.
Lyncus, 245, 246.
Lyssiannissa, Tab. I, 32.

INDEX. 391

MACHAI, Tab. K, 13.
Machaon, 349.
Mæander, Tab. C, 16.
Mænades, 188.
Magnes, 371, 373.
Maia, 268, 366.
Mars. See ARES.
Marsyas, 151.
Maryandynus, 244.
Medea, 240, 256, 346, 373.
Medus, 373.
Medusa, Tab. I, 63; descp. 303.— 131, 227.
Megæra, Tab. H, 3; descp. 279.
Megara, 219.
Melampus, 373.
Melas, 372.
Meleager, 343, 345, 372.
Melete, 177.
Melia, 193.
Meliades, 187.
Meliæ, Tab. A, 33; descp. 57 and 278.
Melian Nymphs. See MELIÆ.
Melicertes, or Melkart. See HERACLES.
Melicertes, 244, 345, 373.
Melite, Tab. I, 33.
Melobosis, Tab. C, 49.
Melpomene, 182.
Memnon, Tab. E, 13; descp. 259. —353.
Memphis, 224, 374.
Menelaus, descp. 348.—377.
Menestho, Tab. C, 50.
Menippe, Tab. I, 34.
Menœtius, Tab. G, 3; descp. 267. —67, 305, 371, 379.
Mentha, 103.
Mercury. See HERMES.
Mermerus, 373.
Merope, descp. 268.—373.

Messene, 379.
Mestor, 208.
Metanira, 107, 109.
Metharme, 295.
Metion, 237.
Metis, Tab. C, 48; descp. 127.
Midas, descp. 332.—151.
Milanion, 344.
Minerva. See PALLAS ATHENA.
Minos, Tab. B, 39; descp. 225.— 102, 375.
Minotaurus, descp. 225.—203, 340.
Minyas, 373.
Mithra, 254.
Mneme, 177.
Mnemosyne, Tab. A, 28; descp. 260.—67.
Mœra. See MOROS, also p. 367.
Mœræ, Tab. B, 21, also Tab. K, 6; descp. 315.—343.
Moloch, 60.
Molossus, 379.
Momus, Tab. K, 11; descp. 320.
Moon. See SELENE.
Moros, Tab. K, 5; descp. 313.—76, 283, 353.
Morpheus, Tab. K, 9; descp. 320.
Mors. See THANATOS.
Musæ, Tab. B, 23; descp. 175.— 148, 149, 304, 354.
Muses. See MUSÆ.
Mut, 65.
Mylitta, 284, 290.
Myrmidons, 194.
Myrtilus, 90, 173.

NAIADES, 188, 250.
Naīarque, 78.
Napææ, 188.
Narcissus, 189.
Nature-powers, Tab. A, 3; descp. 47 and 48.—61.

Nauplius, Tab. B, 49; descp. 238.
Nausicaa, 359.
Nausithous, Tab. B, 52; descp. 241.
Neikea, Tab. K, 13.
Neith, 138.
Neleus, Tab. B, 50; descp. 239, 345, 373.
Nemea, Tab. B, 26.
Nemean Lion, Tab. J, 8; descp. 211 and 307.
Nemertes, Tab. I, 35.
Nemesia, 318.
Nemesis, Tab. K, 7; descp. 317.—189.
Neoptolemus, 354.
Nephele, 345, 373.
Neptune. See POSEIDON.
Nereides, descp. 298.—120, 188, 227, 366.
Nereus, Tab. I, 2; descp. 297.—117, 214, 365.
Nesaie, Tab. I, 37.
Neso, Tab. I, 36.
Nessus, Tab. C, 18.
Nessus, 219.
Nestor, 239, 349, 373.
Nicippe, 377.
Night. See NYX.
Night, Starry. See ASTERIA.
Nike, Tab. F, 12; descp. 265.—68, 80, 82, 86.
Nilus, Tab. C, 17.—224.
Niobe (dr. of Phoroneus), 193, 374.
Niobe (dr. of Tantalus), descp. 193.—86, 164, 377.
Nisus, 339, 378.
Notus, 261.
Nutpe, 65.
Nycteus, 241, 192.
Nyctimus, 376.

Nymphæ, Tab. B, 25; descp. 186.—365.
Nymphæa, 186.
Nymphs. See NYMPHÆ; also MELIÆ.
Nyx as Nature-power, Tab. A, 6; descp. 49.—48.
Nyx as Night-goddess, Tab. K, 1; descp. 311.—101.

OCEANIDS, 188.
Oceanus, Tab. A, 21; descp. 248.—58, 67, 93, 101, 106, 117, 258, 365, 374.
Ocypete, Tab. I, 57; descp. 301.
Ocyroë, Tab. C, 51.
Odysseus. See ULYSSES.
Œdipus, 309, 376.
Œneus, 164, 219, 372.
Œnomaus, 86, 90.
Ogygus, Tab. K, 12.
Olympian Games, descp. 84.—213, 231.
Omphale, 218.
Oneiros, Tab. K, 9; descp. 320.—367.
Oneus, descp. 342.—164.
Ops, 65.
Orchomenus, 373.
Oreades, 188, 332.
Orestes, descp. 357.—151, 161, 350, 377.
Orion, 241, 258.
Orithyia, 237, 373.
Ornytion, 373.
Orpheus, 190, 303, 323, 345.
Orphic Philosophy, descp. 207 and 294.—201, 205, 276.
Orseis, 371.
Orthrus, Tab. J, 6.—214.
Oryithus, 244.
Osiris, 201, 206, 224, 254, 295.

INDEX.   393

Ossa, 367.
Otos, Tab. B, 60; descp. 246.—141, 366.
Oure, Tab. A, 10; descp. 51.—50.

PÆAN, 363, 372.
Pa-hra, 258.
Paieon. See PÆAN.
Pallantides, 340.
Pallas (son of Pandion II.), 339, 378.
Pallas, Tab. F, 11; descp. 264.
Pallas Athena, Tab. B, 13; descp. 127.—94, 126, 140, 185, 207, 215, 228, 242, 275, 344, 358, 363, 364.
Pan, descp. 329.—64, 151.
Panathenæa, 136.
Pandia, Tab. B, 26.
Pandion (son of Erichthonius), 132, 236, 378.
Pandion II. (son of Cecrops), 339, 378.
Pandion (son of Phineus), 378.
Pandora, descp. 273.—136.
Pandorus, 237.
Pandrosos, 132, 378.
Panisci, 331.
Panope, Tab. I, 38.
Parcæ. See MŒRÆ.
Paris, descp. 347; Judgment of, 287, 298, 380.
Parthenius, Tab. C, 19.
Pasiphaë, Tab. E, 6; descp. 256 and 225.
Pasithea, 184.
Pasithea, Tab. I, 39.
Pasithoë, Tab. C, 52.
Patroclus, 231, 249, 349, 352, 379.
Pedile, 269.
Pegasus, Tab. I, 65; descp. 304.—341.
Peiras, 193, 194, 374.
Peisidici, 371, 372.

Peitho, 184, 287.
Pelasgus, Tab. B, 29.—374, 376.
Peleiades, 72, 78.
Peleus, 287, 298, 345, 379.
Pelias, Tab. B, 50; descp. 239.—344, 373.
Pelops, descp. 196.—86, 90, 195, 377.
Penelope, 360, 379.
Peneus, Tab. C, 21.
Penthesilea, 353.
Pentheus, 243, 376.
Pephredo, Tab. I, 62.
Pereires, 371, 373.
Peribœa, 372, 377, 379.
Periclymenus, 239, 373.
Perieres, 379.
Perimede, 371, 372.
Periphetes, 339.
Pernicious Winds, Tab. J, 3; descp. 306.—261.
Pero, 239, 373.
Perse. See PERSEIS.
Perseis, Tab. C, 56.—366.
Persephone, Tab. B, 14; descp. 104 and 111.—101, 127, 174, 189, 197, 284, 363.
Perses, Tab. E, 7.
Perses, Tab. F, 9; descp. 262.
Perseus, Tab. B, 40; descp. 226.—208, 375.
Petroie, Tab. C, 57.
Phædra, 225, 375.
Phaënna, 184.
Phaëthon, Tab. E, 8; descp. 256.
Phaëthusa, Tab. E, 9; descp. 256.—366.
Phantasos, 320.
Phasis, Tab. C, 20.
Pheres, 373.
Pherousa, Tab. I, 40.
Philæus, 379.
Philammon, 158.

Philoctetes, 220, 349.
Philomela, 237, 378.
Philonoma, 247.
Philotes, Tab. K, 13.
Phineus, descp. 242 and 244.—345, 378.
Phlegyas, 373.
Phobetor, 320.
Phobos, 141, 367.
Phocus, 379.
Phœas, 226.
Phœbe, Tab. A, 24; descp. 251.—58.
Phœbe (dr. of Leucippus), 379.
Phœbe. See ÆGLE.
Phœbus Apollo, Tab. B, 18; descp. 145 and 210.—86, 120, 136, 143, 179, 217, 231, 247, 251, 254, 358, 363, 364, 373, 378.
Phœnix, Tab. B, 57; descp. 224.—242.
Phonoi, Tab. K, 13.
Phorcys, Tab. I, 58; descp. 301.—366.
Phoroneus, 193, 373.
Phryxus, 345.—373.
Phyleus, 213.
Phyto, 269.
Pierus, 178, 304.
Pirithous, Tab. B, 34; descp. 197.—91, 215, 345.
Pisinoë, 303.
Pittheus, 377.
Pleiades, Tab. G, 7; descrip. 268.—188.
Pleione, 268.
Pleuron, 372.
Plexaure, Tab. C, 53.
Plexippus, 378.
Plusia, 177.
Pluto. See HADES.
Pluto (a nymph), Tab. C, 55.—377.

Plutus, 117.
Podalirius, 349.
Podarge, 367.
Pœas, 220, 226.
Pœna, 317.
Pollux, Tab. B, 41; descp. 228.—189, 343, 345, 372.
Polybus, 309.
Polycaon, 379.
Polydectes, 227, 228.
Polydectus, 244.
Polydora, Tab. C, 54.
Polydorus, 243.
Polydorus, 244, 376.
Polymnia, 181.
Polynices, 310, 376.
Polynome, Tab. I, 42.
Polyphemus, Tab. B, 47; descp. 238.
Polyphemus, Tab. B, 48; descp. 238.—56.
Polyxo, 269.
Ponos, Tab. K, 13.
Pontoporia, Tab. I, 41.
Pontus, Tab. A, 11; descp. 51 and 297.—50, 117, 248.
Porphyrion, Tab. H, 1; descp. 277.
Porthaon, 372.
Portheus. See PORTHAON.
Poseidon, Tab. B, 11; descp. 69 and 117.—55, 67, 80, 90, 94, 129, 130, 131, 133, 135, 141, 217, 225, 227, 239, 240, 303, 363, 364, 372, 373, 374.
Potamides, 188.
Pothos, 287.
Priam, descp. 347.—217, 380.
Prithivi, 53.
Procne, 237, 378.
Procris, 237, 378.
Procrustes, 339.
Prœtus, 246, 341, 375.
Promachus, 373.

INDEX. 395

Prometheus, Tab. G, 9; descp. 270.
—81, 136, 235, 266, 321, 371.
Pronöē, Tab. I, 43.—372.
Proserpine. See PERSEPHONE.
Proteus, 120, 366.
Proto, Tab. I, 44.
Proto, Tab. I, 45.
Protogenia, 371.
Protomedia, Tab. I, 46.
Psamanthe, Tab. I, 47.—379.
Psyche, descp. 276 and 293.
Psychopompos, 172.
Pthah, 235.
Pyanepsia, 341.
Pygmalion, 294.
Pylades, 357.
Pyriphlegethon, 102.
Pyrrha, Tab. G, 12; descp. 277, 371.
Pyrrhus, 379.
Python, descp. 149.—156.

RA, 156, 254.
Ra, Amon, 89.
Reshiph-Mical, 156.
Rhadamanthus, Tab. B, 39; descp. 226.—101, 102, 375.
Rhea, Tab. A, 20; descp. 61.—58, 60, 66, 69, 91, 107, 115, 125, 365.
Rhesus, Tab. C, 22.
Rhexenor, 241.
Rhode, Tab. B, 46.
Rhodia, Tab. C, 58.
Rhodius, Tab. C, 23.
Rhœtus, Tab. H, 1; descp. 277.
River-goddesses, Tab. C.
River-gods, Tab. C.
Rivers, 248 and 249.

SALMONEUS, 371, 373.
Sama, 103.
Sangarius, Tab. C, 24.
Sao, Tab. I, 48.

Sarameya, 172.
Saripolis, 143.
Sarpedon, Tab. B, 39; descp. 226.—375.
Sarpedon, Tab. B, 42; descp. 231.—373.
Sati, 97.
Saturn. See CRONUS.
Saturnalia, 60.
Satyrs, descp. 333.—332.
Scamanders, Tab. C, 25; 365.
Scylla, Tab. I, 59; descp. 302.
Seasons. See HORÆ.
Seb, 60.
Seirenes, Tab. I, 60; descp. 302.—366.
Selene, Tab. E, 10; descp. 257.—196, 253.
Selli, 75, 78.
Semele, 202, 243, 244, 376.
Serapis, 103.
Sileni, 334.
Silenus, descp. 334.—202.
Silver Age, 261, 278.
Simois, Tab. C, 26.
Sinis, 339.
Sinon, 356.
Sirens. See SEIRENES.
Sisyphus, 371, 373.
Sleep. See HYPNOS.
Sol. See HELIOS.
Somnus. See HYPNOS.
Sparta, 197, 379.
Sparti, 243.
Spercheus, 249, 365.
Sphinx, Tab. J, 9; descp. 307.—86, 116.
Spio, Tab. I, 49.
Sterope, 268.—90.
Steropes, Tab. A, 17; descp. 55.
Sthenebœa, 341.
Sthenelus, 349.

Sthenelus, 228, 375.
Stheno, Tab. I, 63.—227, 303.
Strymon, Tab. C, 27.
Stymphalides, 212.
Styx, Tab. C, 59; descp. 68.—101, 265.
Styx, a river, 94, 101, 102, 149.
Sun. See HELIOS.
Sylphs, 188.
Symplegades, 190, 346.
Syrinx, 332.

TALUS, 226, 234.
Tammuz. See ADONIS.
Tantalus, Tab. B, 31; descp. 195.—90, 377.
Taras, Tab. B, 55; descp. 241.
Tartarus, Tab. A, 5; descp. 48 and 313.—49, 67, 68, 101, 149.
Tartarus, as prison, 49, 67, 68, 101, 102.
Taygete, 268.
Tegeates, 376.
Telamon, 347, 379.
Telchines, 324.
Teledice, 373.
Telegonus, 225.
Telemachus, 360, 375.
Telephus, 223, 349, 350, 376.
Telestho, Tab. C, 62.
Tellus, 53.
Tenes, 247.
Tengri, 54.
Tentamidus, 228.
Tereus, 237, 378.
Terpsichore, 181.
Terra, 53, 126.
Tethys, Tab. A, 22; descp. 248 and 249.—58, 93, 106, 365, 374.
Teucer, 191, 379.
Thalassa, 323.
Thalia, descp. 185.

Thalia, Tab. I, 50.
Thalia (a Muse), 182.
Thallo, 174.
Thamyris, 178.
Thanatos, Tab. K, 8; descp. 318.—101, 173, 231, 311, 367.
Thasus, descp. 242 and 244.
Thaumas, Tab. I, 55; descp. 299.
Thelxiepia, 302.
Thelxino, 177.
Themis, Tab. A, 30; descp. 173 and 266.—67, 148, 149, 276, 363.
Themisto, Tab. I, 51.—373.
Thersander, 349, 373.
Thersites, 353.
Thesauri, 86.
Theseus, descp. 339.—91, 131, 136, 197, 203, 214, 215, 229, 323, 339, 345, 375, 378.
Thesmophoria, 115.
Thestius, 372.
Thetis, Tab. I, 52; descp. 298.—94, 233, 275, 351, 353, 366, 379.
Thia, Tab. A, 26; descp. 252.
Thoë, Tab. C, 60.
Thoosa, 366.
Thoth, 172.
Thyene. See DIONE (dr. of Atlas).
Thyestes, 377.
Thynus, 244.
Thyone. See SEMELE.
Tien, 54.
Timandra, 379.
Tiresias, 255, 310.
Tiro, 89.
Tisiphone, Tab. H, 3; descp. 279.
Titaia, 56.
Titania, 53.
Titanic Groups, Tab. A, 18; descp. 56, 57, 58, 100.
Titanic War, Tab. B, 4; descp. 67.—53, 81, 120, 249, 260, 261, 332.

INDEX.

Titanomachia. See TITANIC WAR.
Titans, descp. 56.—53, 54; rebellion of, 57, 59, 207; marriage of, 57.
Tithonus, 258, 353.
Tityus, 150.
Tomouri, 75, 78.
Triformis, 263.
Triptolemus, 107, 109.
Triton, Tab. B, 46; descp. 238.—120.
Tritons, 120.
Trœzen, 377.
Trojan War, descp. 218 and 347.—81, 89, 93, 98, 122, 138, 139, 142, 156, 166, 172, 223, 231, 284, 287, 299.
Trophonius, 241.
Tros, 191, 192, 380.
Tyche, Table C, 61; descp. 317 and 325.
Tydeus, 372.
Tyndareus, 229, 372, 379.
Typhaon, Tab. J, 2; descp. 306.
Typhœus, Tab. J, 1; descp. 68 and 306.
Tyr, 89.
Tyw, 239, 373.

ULYSSES, descp. 349.—238, 255, 302, 349, 350; return of Odysseus, 359, 375.
Urania, Tab. C, 63.
Urania (a Muse), 183.

Uranus, as Heaven-Father, Tab. A, 12; descp. 53 and 57.—50, 60, 70.
Uranus, as Nature-power, Tab. A, 9; descp. 50.
Ushas, 138.

VARUNA, 54.
Venus. See APHRODITE.
Vesta. See HESTIA.
Victory. See NIKE.
Vulcan. See HEPHÆSTUS.

WINDS. See ANEMOI; also PERNICIOUS WINDS.

XANTHO, Tab. C, 64.
Xantippe, 371, 372.
Xenodice, 225.
Xeuxo, Tab. C, 65.
Xuthus, 277, 367, 371, 378.

ZELUS, Tab. F, 12; descp. 265.—68, 80.
Zephyrus, descp. 261.—151, 366.
Zetes, 345, 378.
Zethus, Table B, 28; descp. 192.
Zeus of Dodona, descp. 70 and 77.—54, 82, 100.
Zeus, son of Cronus, Tab. B, 7; descp. 66, 69, and 70.—55, 60, 94, 108, 252, 256, 266, 270, 281, 287, 295, 345, 351, 363, 364, 371, 372, 373, 374, 375, 376, 377, 379, 380.
Zeuxippe, 378.

THE END.

www.ingramcontent.com/pod-product-compliance
Lightning Source LLC
Chambersburg PA
CBHW030427300426
44112CB00009B/891